The Social Effects of Native Title:
Recognition, Translation, Coexistence

Benjamin R. Smith and Frances Morphy (Editors)

E PRESS

Centre for Aboriginal Economic Policy Research
The Australian National University, Canberra

Research Monograph No. 27
2007

Published by ANU E Press
The Australian National University
Canberra ACT 0200, Australia
Email: anuepress@anu.edu.au
This title is also available online at: http://epress.anu.edu.au/c27_citation.html

National Library of Australia
Cataloguing-in-Publication entry

The social effects of native title : recognition,
translation, coexistence.

Includes index.

ISBN 9781921313516 (pbk.)
ISBN 9781921313523 (online)

1. Native title (Australia) - Social aspects. I. Smith,
Benjamin Richard. II. Morphy, Frances, 1949- .

346.940432

All rights reserved. No part of this publication may be reproduced, stored in a retrieval system or transmitted in any form or by any means, electronic, mechanical, photocopying or otherwise, without the prior permission of the publisher.

Cover design by Brendon McKinley.

This edition © 2007 ANU E Press

Contents

Notes on contributors	vii
Abbreviations and acronyms	xi
1. The social effects of native title: recognition, translation, coexistence	1
Benjamin R. Smith and Frances Morphy	
2. Performing law: The Yolngu of Blue Mud Bay meet the native title process	31
Frances Morphy	
3. Claim, culture and effect: property relations and the native title process	59
Katie Glaskin	
4. Some initial effects of pursuing and achieving native title recognition in the northern Kimberley	79
Anthony Redmond	
5. 'We're tired from talking': The native title process from the perspective of Kaanju People living on homelands, Wenlock and Pascoe Rivers, Cape York Peninsula	91
David Claudie	
6. Towards an uncertain community? The social effects of native title in central Cape York Peninsula	117
Benjamin R. Smith	
7. Native title and the Torres Strait: encompassment and recognition in the Central Islands	135
Julie Lahn	
8. 'No vacancies at the Starlight Motel': Larrakia identity and the native title claims process	151
Benedict Scambary	
9. What has native title done to the urban Koori in New South Wales who is also a traditional custodian?	167
Dennis Foley	
10. Beyond native title: the Murray Lower Darling Rivers Indigenous Nations	185
Jessica Weir and Steven Ross	
11. The limits of recognition	203
Manuhuia Barcham	

12. History, oral history, and memoriation in native title   215
James F. Weiner

List of Figures

2.1.	The ritual space of the court	34
2.2.	The 'translation' steps in a witness statement	39
2.3.	The opening ceremony: approach to the court	45
2.4.	The opening ceremony: in the court	46
2.5.	The court at the edge of the Yolngu law space	47
2.6.	The return from the Yolngu law space	47
2.7.	Mungurru on a calm day	51
2.8.	Mungurru on the day of the 'view'	51
5.1.	Kaanju homelands showing clan estates	93
8.1.	Itinerant protestors in Darwin	159
8.2.	Cover of *Kujuk*	160
8.3.	Cover of *Longgrass*	161
10.1.	The Indigenous nations of the Murray–Darling system	186

Notes on contributors

Manuhuia Barcham

Manuhuia Barcham is the Director for the Centre for Indigenous Governance and Development at Massey University, New Zealand. His recent work has looked at the governance of indigenous organisations in Australia, Canada and New Zealand. The Australian work has focused on work with Noongar in southwest Western Australia and with urban Aboriginal groups in Sydney and Melbourne.

David Claudie

David Claudie is a Traditional Owner for Kaanju Ngaachi, some 840 000 hectares of culturally and biologically significant country centred on the Wenlock and Pascoe Rivers in central Cape York Peninsula. He is the Chairman of the Chuulangun Aboriginal Corporation, the peak body for land and resource management, homelands and economic development for Kaanju homelands. In 2003 he was the Inaugural Indigenous Visiting Fellow at the Centre for Aboriginal Economic Policy Research, The Australian National University and was Visiting Fellow again in 2005. He has published and presented a number of papers in the area of Indigenous land management, land tenure and Indigenous policy.

Dennis Foley

Dennis Foley is an Endeavour Fellow and a Fulbright Scholar lecturing at the Australian Graduate School of Entrepreneurship. His blood connection is with the Gammeray, the Gatlay and the Gaimai. His father is a descendant of the Capertee/Turon River people, of the Wiradjuri. Dennis identifies as a descendent of the Gai-mariagal people. He is the author of *Repossession: of Our Spirit*, an ethnographic study of his family, and *Successful Indigenous Australian Entrepreneurs: A Case Study Analysis*.

Katie Glaskin

Katie Glaskin has worked as an applied anthropologist in the area of native title, largely in the Kimberley region, since 1994. In 2002, she was the recipient of the inaugural Berndt Foundation Post Doctoral Research Fellowship at the University of Western Australia, where she is currently a Senior Lecturer. With James Weiner, she co-edited *Custom: Indigenous Tradition and Law in the Twenty-First Century* (*The Asia Pacific Journal of Anthropology* Special Issue 7(1), 2006) and *Customary Land Tenure and Registration in Australia and Papua New Guinea: Anthropological Perspectives* (Asia-Pacific Environment Monograph Series, ANU E-Press, 2007).

Julie Lahn

Julie Lahn is an anthropologist at the Centre for Aboriginal Economic Policy Research, The Australian National University. Her work on Australian Indigenous issues addresses a number of core themes including morality, relatedness, marine resource use, religion, repatriation, and native title and land rights. She has worked with Torres Strait Islanders since 1994, when she conducted her doctoral research. She has been an anthropological consultant since 1998 and has prepared numerous reports documenting the native title interests of Torres Strait Islanders and more recently those of Aboriginal people in southwest Cape York.

Frances Morphy

Frances Morphy is a Fellow at the Centre for Aboriginal Economic Policy Research, The Australian National University. She is an anthropologist and linguist whose research since 1974 has largely focused on the Yolngu people of north east Arnhem Land. In the late 1990s and early 2000s she assisted in the preparation of the Blue Mud Bay native title claim, and wrote the linguistic report in support of the claim. She is co-editor (with Jon Altman and Tim Rowse) of *Land Rights at Risk? Evaluations of the Reeves Report* (CAEPR Research Monograph No. 14, 1999), and co-editor (with Bill Arthur) of the *Macquarie Atlas of Indigenous Australia: Culture and Society through Space and Time* (2005).

Anthony Redmond

Anthony Redmond has worked in the northern Kimberley region with Ngarinyin people and their near neighbours since 1994. During this time he has conducted both academic research (into transforming local economies, the relationships with pastoralists, traditional cosmology, sung traditions and bodily experience of time and country) as well as applied native title research. His most recent works have been treatments of death and grieving, the comic in everyday Ngarinyin life, the social and ritual importance of body fat, and a phenomenology of travelling in community trucks. Anthony is currently a Visiting Research Fellow at the Centre for Aboriginal Economic Policy Research, The Australian National University.

Steven Ross

Steven Ross is a Wamba Wamba man from Deniliquin in southern New South Wales, with cultural and familial connections to the Muthi Muthi and Wiradjuri Nations. He has been the coordinator of the Murray Lower Darling Rivers Indigenous Nations since late 2003, having previously worked for the NSW Cabinet Office, NSW Department of Aboriginal Affairs and NSW Attorney General's Department. A graduate in Government and Public Administration from the University of Sydney, he also studied at the University of Edinburgh in 2002, as a British Council Chevening Scholar.

Benedict Scambary

Benedict Scambary is an anthropologist with over 10 years experience working with the Native Title Act in the Northern Territory. As an employee of the Northern Land Council he was involved in the coordination of the Larrakia native title claims over Darwin. He has recently completed a PhD in anthropology through the Centre for Aboriginal Economic Policy Research, The Australian National University.

Benjamin R. Smith

Benjamin Smith is a Research Fellow at the Centre for Aboriginal Economic Policy Research, The Australian National University. His research interests include the social effects of customary land claims, the relationship between Indigenous Australians and the state, and the intercultural character of contemporary Indigenous life-worlds. He has carried out both academic and applied research with Aboriginal people in Cape York Peninsula and other locations across northern Queensland. His recent publications include '"More than love": locality and affects of indigeneity in Northern Queensland' (*The Asia Pacific Journal of Anthropology*, 7(3), December 2006) and '"We got our own management": local knowledge, government and development in Cape York Peninsula' (*Australian Aboriginal Studies* 2005/2).

James F. Weiner

James F. Weiner has held academic appointments at the ANU, the University of Manchester and the University of Adelaide. Since 1998 he has been a full-time consultant anthropologist in the fields of native title, social mapping in Papua New Guinea (where he has conducted over three years of fieldwork), and cultural heritage in Australia. He is the recent co-editor of *Customary Land Tenure and Registration in Australia and Papua New Guinea: Anthropological Perspectives* (ANU E Press, 2007), and of *Custom: Indigenous Tradition and Law in the Twenty-First Century* (*The Asia Pacific Journal of Anthropology*, vol. 7(1) 2006).

Jessica Weir

Jessica Weir is a Visiting Research Fellow in the Native Title Research Unit at the Australian Institute of Aboriginal and Torres Strait Islander Studies. A human geographer, her research focuses on ecological and social issues, particularly water and ecological devastation, and the relationship between Indigenous representative structures and natural resource management institutions. She is currently completing her PhD thesis at the Fenner School of Environment and Society, The Australian National University, on 'Murray River Country: An Ecological Dialogue with Traditional Owners'. This project is supported by a research agreement with the Murray Lower Darling Rivers Indigenous Nations.

Abbreviations and acronyms

ABC	Australian Broadcasting Commission
AIATSIS	Australian Institute of Aboriginal and Torres Strait Islander Studies
ALA	*Aboriginal Land Act 1991* (Qld)
ALP	Australian Labor Party
ALRA	*Aboriginal Land Rights (Northern Territory) Act 1976* (Cwlth)
ATSIC	Aboriginal and Torres Strait Islander Commission
BDAPR	*Batavia Downs Aspirations Planning Report*
CAEPR	Centre for Aboriginal Economic Policy Research
CDEP	Community Development Employment Projects
CEO	Chief Executive Officer
CLP	Country Liberal Party
CYLC	Cape York Land Council
DNRM	Department of Natural Resources and Mines (Qld)
DSE	Department of Sustainability and the Environment (Vic)
FCAATSI	Federal Council for the Advancement of Aborigines and Torres Strait Islanders
ILC	Indigenous Land Corporation
ILUA	Indigenous Land Use Agreement
IPA	Indigenous Protected Area
LNAC	Larrakia Nation Aboriginal Corporation
LRA	*Land Rights Act No. 42 1983* (NSW)
Mabo (No. 2)	*Mabo v Queensland (No. 2)* [1992]
MLDRIN	Murray Lower Darling Rivers Indigenous Nations
NLC	Northern Land Council
NNTT	National Native Title Tribunal
NTA	*Native Title Act 1993* (Cwlth)
NTRB	Native Title Representative Body
PBC	Prescribed Body Corporate
PGA	Pastoralists' and Graziers' Association
TSILA	*Torres Strait Islander Land Act 1991* (Qld)
TSRA	Torres Strait Regional Authority
Wik	*Wik Peoples v State of Queensland* [2004]
WRIMP	Wimmera Indigenous Resource Management Partnership
Yorta Yorta	*The members of the Yorta Yorta Aboriginal Community v The State of Victoria & Ors* [1998]

1. The social effects of native title: recognition, translation, coexistence

Benjamin R. Smith and Frances Morphy

Native title has had a profound social impact in Australia. Its effects have been felt from the local level through to the national level ever since the success of the Mabo No.2 case in the Federal Court. But despite the involvement of large numbers of anthropologists in the field of native title practice (alongside lawyers, historians, archaeologists and others trained in the social sciences and humanities) there has been surprisingly little reflection on the social effects of native title. Native title law and native title claims, negotiation of Indigenous Land Use Agreements (ILUAs) and other processes associated with the *Native Title Act 1993* (Cth) (NTA) and its amendments all present themselves as candidates for analysis by social scientists. But although there is now an extensive literature on native title, almost all of this literature is concerned with Native Title *practice*.[1] Far fewer scholars and practitioners—many of whom are publishing academics as well as consultants or employees of various agencies engaged in native title work—have engaged with native title as a social phenomenon potentially (we would argue necessarily) deserving of critical reflection.

This collection seeks to make a contribution towards the study of the *social effects* of native title. Based on a workshop which took place in November 2005 at The Australian National University, convened by the Centre for Aboriginal Economic Policy Research, the collection includes papers by anthropologists, claimants and other practitioners and scholars dealing with the direct and indirect effects of native title on particular places and people. In particular the collection provides a range of responses to widespread complaints by Aboriginal Australians and Torres Strait Islanders that native title delivers little in the way of meaningful recognition of customary property rights (or the systems of 'law and custom' in which these rights are embedded), that where such 'recognition' occurs it

---

[1] There is, however, a more developed anthropological literature—which includes a significant critical dimension—on Australia's various State and Territory Aboriginal Land Rights Acts; see, for example, Berndt and Berndt (1984); Hiatt (1984); Merlan (1998); Morphy and Morphy (2001); Rumsey (1989); Smith (2003). Although they maintain a focus on Native Title practice, Sutton (2003) and Toussaint (2004) both make valuable contributions to the anthropological theorisation of native title, whilst Povinelli (2002) contains a significant critique of the social effects of Native Title. A number of the papers in Sullivan and Bauman (2006) (in particular Bauman 2006a; Correy 2006; Langton, et. al. 2006) also discuss the social effects of native title. Likewise, much of the work undertaken by the Native Title Research Unit (NTRU) at the Australian Institute of Aboriginal and Torres Strait Islander Studies is relevant to the social effects of native title. In particular, the work of the NTRU's Indigenous Facilitation and Mediation Project has examined the conflict and unsustainable outcomes arising out of poor decision making and management within the native title process (see Bauman 2005, 2006b; Bauman and Williams 2005).

mistranslates and transforms local Aboriginal 'cultures of connection' to land, and that native title produces unnecessary conflict both between Indigenous groups, and also between claimants and other parties.

A critical examination of the effects or impacts of native title seems particularly timely. Following the Federal Government's 1998 amendments to the NTA (the '10 point plan') and the development of native title case law, native title has increasingly been seen as disappointing or even dangerous by many Indigenous Australians. As Lahn (Chapter 7) notes, the initial optimism that surrounded the Mabo decision has given way to a perception of relatively few benefits or even 'further dispossession' flowing from the NTA. Certainly, a number of prominent Indigenous commentators have questioned the trajectory taken by native title law. Noel Pearson, for example, has been extremely critical of the way that native title has come to take its meaning from the NTA and its amendments, writing that the High Court's decision relating to the Miriuwung-Gajerrong people

> has killed off any possibility that the common law of Australia would continue to provide the parameters for reconciliation between the sovereign claim of the Crown and the rights of indigenous peoples as the original occupants of their traditional homelands ... [t]he High Court incorrectly, and with the consent of the Aboriginal parties appearing before it, treated native title as a creature of the Native Title Act rather than understanding that this legislation was never intended to change the concept of native title at common law (Pearson 2002).

For Pearson, this decision 'short-changed' Aboriginal Australians, being based on an 'anthropological rather than common law' conception of native title. Pearson's comments, however, mask the fact that many anthropologists have themselves been critical of the direction taken by native title. But if we take his comments on an 'anthropological conception' to indicate a prescriptive rather than 'open' form of recognition, then they draw our attention to the *effects* of native title in delimiting and forcefully re-shaping the character of Indigenous ties to traditional lands.

There have also been increasing criticisms of native title from across the political spectrum. The Howard Government has been vehement in its ongoing criticism of native title, arguing both that native title has failed to deliver tangible benefits to Aboriginal people, and that it has significantly impacted economic development, particularly in 'regional' Australia. This continuing governmental critique has also led to practical interventions, most notably the Federal government's '10 point plan', developed in response to the success of the Wik and Wik Way peoples' native title claim in western Cape York Peninsula. More recently, the Howard government has sought to overhaul the native title system to ensure the faster and more efficient processing of native title claims. In so doing, the government has inquired into the effectiveness of representative Aboriginal and Torres Strait Islander bodies, the relationship between the Federal Court and the National Native Title Tribunal, the effectiveness of Native Title Tribunal mediation, and the ways in which prescribed bodies corporate operate. On the basis of their continuing criticisms and interventions, it remains unclear to what degree the Howard government wishes to improve the functioning of Australia's native title system and its ability to produce tangible effects, and to what degree the government wishes to further lessen native title's impacts on the status quo.

In this collection, we identify three main effects of native title. Firstly, a number of the papers deal with the issue of *recognition*—the ways in which the native title process establishes particular groups of Indigenous Australians as (potential) 'native title holders'. As a number of the papers suggest, rather than simply recognising pre-existent social groups and importing wholesale the manner in which traditional law and custom operate in local Indigenous contexts into the 'mainstream' or the 'intercultural' context of native title, the process of 'recognition' is necessarily partial and transformative. The 'effects' of native title thus include the ways in which 'recognition' operates as a particular social and cultural process.

Secondly, several of the papers explore the closely linked theme of *translation*. Anthropology—deeply embedded, in Australia, in the practice of native title and its social effects—is often spoken of (more or less problematically) as a discipline that specialises in 'cultural translation'.[2] But translation is never a simple or direct process. For translation to be possible in any simple sense there must be commensurability between the terms of the two systems—linguistic or cultural—between which the act of translation is taking place. In practice, in translating a language—or a set of culturally inflected forms and practices—there is almost always a transformation. This goes largely unrecognised in the native title process, which in some respects can be viewed as an exercise in 'enforced commensurability' (Morphy, Chapter 2, and see Povinelli 2001). A number of the papers in this collection explore the effects of such translation-induced transformations both within the native title process itself (for example, in the courtroom or in the process leading to a consent determination[3]) and in the effects that 'flow on' from the native title process (in the existence and practice of codified native title 'rights and interests', and in acts of 'misrecognition', for instance).

---

[2] The anthropological 'translation process' involves the construction of a meta-language in terms of which comparison between two cultural forms can then be framed. Morphy (Chapter 2) distinguishes this process as explication rather than translation.

[3] As one of the readers for the ANU E Press notes, the settling of a native title claim by consent and a determination of native title following a full trial involve markedly different processes which will likely lead to different—although not completely distinct—social effects.

Lastly, this collection explores issues relating to *coexistence*—the ways that particular individuals, groups and 'peoples' live together. This includes both the coexistence of different Indigenous groups or factions, who may either cooperate with and support or contest claims to native title by other Aboriginal people or Torres Strait Islanders, as well as the coexistence of Indigenous and non-Indigenous or 'settler' Australians. Taken together the papers reveal that the circumstances of coexistence vary considerably from place to place and context to context. More broadly, the papers also consider the implications of coexistence at broader levels—between State and Territory governments and Indigenous populations for example. In all of these instances, coexistence has been deeply affected by the 'native title era', in both positive and negative ways.

Recognition

> [T]here is a profound irony involved in the idea of recognition: the very desire that makes that ideal so compelling—the desire for sovereign agency, for an antidote to the riskiness and intermittent opacity of social life—may itself help to sustain some of the forms of injustice that many proponents of recognition rightly aim to overcome.
>
> (Patchen Markell, *Bound by Recognition,* p. 5)

As Manu Barcham (Chapter 11) notes, the last 20 years have seen unprecedented levels of recognition given to the Indigenous peoples of Australia. Citing Fraser's (1995) claim that the politics of recognition has replaced the politics of redistribution in Anglo-American counties, Barcham cautions that recognition involves particular social and cultural transformations which may produce problems as well as benefits for Indigenous people.

These problems of recognition are insightfully identified by the political philosopher Patchen Markell. Markell (2003)—building on Hegel's account of the 'struggle for recognition', and responding to the recent explosion in the politics of recognition—identifies two interrelated grounds for concern about such a politics. Firstly, he suggests that we might take note of a strand of political thought, running from Tocqueville to Arendt, that cautions against the idea that we might be able to achieve certainty in social and political relations. Rather than being problematic, or even pathological, 'uncertainty' may well name an irreducible condition of human life. As several of the authors in this collection note, the desire for certainty has been at the heart of responses to the advent and development of native title. Moreover, it may well be that indeterminacy is even more important within the context of Indigenous cultural production than in other social and political contexts (see Smith 2003b). Even if this is not the case, Markell cautions us against a desire for certainty, through recognition, that may 'blind us to certain ineliminable, and perhaps also valuable, aspects of our own situation' (2003: 4).

Noel Pearson's (1997) model of the 'recognition space' allows us to explore the
operation and the perhaps problematic effects of recognition on the basis of
native title in Australia. Pearson's model—from which he has now
resiled—presents native title as existing in the overlap between distinct fields
of Aboriginal law and Australian law. This model has continued to be touchstone
for those seeking to understand this process, in particular through the work of
David Martin and Christos Mantziaris (see Mantziaris and Martin 2000; Martin
2004) cited by several of the contributors to this collection.

For Martin, the recognition space also involves a process of translation (see
below) and a hegemonic, rather than equal interplay between the two forms of
property law that coincide in this space. Further, Martin also notes that the
recognition space is only one aspect of a complex series of interconnections
between Indigenous and non-Indigenous sociocultural forms (see also Smith,
Chapter 6).

In his review of Mantziaris and Martin's (2000) book—which contains their
account of the recognition space—Weiner (2003) claims that anthropologists
need to be more critical of 'the legalistic appropriation of anthropological and
ethnographic methodology' and deal with native title as a 'total social fact' (see
also Lahn, Chapter 7)—that is, as a social phenomenon which re-shapes the local
and broader social contexts with which it articulates. Martin (2003: 3) has, in
turn, replied to Weiner's critique, arguing that his and Mantziaris's use of the
'recognition space' concept, criticised by Weiner as over-simplifying the complex
interactions between Indigenous Australians and the wider society within which
they are now encompassed, was for the limited purpose of identifying the
difference between Aboriginal law and custom, and native title rights and
interests that develop through the legal process of recognition. Taken together,
Mantziaris and Martin's book and Weiner's critique are both of great use in
understanding the processes of recognition operating within the native title
process.

Another account of recognition in the native title context is provided by Patton
(1995, 2000), who presents a critical account of the operation of native title
law—that is, of native title as a 'social fact' in Weiner's terms. For Patton,
recognition is understood as part of a wider process of reterritorialisation in
response to the threatened rupture of the fabric of the settler nation-state in
Mabo No.2 and its aftermath. But this process remains ambiguous. While it
involves the transformative 'capture' (rather than simply recognition) of
Indigenous law by the common law of the settler state, it also bears the potential
of a commensurate capture of the state by indigenous law and custom, a
'becoming-indigenous of the common law to the extent that it now protects a
property right derived from indigenous law' (Patton 2000: 129, cited in Smith,
Chapter 6).

Of course, many Indigenous claimants recognise these problems. As Morphy (Chapter 2) notes, the Yolngu of North-East Arnhem Land came to see the operation of native title as part of an ongoing process of colonisation, having brought with them to the arena a sense of being 'encapsulated but not colonised'. Morphy argues that this does not involve a state of 'false consciousness' on the part of Yolngu claimants; rather, they recognised the power relations at play in the 'recognition space', but simultaneously problematised the legitimacy of the state's assertions, and insisted on the continuation of other social domains in which their own law and custom remain autonomous from the state, and dominate the construction of social action.

In southern Australia too, Aboriginal people continue to express concerns about the non-Indigenous determination of the character of native title, and the compromises and effects of native title claims. Whilst some of the Aboriginal people of the Murray and Lower Darling Rivers have chosen to pursue native title claims, their recognition of the limited—and increasingly narrow—character of 'recognition' offered by native title has led to the formation of an Indigenous alliance, the Murray Lower Darling Rivers Indigenous Nations (MLDRIN), to pursue more meaningful recognition outside the ambit of the Native Title Act (Weir and Ross, Chapter 10). For the members of MLDRIN, traditional ownership pre-exists and extends far beyond the limited recognition of rights and interests available as 'native title holders'. In negotiating agreements and partnerships outside of the native title framework, MLDRIN's members see themselves as gaining forms of recognition that come far closer to recognising them as 'self-determining' traditional owner groups than would be possible under the NTA, and which do not subject them to 'another colonial validation process'. But MLDRIN's members also see advantages in the native title system. In particular, native title is seen as a means to gain broader recognition of Indigenous rights, despite the risk of a commensurate loss of recognition where claims are unsuccessful.

Although Aboriginal people may recognise the complexities of being party to the native title process, the question of false consciousness, however uncomfortable, cannot be ignored. Many Aboriginal people, for example, continue to understand native title as being bound to continuing Indigenous sovereignty and maintain that they are able to hold a part of their sovereign selfhood at a reserve from their articulations with the state and the 'mainstream'. From the perspective of the courts enacting the native title process however—as Morphy (Chapter 2) rightly notes—sovereignty is not at issue with regard to the NTA. The High Court has already rejected the use of Native Title as 'a vehicle to claim indigenous legal and political sovereignty' (Mantziaris & Martin 2000: 28). To enter into a native title claim, no matter what reservations are voiced by claimants, is to submit to the state's authority over the contemporary existence of indigenous property rights, *even as they exist between Indigenous Australians*.

Whatever its potential 'symbolic' or 'practical' benefits, native title—at least as it exists under the NTA—involves the 'radical enactment of sovereignty' over colonised subjects (see also Lahn, Chapter 7). Further, the ability of Aboriginal people anywhere in Australia to think of themselves in a manner autonomous from the state and the mainstream remains open to question. It seems likely that many, if not all forms of contemporary Indigenous identity are at least inflected by forms of identity making—and the 'politics of recognition'—that are deeply tied to the 'encapsulating' mainstream both nationally and internationally.

From this perspective, Aboriginal claims of autonomy from an encapsulating nation-state seem problematic. As Weir and Ross (Chapter 10) rightly note, it is impossible to unpick the assertions of Indigenous group identity in the Murray-Darling region from the intercultural environment within which it came into being and continues to operate. Whilst it may be true that MLDRIN has a distinct character as a result of having emerged as the result of contemporary Indigenous social action (albeit with roots in ongoing 'custom and tradition'), both the kinds of group identities that coalesce within MLDRIN and the ways it operates as 'traditional owner' organisation are undoubtedly inflected by 'complex historical processes of interaction' between Aboriginal people and settler society (Weir and Ross, Chapter 10, citing Tully 2004). Both the forms of recognition offered to Indigenous Australians *and* the desire for recognition itself today form part of the intercultural existence of Aboriginal Australians and Torres Strait Islanders in the context of the nation-state (and, beyond Australia, the international context which is often cited by Indigenous Australians as a source of potential recognition beyond the limited forms offered by Australian governments).

One of the most common complaints Aboriginal Australians make about the native title process—itself based in a sense of autonomy and a desire for self-determination—is that native title involves 'Aboriginal people having to prove our right to "them" [i.e., to settler Australians and 'their' legal system]'. From this perspective, native title is again seen not just as a system of recognition, but also as a system of continuing colonial domination—Aboriginal people have to prove *their* 'rights', whilst settler law not only remains unquestioned, but also retains the authority to rule over the acceptability of Indigenous claims (cf. Morris 2003). Nonetheless, the desire of many Aboriginal people to gain recognition in the eyes of Australian law as 'traditional owners' puts many people in a position in which they must necessarily endure this process and its perceived inequities or questionable authority in order to protect their interests and continue to benefit from their connection to their country.

The authority of the non-Indigenous system of law in the native title context is evident in Morphy's description of the court proceedings in the Blue Mud Bay Native Title Claim (Chapter 2). Morphy notes the existence of elaborate court rules which determine who gets to speak, in what way, and at what points. This discursive structure emphasises the authority of the Judge, who can choose to speak freely at any time. But the Yolngu claimants, who are the most knowledgeable about their own system of 'laws and customs', have the most severely curtailed rights to speak in the space of the court. As Morphy notes, the court rules which structure the admissibility (or not) of various kinds of discourse (and of various speakers) 'seems designed … to emphasise the power of European law by systematically constraining the ability of the knowledgeable practitioners to express that law clearly *in its own terms and in its fullness*'. The result of these rules is that Yolngu law is 'present, but not enacted' in the court, 'rather, it is explicated through the mediating discourse of examination and cross-examination', which constrain the way in which Yolngu law is represented, forcing it to become merely subsidiary to both the terms and authority of European law.

The authority that inheres in the 'ritual space of the court' is also made evident in other ways. As Pierre Bourdieu has demonstrated, the organisation of particular social spaces is deeply connected to—and reproductive of—socio-religious structures. Like the Kabyle house analysed by Bourdieu (1977), the European courtroom, constructed according to an established set of rules, brings those attending the court into a spatial field saturated by particular cultural orientations. Whilst many such spaces appear as apparently culturally-uninflected or neutral to those whose own selfhood is established in the socio-cultural milieu from which the space is drawn, Morphy's identification of the courtroom as a 'ritual space' makes it clear that its intrinsic meanings are experienced as forceful even by those—the Judge, court officials, lawyers—to whom it is familiar. For other participants—in particular, the Yolngu claimants—the court is alienating not because of a simple cultural disjuncture, but because this disjuncture is one inextricably tied to the ritual performance of power in the person of the Judge and the legal apparatus he or she represents. Thus even before the court makes its authority evident through disciplining speech, this authority is established *prima facie* by the courtroom itself. As a literal manifestation of the supposed 'recognition space' of native title, the courtroom makes it abundantly clear to all participants—and to Aboriginal claimants in particular—that any such recognition will take place on the basis of particular cultural foundations, and under the authority of the Australian legal system.

As Morphy makes clear, however, although Yolngu claimants were forced to accommodate the court's authority within the native title process, they were also able to make their own system of law visible within the space of the court. Moreover, events that occurred during the court hearings were taken by the Yolngu claimants to be evidence of the power of an autonomous system of ancestral law that continues to inhere in country regardless of the attempts of Australian law to superimpose itself on Yolngu homelands.

Yolngu claimants successfully endeavoured to make their own law evident in the court through performing a ceremony to 'welcome' the judge and the court. Such performances, of course, continue to be an enactment of the local authority of particular Aboriginal groups. In participating in this ceremony (and a later performance of Yolngu law at Blue Mud Bay itself) the court implicitly acknowledged the ownership and *authority* of the clans conducting the welcome. Further, as Morphy notes, the ceremony *spatially* disrupted the court space, displacing most of the court officials and other non-Yolngu. This spatial displacement—notably not including the judge—made further implicit demonstration of the delimited nature of Yolngu claimants' accession to the court's authority.

The court's authority was further undermined, from a Yolngu perspective, by events that occurred during 'site visits' within the claim area. In particular, unusually rough conditions during a boat trip were interpreted by Yolngu claimants as a manifestation of local ancestral beings' displeasure. The evident power of these beings was evidence, for Yolngu, of incommensurability between 'European' and 'Yolngu' law. Whilst the court might insist on its own authority and power to shape the conditions of recognition within its own 'recognition space', the power of Yolngu ancestors made it evident that the court proceedings were unable to affect the ancestral power that underlies the Yolngu law and custom on which the court sought to operate.

The problem is, of course, that the NTA has extended the power of the Australian legal system further into Aboriginal lives. Even for the Yolngu of Blue Mud Bay, the power of local ancestral beings has only been able to translate into restricted intercultural rights with regard to the waters of the claim area. And these rights have themselves been objectified and transformed by the native title process.

The process of recognition entails the objectification, codification and hence reification of certain aspects of cultural practice as property rights under native title. This can lead to tension between the resulting textualised reifications of customary tenure and local Indigenous practice, as is demonstrated in the papers by Claudie (Chapter 5) and Foley (Chapter 9). For Claudie, native title process generates and supports structures that are at odds with local Indigenous land tenure and governance systems despite its supposed basis in recognising 'traditional law and custom'. In central Cape York Peninsula, native title claims lodged on behalf of broader language-named identity groups fail to take sufficient account of local principles assigning primary interests in particular areas to specific families or descent groups, or assigning the right to speak authoritatively to country differentially amongst the people associated with a particular area. Although both native title case law and the complexities of connection arguably make it necessary to be broadly inclusive in determining a claimant group in this region, such broad-based claims then allow for the possibility of the assertion of interests by members of the claimant group at odds with local Aboriginal law and custom.

Foley makes similar criticisms in relation to the effects of both the New South Wales *Land Rights Act 1983* and the NTA. In Foley's opinion, the New South Wales Act enabled a 'land grab' by local Aboriginal Land councils, often without the involvement or consent of local Aboriginal people. These land councils are perceived as being duplicitous in advertising and organising meetings, and excluding other Aboriginal people, in order to meet the needs of members exercising control over the council. If some land councils have been remiss in serving their constituents or clients, a number of Aboriginal people believe that others may have purposefully manipulated their role for personal benefits.

In the particular case discussed by Foley, the situation is made more complex by the fact that those Aboriginal people controlling the local land council do not identify themselves as traditional owners of areas which they control. Further, they have denied the continuing existence of any traditional owners in some of these areas, despite dealing with people on the basis of their 'custodianship' of these areas in other contexts. Foley argues that the current land council system needs to be revised to include traditional owners or custodians on executive committees, greater transparency in the operation of the land rights system, a land sales register created to protect those Aboriginal people who are not members of the local land council, and a review undertaken of who is able to act authoritatively in 'cultural heritage' matters (such as site clearance in advance of development projects).

In other instances, the dynamics of identification and objectification within the native title process—as well as in 'land rights' legislation—may have less problematic outcomes from the perspective of 'local' claimants. In Chapter 7, Lahn describes the way that native title claims produce new social groupings in response to the terms of the NTA and its interpretations. Lahn describes the situation on the Island of Warraber in the Torres Strait, where there are two contrasting modes of Indigeneity—*netiv* ('native') and *porena* ('foreigner').

Although all Warrabeans can trace both native and foreigner forebears, a local emphasis on patrilineal descent means that the majority assert a *porena* identity. A successful claim under the *Torres Strait Islander Land Act 1991* (TSILA) proceeded on the basis of 'customary affiliation'. However, the relatively open definition of key terms in the TSILA allowed recourse to local accounts of *Ailan kastom* ('Island tradition'), leading to a claim by a 'clan' group whose membership depended on either consanguineal *or* affinal ties (i.e. 'blood'/'descent' ties *or* ties through marriage) to families identified with a Vanuatan forbear. The principles of membership allowed for the emergence of an 'inclusive and seamless' claimant group.

Following TSILA claim, Warraber residents initiated a NT claim. However, as Lahn notes, '[t]he Native Title Act demanded a demonstration of emplaced social identity that was subject to much more sharply delimited terms of authenticity and legitimacy than [in the] TSILA'—in particular by emphasising specific forms of continuity with the colonial past. Lahn, who worked on the ensuing native title claim, notes that despite the superficially straightforward nature of producing a connection report in this context (e.g. identifiable Warraber ancestors present at annexation in 1872), the Warraber native title claim faced a fundamental problem. The laws and norms that shape the native title process 'marginalised and potentially stigmatised' the local principles that underlay the 'clan' identity which provided the focus for the TSILA claimant group. The principal ancestral figure in the previous TSILA claim was *not* a Torres Strait Islander and had never resided on Warraber, a situation that infringes what have come to be regarded as key requirements for the consent determination of native title in the State of Queensland.

As a result, a new group identity was asserted for the purposes of the native title claim, based on a number of *netiv* forebears (most of whom were women) and a collective identity as *Warraberalgal* ('people belonging to Warraber'). This new group accorded with the conditions for successful native title, but did so through departing from the normative local emphasis on male forebears and the established *porena* forebear-focused Gau Clan identity. As Lahn notes, the *Warraberalgal* native title claimant grouping marked native title as a realm of *intercultural* production, where an emergent group (and the linked local process of collective representation) was determined as much by the formal and informal expectations of the state as by continuities in local law and custom.

The contemporary and historical complexities of group identities are often elided in native title claims. This is ironic, given that native title has emerged as a historical context of particular import in the refiguring of local identities and groups. Whilst the need to 'get a claim over the line' is often seen as impeding a critical examination of regional histories of the articulation of Aboriginal identities, the papers in this collection point towards a rich and relatively under-examined aspect of Indigenous Australian life-worlds and their articulation with the Australian 'mainstream'. As the papers here indicate, native title can be the context for the development of new groups, the resurgence of 'undergrounded' Aboriginal identities (Sutton 2003) and the transformation of extant social categories in a changing intercultural context.

Here the effects of native title are shaped by the relatively conservative and limited forms of recognition it offers, forms that nonetheless have radical effects on both the 'content' of native title and the local social fields in which it acts. Like all social milieus—in particular those which have emerged from a recent history of colonialism—the life-worlds of Aboriginal Australians are founded in the interplay of received forms of knowledge and action ('traditional law and custom') and historical changes and interactions (see Smith, Chapter 6). However, native title tends to engage poorly with such histories, emphasising what is perceived to be traditional and excluding or rejecting what has been subject to profound historical impacts. One key effect of native title has been to crystallise local distinctions between 'traditional' and 'historical' people on this basis. As a result, a number of Indigenous settlements have experienced increased levels of conflict and stress as families who regard the settlement as their home find that they are being identified as 'second class citizens' in relation to those who identify and have perhaps succeeded in being recognised as 'traditional owners'.

However, as Foley and Claudie's papers suggest, this emphasis on the 'traditional' occurs in particular and limited ways. The 'traditional' recognised within the native title process may be at odds with what local Aboriginal groups or individuals regard as 'proper' law and custom, allowing 'outsiders' or those considered to have little or no traditional authority position themselves as 'traditional owners', and marginalising those who regard themselves as truly authoritative or entitled.

The distinction between tradition and history is also explored in Weiner's paper (Chapter 12), which suggests that the distinction represents an ongoing inability of anthropologists (and of the native title system more generally) to grapple with the relationship between cultural change and continuity as a result of differentiating social structure (or 'tradition') from historical processes and subjective experience. This problem is compounded where Aboriginal people insist on the unchangeability of the Law, a commensurate refusal of a constitutive relationship between culture and history.

Weiner notes that in a number of native title claims, issues of connection have been approached through a separation of accounts of historical occupation and activity on the one hand, and the cosmological reckoning of connection on the other. As he rightly points out, this bifurcate approach handicaps the possibility of presenting the two aspects of Indigenous connections as deeply imbricated in one another. In limiting the anthropologist's (and other 'experts') presentation of the iteration of 'traditional law and custom' through a history of practical engagements with 'country', this approach also limits the possibilities of arguing for the interweaving of change and continuity that likely exist across *all* of 'Indigenous Australia'. Further, to not link the two, from the perspective of social science 'expertise' is disingenuous—as Weiner notes, the distinction, in social science terms, is 'insupportable and factitious'.

For Weiner, the connections between history and anthropology have become increasingly hard to develop given the increasing acceptance of what he calls 'the project of mythopoeia' or 'memoriology', a blurring of the distinction between myth and history which leads to essentialist constructions of enduring cultural identities (see also Smith 2006). He notes the widespread use of oral history in native title claims as an alternative to (often absent) written records of previous Aboriginal social action. As Weiner notes, oral histories are often counterposed to 'objective history', polarising Aboriginal and non-Indigenous positions; proponents of Aboriginal rights simultaneously insist on the lack of difference between oral histories and written histories, equating them simply as equivalent kinds of texts. In insisting that this equivalence should be refused, Weiner does not seek to denigrate oral history. Rather, he draws our attention to the ways in which oral histories are aspects of the cultural constitution of identity. A particular kind of meaning-making that emerges from the interplay of event and human apperception, oral history, like other forms of mythic iteration, can be usefully examined by anthropologists assessing the continuities of law and custom in a particular milieu.

Building from Weiner's argument, it may be that anthropologists working in the field of native title might usefully examine the construction of the claimant group—and the arguments or reasons cited by claimants for this construction—as evidence for particular (and perhaps ongoing) forms of 'customary' practice. Doubtless, the desire evident both amongst anthropologists and other professionals working in the field of native title to present less processual accounts of group-ness limit the acceptability of this approach, providing further evidence of the kinds of bad faith that are evident in native title practice. Such an approach also involves a greater commitment to lengthy ethnographic research, which few NTRBs would be able or willing to support. Nonetheless, as Weiner argues—and as Lahn's case study (Chapter 7) also suggests—a defensible anthropological analysis of 'law and custom' must necessarily take account of the various forms of conjuncture (both between settler and indigenous histories, and between indigenous groups themselves) through which current Indigenous connections to country have been constituted. The problem remains whether such accounts will not open the claimants to challenges that may well lead to a finding of a 'loss of continuity' by courts that are less able or willing to accept such accounts of connection.

This ability of the courts to determine the extinguishment of native title is a major concern of native title practitioners, whether such extinguishment occurs on the basis of radical transformation of local Aboriginal law and custom or the development of settler property rights in a given area (in particular the granting of freehold tenure). As Lahn notes, rather than recognition *per se*, native title's principal effect may be the delimitation of Indigenous relations to land, or the endorsement of claims of extinguishment (see also Morris 2003). Further, as Wolfe (1999: 202) argues, the forms of 'repressive authenticity' demanded by native title displace the burden of historical extinguishment from the expropriating agency of the state to the character of the claimant group.

The outcome of the Yorta Yorta claim looms large in the native title landscape as the paradigmatic determination of the historical extinguishment of native title. In the Yorta Yorta claim Olney J found that the 'tide of history' had washed away any substantial continuity in law and custom among the claimants and their forebears (see Weir and Ross, Chapter 10).[4] The Yorta Yorta case made it clear that Aboriginal claimants—in particular those in the 'settled south' of Australia—would be subject to extremely conservative and limited grounds for recognition of their law and custom, although the recent finding in the Noongar case makes it clear that, in some cases at least, native title is able to be recognised in the 'south', albeit in extremely limited forms.

Following Yorta Yorta it has become evident that native title, as it exists under the Native Title Act, may be at odds with a continuing local system of Aboriginal law and custom pertaining to a particular area. Scambary (Chapter 8) notes that the Larrakia people of Darwin, like the Yorta Yorta, have been unable to gain legal recognition of native title rights and interests despite the court's recognition of the Larrakia community as 'a vibrant, dynamic society which embraces its history and traditions'. In the Larrakia claim, the effects of the settlement of Darwin, the arrival of other Aboriginal people into the area and the impacts of government policy proved enough for Mansfield J to find that the claimants had failed to maintain the required form of traditional and cultural continuity. As Scambary notes, this decision seemingly demonstrates the inability of the NTA to recognise a 'vibrant' society, with clear connections to its history and customs as native title holders.

Like the Warraber claim described by Lahn, the Larrakia native title claim was preceded by a land rights claim (under the Northern Territory's Aboriginal Land Rights Act (ALRA)), which led to the coalescence of a particular named group asserting customary ownership of the land in question. Unlike the TSILA claim, however, the Kenbi ALRA claim fed into the production of a series of disjunct, competing groups asserting traditional rights over parts of the wider Darwin region. Competition between Larrakia factions included the establishment of separate corporations and public contestation at opening ceremonies of other Larrakia groups' credentials. The establishment of an umbrella organisation—the Larrakia Nation Aboriginal Corporation—intended to provide a corporate identity for Larrakia factions also had the unintended result of supporting Mansfield J's determination of extinguishment, being cited as evidence for the radical transformation of traditional decision-making processes.

Dissatisfaction with the limits of recognition of customary land tenure and other aspects of Indigenous Australians' connections to their country have led an

---

[4] As one of the referees for the ANU E Press notes, although the Yorta Yorta case has become the focus for much discussion of the 'tide of history' in relation to native title, the more recent Larrakia and Wongatha judgements have led to further developments on this issue.

increasing number to seek alternatives to the native title system.[5] In central Cape York Peninsula, for instance, Kaanju people's dissatisfaction with native title—discussed in Claudie's paper (Chapter 5)—has led to alternative strategies for the recognition of Kaanju aspirations for land management. In particular, Kaanju people have developed a proposal for an Indigenous Protected Area (IPA) under Federal environmental legislation, which they have used as the basis for partnerships with various governmental, non-governmental and private sector organisations to gain recognition of their indigenous system of governance and management (see Smith and Claudie 2003). The Yolngu are also following this course, with the recent declaration of stage 1 of the Laynhapuy IPA in the Blue Mud Bay area. Similarly, members of several Aboriginal traditional owner groups from the Murray and Lower Darling Rivers in south-eastern Australia, as well as the Wotjobaluk of the Wimemera-Mallee country (see below),[6] have negotiated agreements with the Victorian government and other 'mainstream' agencies outside of the NTA. In the case of the Murray and Lower Darling Rivers groups, this course of action has been taken partly in response to the failure of the Yorta Yorta people (who are one of the Indigenous 'nations' on the Murray River system) to have native title rights and interests recognised (see Weir and Ross, Chapter 10). All of these cases demonstrate an increasing desire of Aboriginal groups (and government agencies) to circumvent the NTA and find other routes to developing meaningful and substantial forms of recognition of traditional ownership that lead to tangible social, economic and environmental outcomes.

In many cases, the 'business' of recognition may be impeded by the complex dealings between parties representing Aboriginal claimants and other stakeholders in the native title process. Claudie (Chapter 5) outlines perceived failings by a regional land council, which was seen to be responsive rather than proactive in its engagements with the State government. As Claudie points out, these frustrations are (in part, at least) explicable as the result of limited resources and staff, such that land councils are unable to progress all but the most pressing matters at any given time. Even where the reasons for such delays are explained to claimants (and this is not always the case), they do little to persuade Aboriginal people that they are being well served by the native title process.

Doubtless it is these kinds of complexities, in addition to the limited outcomes available in most (although not all) cases, the unpredictable outcomes of court decisions, the lengthy negotiations that may eventually lead to a consent

---

[5] Although they are a part of the native title system, Indigenous Land Use Agreements (ILUAs) have also become increasingly important as an alternative means of addressing the limited ability of a determination of native title to meet the aspirations of 'traditional owners' and other parties across Australia.

[6] In the November 2005 workshop, where earlier versions of the papers collected here were presented, members of the Wotjobaluk people, in collaboration with employees of State government agencies, described the outcomes they have managed to negotiate beyond the determination of native title. Unfortunately this paper (Beer et al. 2005) was not able to be included in the present collection.

determination, and the kinds of intra-Indigenous and local conflicts that develop in the native title context which have led to the seeking of alternative routes for recognition of indigenous ties to land. Nonetheless, it is unclear how many of these alternatives would be available without the pressure exerted on other partiers by native title claims. In any case, it is clear that we are now dealing with a complex and evolving system of recognition, within which Aboriginal people and Torres Strait Islanders are increasing their ties with 'mainstream' agencies and organisations—and the rest of Australian society—whilst retaining distinct identities as members of particular Indigenous groups.

Translation

> Any translation inherently compromises the original
>
> (John McWhorter, *The Power of Babel*, p. 38)

Translation is a key element of the native title process. As Mantziaris and Martin note, 'native title involves a process of translation from indigenous "relations" defined by traditional law and custom to native title rights and interests enforceable within the Australian legal system. This process of translation becomes difficult, or impossible, when the terms of the translation are incommensurable' (2000: 29; see also Morphy, Chapter 2).

The linked issues of translation and incommensurability are deeply imbricated in the effects of native title. Whilst such incommensurability is neither inevitable nor uncircumventable, several of the papers in this collection suggest that translation and incommensurability *do* present problems in the context of native title processes, and that these problems are compounded by the force and authority brought to bear by the native title system, to the benefit of some parties and the detriment of others. Povinelli (2001) draws attention to the issue of power relations in determining 'linguistic distortion (commensurability and incommensurability)', citing Asad's comment that insofar as 'the languages of the Third World societies ... are "weaker" in relation to Western languages ... they are more likely to submit to forcible transformation in the translation process than the other way round' (Asad 1986: 157–8, cited in Povinelli 2001: 324). In the native title context, it is Indigenous terms and social forms that are required to submit to transformation, in a process that Morphy (Chapter 2) terms 'enforced commensurability'. The Yolngu 'insistence on difference' can be seen as a form of rhetorical resistance to this process.

Lahn's case study (Chapter 7) provides a clear example of forcible transformation. The English-based Torres Strait Creole terms *'neitiv'* and *'porena'* both reference types of indigeneity acknowledged by Torres Strait Islanders, but 'this situation is a difficult one to render in English, which lacks adequate means to characterise such a contrast in a way that still affirms an embracing state of indigeneity'. English's problem is turned back onto the Warraberan native title applicants, who had previously pursued a successful land claim under the TSILA under a collective representation, the Gau clan, which stressed patrilineal descent from *porena* ancestors. In their native title case, in the context of a regime which 'marginalised and potentially stigmatised' *porena* indigeneity, the applicants were forced to adopt an alternative form of collective representation as *Warraberalgal* 'people belonging to Warraber' who traced descent primarily through *neitiv* female ancestors.

Another example of the problems of 'translation' in the context of native title is provided by Morphy (Chapter 2) in her analysis of the workings of the court in the Blue Mud Bay Native Title claim. In the Blue Mud Bay case, the court's hearing of evidence relied partly on 'witness statements', prepared statements that are intended to assist the court by reducing the amount of time taken up by hearing evidence, ensuring the applicants' case is well-articulated and allowing other parties time to consider their response. Morphy—who acted as an expert assisting the court in this case—discusses her concerns that the written form of such statements potentially disadvantaged Aboriginal witnesses. The perceived disadvantage lay with potential problems of understanding and translation. In the Blue Mud Bay case, Selway J was not inclined to take such claims into consideration, noting the 'intelligence and relative sophistication [with regard to the workings of European society]' demonstrated by most of the Yolngu witnesses. Nonetheless he did note 'potential issues arising from translation between Yolngu language and English'.

Morphy argues that, rather than simply 'translation', the preparation of witness statements involves a complex process in which a Yolngu concept, which may have no direct equivalent in English, is presented in the context of an English statement. This statement is later glossed by Land Council lawyers (in the form of an affidavit), replacing the terms in Yolngu-matha with what are taken to be commensurate terms in English. This affidavit is, in turn, presented back to the witness, often with a translator present, and sworn as his or her own statement. Unfortunately two key presumptions in this process—that there are simple equivalents for words/concepts drawn from one language in another language, and that the words use to gloss Yolngu terms have the same meaning for the witness and for the court—do not hold. Rather, the process of replacing a term in Yolngu-matha with an English term obscures the particular meaning of the Yolngu term within its own cultural context. Further, the use of number English terms in the legal context (e.g. 'permission') in witness statements commit the Yolngu witness to legal claims whose particular meanings are invisible to the witness and potentially at variance with the claims they were trying to make in their original statement. This can present particular problems when witnesses are cross-examined on the contents of 'their' statements, which can lead to apparent differences or contradictions between the witness's response and 'their' earlier statement, potentially undermining their case. Alternatively, the potential disjuncture between the language of a witness statement and the witness's oral evidence can also be used to cast doubt on the provenance of the written statement, and its admissibility as evidence in the proceedings.

Markell argues that a politics of recognition—including one based on notions of difference—may lead to the continuation or extension of deep-seated relations of inequality and power (2003: 4-5). In situations of cultural difference, the inequalities effected by 'recognition' may include forms of misrecognition that although superficially cognisant of (or based on) difference, in fact manifest ethnocentric and transformative engagements with disempowered groups. It could be argued that the source of this misrecognition in Australian native title is the insistence on translatability through a process of enforced commensurability. Several of the papers in this collection suggest that misrecognition of this kind is, indeed, common in the native title context, a suggestion likely to cause some discomfort for those anthropologists—among others—who have seen involvement in native title claims as a means to further social justice in relation to Indigenous Australians.

In Chapter 3, Glaskin examines the transformative impacts of native title, drawing on her research with Bardi and Jawi people in the northwest Kimberley. For Glaskin, native title does not simply recognise, but rather *codifies* Aboriginal property rights. Indeed, the native title process demands that claimants themselves articulate and objectify aspects of their property relations. These include aspects of Aboriginal cultural practice that are normatively implicit, and Glaskin argues that the discursive reification of these aspects of cultural practice, and the ensuing 'dialectics of articulation', will likely have considerable impact on the social lives of Bardi and Jawi claimants.

Following Wagner (1981[1975]), Glaskin suggests that any 'self-conscious' articulation of 'culture' will be constrained by the strictures of identity. In the case of native title claims, self-conscious definitions may well 'feed back' into the identities of native title holders in the manner identified by Hirsch (2001) as the 'looping effect of human kinds', which occurs 'especially where such objectification becomes reified or codified in some form'. Whilst Bardi and Jawi people have long reified aspects of their law and culture—in particular in ritual or religious knowledge and practice—the forms of reification involved in native title claims are likely to have very different effects to these indigenous practices of reification. Detached from the field of the 'inner workings' of Bardi and Jawi society, the intercultural or 'conjunctural' field of native title demands forms of reification alien to local practices of cultural production. In particular, the composition of a prescribed body corporate, a necessity following a successful native title claim, meant that Bardi and Jawi people found themselves attempting to objectify their traditional cultural principles or 'rules' to shape the workings of the new corporation. Glaskin notes that the codification of principles and processes within portions of the draft constitution represented a transition from the previously informal and negotiative enactment of the local Aboriginal jural public. The native title process is leading to an explicit formulation of the principles of customary law. This textual codification seems likely to 'transform 'social values and practices' by freezing these at a given point in time and thereby 'encouraging stasis in the system', with the system itself likely to 'dialectically evolve with reference to these representations' (Glaskin, Chapter 3, citing Mantziaris and Martin 2000: 43; see also Smith 2003b). Moreover, this process of textualisation may potentially lead the resolution of questions of interpretation of local laws and customs—questions whose articulation lies at the heart of the enactment of Aboriginal 'law'—to be taken over to a greater or lesser extent by outside experts, including lawyers and anthropologists.

Glaskin suggests that the articulation of textualised reifications of Aboriginal law and custom may also lead to increased conflict between Aboriginal groups or factions. Similarly, Barcham (Chapter 11) suggests that the 'neo-traditional corporate constructs' that emerged in response to recent policies regarding Māori property and resource rights led to a number of acrimonious court battles between *iwi* ('tribal') groups and representatives of urban Māori. Like Glaskin, Barcham suggests that the articulation between 'frozen' or reified versions of Indigenous society and the ongoing iterations of local Indigenous practice may become increasingly problematic.

Coexistence

> [N]ot being able to say 'we' is what plunges every 'I,' whether individual or collective, into the insanity where he cannot say 'I' either. To want to say 'we' is not at all sentimental, not at all familial or 'communitarian.' It is existence reclaiming its due or its condition: coexistence.
>
> (Jean-Luc Nancy, *Being Singular Plural*, p. 42)

One of the most important social effects of native title has been its impact on coexistence. Since the initial success of the Mabo No. 2 claim and the passing of the NTA, native title has been labelled as a threat to co-existence. Such claims are exemplified by the statements made following the passage of the Act by the then Deputy Prime Minister Tim Fischer's about the threat to Australians' backyards (claims echoed in the Attorney-General Philip Ruddock's recent claims that the Noongar native title case in Perth represents a threat to beaches and parks around Australia).

In Chapter 6, Smith discusses the relationship between Aboriginal people and pastoralists in central Cape York Peninsula, at the eastern fringes of the Wik claim area. Until recently, these relationships have remained extremely close, but also deeply marked by the history of indentured labour relationships between Aborigines and settlers. But a decline in Aboriginal employment following the 'freedom' of the 1970s has weakened—although not removed—these ties, which were further strained by the advent of land rights and the NTA). Non-Indigenous pastoralists' responses to the Wik claim were initially extremely negative, and many claimed that the recognition of native title rights and interests in the area of their pastoral leases would bankrupt them. However, following the Howard government's 10-point plan and a growing understanding of the practical effects of native title, many (although not all) of the region's pastoralists became more willing to negotiate ILUAs and support a determination of limited native title rights in their lease areas. In so doing, a number of the pastoralists publicly asserted their desire to re-develop ties with local Aboriginal families, whilst also stressing their need for control of activities in their lease areas and their desire for privacy.

This mixture of solicitation of social relationships and assertion of the need for control and privacy is at least superficially reminiscent of the now widely-recognised dynamic between autonomy and relatedness that lies at the heart of Aboriginal social relations (Martin 1993; Myers 1986). Certainly the pastoralists' asserted needs were recognised by the Aborigines with whom they were negotiating proposed ILUAs—not least because most of the Aborigines were themselves familiar with the requirements of running a cattle station. But Smith argues that there are more than superficial parallels or particular historical ties at play in such situations. Rather, the intercultural space of negotiation between Aborigines and settlers in remote Australia itself subsists within a more general human orientation to relations with and between other persons. Perhaps the most successful approach made by the settlers in the context of the ILUA negotiations was an emphasis on face-to-face and informal negotiation of ongoing coexistence rather than on formal legal structures. This inter-personal emphasis resonates strongly with the indeterminate or 'uncertain' but heavily interactive character of local Aboriginal sociality in a manner that reassured the Aboriginal claimants that a meaningful social outcome was possible as part of the agreement-making process. Nonetheless, there was some ingenuousness to the pastoralists' claims—their insistence on informal relations took place against the backdrop of a formal agreement that they were assured allowed them near-absolute control over when and where Aborigines could make use of country within their leases. And it seems certain that there would have been no such negotiations unless the NTA had impelled the settlers to 'come to the table' in the first place. Thus whilst meaningful 'informal' coexistence (and, arguably, a measure of social justice) may yet emerge from the Wik decision, it has taken the *formal* force of the law to bring this about.

Redmond's paper (Chapter 4) similarly addresses the topic of 'pathways out of the near-hegemonic relations of the past' in the context of the native title process. In the Northern Kimberley, the suppressed memories of historical oppression of Aboriginal people by European pastoralists were laid bare in the adversarial process of the pursuit of native title. Nonetheless, as in central Cape York Peninsula, Aboriginal and non-Indigenous parties in the native title process were both required to and in many cases remain desirous of continuing to co-exist in the region.

Like Morphy (Chapter 2), Redmond focuses on the courtroom as the social context within which competing constructions of Aboriginal connections were articulated. In the case of the Ngarinyin peoples' claim, however, the contestation of continuing Aboriginal title included counter-claims made by a number of local pastoralists, many of whom have long-standing social connections with Ngarinyin people. These pastoralists included both an 'elite' contingent, and other pastoralists who represented themselves as 'battlers'. With regard to both sets of pastoralists, the native title claim saw a worsening of social relationships with the Aboriginal claimants. The perceived threat of native title to the pastoralists' interests led to an aggressive challenge to the Ngarinyin claim, accompanied by attempts to exclude claimants from cattle stations, even after a successful determination of native title rights and interests in the areas covered by the pastoralists' leases. The pastoralists were also aggrieved by the manner in which the court proceedings elicited frank accounts of the mistreatment of Aboriginal workers and their families by their white 'bosses', despite Aboriginal attempts to accompany such accounts with reference to the close ties that have continued to exist between the Ngarinyin and their employers.

Despite the context of the courtroom—which, as Redmond notes, might have proved overwhelming for the claimants, given that for most of them it had only ever been experienced as a place of punishment—and the attempts by the respondents' lawyers to trip up and shame the Ngarinyin in cross-examination, the claimants' resilience led to a determination of extensive (and in some cases exclusive) determination of native title. However, the effects of the determination with regard to regional coexistence have been ambiguous. On the one hand, Redmond suggests that native title 'may well open up pathways out of the almost hegemonic relationships of the past'. Further, at least some pastoralists have begun to rekindle relationships with select groups among the claimants. On the other hand, locked gates, the establishment of access protocols which (consciously or otherwise) act to further exclude the Ngarinyin from their homelands, and other forms of resistance to the claimants' win mean that many Ngarinyin feel that little or nothing has changed following the determination.

The hardening of non-Indigenous attitudes to Aboriginal groups in response to claims over traditional homelands is apparently widespread. Scambary (Chapter 8) describes the ongoing politicisation of Indigenous rights in the Northern Territory, where reactionary statements about land rights and native title have proved to be sure-fire vote winners. The Larrakia claim over Darwin has been the target of reactionary politics by both the Country Liberal and Labor parties in the Territory, as well as of a broader public backlash that followed the 1996 lodgement of Darwin area claim. This backlash focused both on fears that the wider public would be excluded from areas such as public beaches and reserves (despite assurances by claimants that they did not seek to exclude non-Larrakia) and fears over hindrances to development. Notably both sets of fears have again surfaced in reaction to the recent successful claim by the Noongar people over the Perth area.[7]

Scambary's paper points to the complexities of co-existence in relation to native title, which affects relationships not only between Aborigines and settlers but also between claimants and other Aboriginal people. With regard to relations with non-indigenes, Scambary outlines the ways in which the Northern Territory government simultaneously opposed the Larrakia Native Title Claim and sought the involvement of the Larrakia Nation in the 'Community Harmony' project, which sought to address the issue of Aboriginal itinerants in Darwin, in part through the development of protocol for Aboriginal people visiting Darwin.

Indigenous 'itinerants', for the most part, have developed fairly good relations with the Larrakia, and many itinerants supported the Larrakia claim. However, Scambary suggests that the relationship between the Larrakia and the itinerants was weakened by the native title process. The native title claim was cited by the Northern Territory government as preventing the grant of title to an established fringe camp area (despite successfully negotiated deals for land use between the Larrakia and non-Indigenous parties) and the ability of the Larrakia to support itinerant interests was weakened by the demands of the native title process. As a result, ties between the Larrakia and itinerant groups became strained. Further, the partnerships that had developed between the Larrakia and the Territory government were wound back when the government decided to retreat from these partnership arrangements in order to bolster support for an upcoming election.

In other cases, a more positive relationship seems to have developed between governments and local Indigenous groups in the native title context. In Victoria, for example, the Wotjobaluk people, despite some reservations, have established successful partnerships with the Victorian Government following the registration and eventual consent determination of a native title claim (Beer et. al. 2005). Building on a government policy of recognition of traditional owners within and beyond the parameters of native title, these partnerships have involved a number of developments that have gone a considerable way to meeting the aspirations of the Wotjobaluk group. These include social and economic

---

[7] It should be noted, however, that on this occasion those politicians opposing the determination appear to have been wrong-footed by the general public of Perth, many of whom welcomed the native title decision, a reaction that further confirms the potential of native title to act as a vehicle for reconciliation between Indigenous and settler Australians.

aspirations (e.g. the preservation of 'oral history' and cultural knowledge, and the development of a financial base for Wotjobaluk activities), partnerships in the management of Wotjobaluk traditional country (including employment in land management and advisory roles and ownership of significant pieces of land), and the recognition of the Wotjobaluk as traditional owners. From the perspective of the Victorian government, it has been important to establish a framework for the acknowledgement of traditional ownership and to seek to resolve conflicts between and within native title and traditional owner groups. Through the development of relationships with these groups it is also clear that the State government has sought to use the native title process as a springboard to facilitate social and economic development for the State's Indigenous people.

Unfortunately, other claimants have not had such a positive experience of dealings with State governments. Claudie (Chapter 5) expresses considerable frustration with regard to the State's actions in a claim over his family's traditional homelands in central Cape York Peninsula. After expending considerable effort to produce a report on Aboriginal aspirations for the claim area, the claimants were left waiting while an opaque 'land evaluation' process was undertaken by the State government. This process was further complicated by mixed messages about the State's willingness to concede the continuing existence of native title over the claim area. And the report—when finally sighted by the claimants—persuaded at least some claimants that the State, rather than being prepared to negotiate in good faith, had already decided how it would deal with the area and was simply seeking to justify this decision through a report of possibly dubious quality despite the demonstrated willingness of the traditional owners to reach a compromise that included the interests of all stakeholders.

In sum, it is clear that the relationship between native title and coexistence is a complex one. On the one hand, the recent reaction to the success of the Noongar claim makes it clear that governmental opposition—and public outcry and misinformation—remain strong in the face of native title claims. And reactions to claims in rural and remote areas give lie to the claim that such opposition is due to the urban setting of the Noongar (and similar) claims. On the other hand, some State governments and other parties—including a number of pastoralists—have developed more accommodating perspectives on native title claims, and have also sought to develop forms of meaningful coexistence which extend beyond the confines of native title rights and interests. Doubtless these agreements are partly based on the levels of 'certainty' that have followed from the Federal government's legislative intervention following the success of the Wik claim in the High Court—and it should be remembered that such 'certainty' does not apply to Indigenous groups whose ability to gain meaningful coexistence on their terms have suffered as a result. But current developments within and beyond native title nonetheless hold some hope for meaningful steps towards coexistence across Australia.

Conclusion

The papers in this collection reflect on the various social effects of native title. In particular, the authors consider the ways in which the implementation of the *Native Title Act 1993* (Cwlth)—and the native title process for which this act legislates—allows for the recognition and translation of Aboriginal law and custom, and facilitates particular kinds of coexistence between Aboriginal title holders and other Australians. In so doing, the authors seek to extend the debate on native title beyond questions of practice and towards an improved understanding of the effects of native title on the social lives of Indigenous Australians and on Australian society more generally.

These attempts to grapple with the effects of native title have, in part, been impelled by Indigenous people's complaints about the NTA and the native title process. Since the Act was passed, many Indigenous Australians have become increasingly unhappy with both the strength and forms of recognition afforded to traditional law and custom under this Act, as well as the socially disruptive effects of the native title process. In particular—as several of the papers in this collection demonstrate—there is widespread discomfort with the transformative effects of recognition within the native title process, effects which can then 'feed back' into other aspects of Indigenous lives.

It seems clear that many of these problems have been compounded by the treatment of native title as 'a creature of the Native Title Act', rather than continuing to treat native title as the common law recognition of Indigenous law and custom. The resulting juridification of native title (Mantziaris and Martin 2000) has increased the degree of transformation that occurs through the process of 'recognition' of native title. This transformative 'violence' of translation occurs not only within the space of the court, but is also apparent in the approach taken by many NTRBs and anthropologists producing materials accounting for the ongoing connection and custom of claim groups. Such materials are often produced in anticipation of the expectations of other parties—in particular, the State and Federal government agencies charged with 'signing off' on consent determinations of native title, or of the judges ruling on native title claims which are decided in the courts. This effect of the native title process has led to one of native title's greatest ironies—in many cases, strong continuities in Indigenous cultural production hamper 'recognition' of native title due to their lack of fit with the NTA, whilst other groups—among whom cultural continuity has been accompanied by the local production of groups and assertions of rights which better 'fit' expectations based on the Native Title Act—find 'recognition' of their rights and interests proceeds more smoothly on this basis.

For the latter groups—those characterised by ongoing connection to 'country' and continuities in cultural production, but also by transformations in the articulation of Indigenous identities and property rights as a result of colonial disruption—native title has, on balance, proved to be a positive social phenomenon, allowing the recognition of Indigenous identity *and* practical benefits to a number of groups. Elsewhere, some Indigenous histories of strong cultural continuity and connection to land—in conjunction with relatively weak forms of colonial tenure—have allowed for the eventual recognition of substantial property rights, even the recognition of exclusive rights in land. But those who fall somewhere between these two positions can find native title particularly frustrating, leading to disappointing practical benefits *and* forms of recognition that are understood to be profoundly disjunct from those which operate in local social lives. And of course—the Noongar case notwithstanding—many Aboriginal people in more settled areas continue to be frustrated by a lack of recognition of their continuing connections to country and the legal determination of the extinguishment of their rights and interests.

Despite these frustrations and limitations, the papers in this collection suggest that the 'native title era' continues to produce positive results for many (although not all) Indigenous Australians, as well as many settler Australians, and arguably for Australian society as a whole. Positive forms of recognition and coexistence have developed not only within the native title process, but also because of its perceived limitations. A range of alternative provisions now mark the determination of Indigenous Australians to redefine their place in Australian society on the basis of their connections to 'country' even where the NTA has provided little or no recognition of these connections. The Act's provision for the production of Indigenous Land Use Agreements without the formal determination of Native Title, the Indigenous Protected Areas scheme, and a range of alternative processes and agreements (including those developed by the Victorian government, and those relationships developed with Indigenous groups in relation to the Murray-Darling system) all mark an increasing willingness by government departments and other public and private bodies to reach arrangements with Indigenous groups which exceed the recognition afforded by the NTA. In retrospect, the development of such alternatives—one more 'effect' of native title, albeit an effect triggered by its limitations—may prove to be just as important as the more positive effects of the native title process both for Indigenous Australians and their settler neighbours.

References

Asad, T. 1986. 'The concept of cultural translation in British social anthropology', in J. Clifford and G. E. Marcus (eds), *Writing Culture: The Poetics and Politics of Ethnography*, University of California Press, Berkeley.

Bauman, T. 2005. 'Whose benefits? Whose rights? Negotiating rights and interests amongst native title parties,' *Land, Rights, Laws: Issues of Native Title*, 3 (2), Native Title Research Unit, Australian Institute of Aboriginal and Torres Strait Islander Studies, Canberra.

Bauman, T. 2006a. 'Nations and tribes "within": emerging Aboriginal "nationalisms" in Katherine', in P. Sullivan, and T. Bauman (eds), *Delimiting Indigenous Cultures: Conceptual and Spatial Boundaries*, Special Issue, *The Australian Journal of Anthropology*, 17 (3): 322-35.

Bauman, T. 2006b. 'Waiting for Mary: process and practice issues in negotiating native title Indigenous decision-making and dispute management frameworks', *Land, Rights, Laws: Issues of Native Title*, 3 (6), Native Title Research Unit, Australian Institute of Aboriginal and Torres Strait Islander Studies, Canberra.

Bauman, T. and Williams. R. 2005. *The Business of Process: Research Issues in Managing Indigenous Decision Making and Disputes In Land*, Report No. 1, Indigenous Facilitation and Mediation Project, Native Title Research Unit, Australian Institute of Aboriginal and Torres Strait Islander Studies, Canberra.

Beer, J., Dalgleish, E., Kennedy, P., Leigh, C. and McLachlan, L. 2005. 'Beyond native title in the Wimmera: the Wotjobaluk, the State and the importance of "doing it local"', paper presented at the workshop *Effects of Native Title*, convened by B. R. Smith and F. Morphy, Old Canberra House, The Australian National University, 1-2 November.

Berndt, R. and Berndt, C. 1984. *Collection of Essays on Aboriginal Land Rights for the Guidance of the Government of Western Australia Aboriginal Land Inquiry 1983–1984*, Special Issue, *Anthropological Forum*, 5(3).

Bourdieu, P. 1977. *Outline of a Theory of Practice* (trans. Richard Nice), Cambridge University Press, Cambridge.

Correy, S. 2006. 'The reconstitution of Aboriginal sociality through the identification of traditional owners in NSW', in P. Sullivan, and T. Bauman (eds), *Delimiting Indigenous Cultures: Conceptual and Spatial Boundaries*, Special Issue, *The Australian Journal of Anthropology*, 17 (3): 336-47.

Fraser, N. 1995. 'From redistribution to recognition? Dilemmas of justice in a 'postsocialist' age', *New Left Review*, 212 (July/August): 68–93.

Hiatt, L. 1984. *Aboriginal Landowners: Contemporary Issues in the Determination of Traditional Aboriginal Land Ownership*, Oceania Monograph No.27, University of Sydney, Sydney.

Hirsch, E. 2001. 'Making up people in Papua', *Journal of the Royal Anthropological Institute*, 7: 241-56.

Langton, M., Mazel, O. and Palmer, L. 2006. 'The "spirit" of the thing: the boundaries of Aboriginal economic relations at Australian common law', in P. Sullivan, and T. Bauman (eds), *Delimiting Indigenous Cultures: Conceptual and Spatial Boundaries*, Special Issue, *The Australian Journal of Anthropology*, 17 (3): 307-21.

McWhorter, J. 2002. *The Power of Babel*, William Heinemann, London.

Mantziaris, C. and Martin, D. F. 2000. *Native Title Corporations: A Legal and Anthropological Analysis*, Federation Press, Sydney.

Markell, P. 2003. *Bound by Recognition*, Princeton University Press, Princeton.

Martin, D. F. 1993. Autonomy and Relatedness: An Ethnography of the Wik People of Western Cape York Peninsula, PhD Thesis, The Australian National University, Canberra.

Martin, D. F. 2003. 'Rethinking the design of Indigenous organisations: the need for strategic engagement', *CAEPR Discussion Paper No. 248*, Centre for Aboriginal Economic Policy Research, The Australian National University, Canberra.

Martin, D. F. 2004. 'Designing institutions in the "recognition space" of native title', In S. Toussaint (ed.), *Crossing Boundaries: Cultural, Legal, Historical and Practice Issues in Native Title*, Melbourne University Press, Melbourne.

Merlan, F. 1998. *Caging The Rainbow: Places, Politics, and Aborigines in a North Australian Town*, University of Hawai'i Press, Honolulu.

Morphy, H. and Morphy, F. 2001. 'The spirit of the plains kangaroo', in T. Bonyhady and T. Griffiths (eds), *Words for Country: Landscape and Language in Australia*, University of New South Wales Press, Sydney.

Morris, B. 2003. 'Anthropology and the state: the ties that bind', in B. Morris and R. Bastin (eds), *Expert Knowledge: First World Peoples, Consultancy, and Anthropology*, Special Issue, *Social Analysis* 47 (1): 137-44.

Myers, F. 1986. *Pintupi Country, Pintupi Self: Sentiment, Place, and Politics among Western Desert Aborigines*, University of California Press, Berkeley.

Nancy, J.-L. 2000. *Being Singular Plural*, Stanford University Press, Stanford.

Patton, P. 1995. 'Post-structuralism and the Mabo debate: difference, society and justice', in M. Wilson and A. Yeatman (eds), *Justice and Identity: Antipodean Practices*, Allen and Unwin, Sydney.

Patton, P. 2000. *Deleuze and the Political*, Routledge, London.

Pearson, N. 1997. 'The concept of native title at common law', in G. Yunupingu (ed.), *Our Land is Our Life*, University of Queensland Press, St Lucia.

Pearson, N. 2002, 'Native title's days in the sun are over', *The Age (Melbourne)*, 28 August 2002.

Povinelli, E. 2001. 'Radical worlds: the anthropology of incommensurability and inconceivability', *The Annual Review of Anthropology*, 30: 319–34.

Povinelli, E. 2002. *The Cunning of Recognition: Indigenous Alterity and the Making of Australian Multiculturalism*, Duke University Press, Durham.

Rumsey, A. 1989. 'Language groups in Australian Aboriginal land claims', *Anthropological Forum*, 6 (1): 69–79.

Smith, B. 2003a. '"All been washed away now": tradition, change and Indigenous knowledge in a Queensland Aboriginal land claim', in J. Pottier, A. Bicker and P. Sillitoe (eds), *Negotiating Local Knowledge: Power and Identity in Development*, Pluto Press, London.

Smith, B. 2003b. 'Whither "certainty"? Coexistence, change and some repercussions of native title in northern Queensland', *Anthropological Forum*, 13 (1): 27–48.

Smith, B. 2006. '"More than love": locality and affects of Indigeneity in northern Queensland', *The Asia-Pacific Journal of Anthropology*, 7 (3): 221–35.

Smith, B. R. and Claudie, D. 2003. 'Developing a land and resource management framework for Kaanju Homelands, central Cape York: opportunities and challenges', *CAEPR Discussion Paper No. 258*, Centre for Aboriginal Economic Policy Research, The Australian National University, Canberra.

Sullivan, P. and Bauman, T. (eds) 2006. *Delimiting Indigenous Cultures: Conceptual and Spatial Boundaries*, Special Issue, *The Australian Journal of Anthropology*, 17(3).

Sutton, P. 2003. *Native Title in Australia: An Ethnographic Perspective*, Cambridge University Press, Cambridge.

Toussaint, S. 2004. *Crossing Boundaries: Cultural, Legal, Historical and Practice Issues in Native Title*, Melbourne University Press, Melbourne.

Wagner, R. 1981[1975]. *The Invention of Culture*, University of Chicago Press, Chicago.

Weiner, J. F. 2003. '*The Law of the Land*: a review article', The Australian Journal of Anthropology, 14 (1): 97–110.

Wolfe, P. 1999. *Settler Colonialism and the Transformation of Anthropology: The Politics and Poetics of an Ethnographic Event*, Cassell, London.

2. Performing law: The Yolngu of Blue Mud Bay meet the native title process

Frances Morphy

> This land was never given up
> This land was never bought and sold
> The planting of the Union Jack
> Never changed our law at all
>
> *Treaty* (1991) Mandawuy Yunupingu with Paul Kelly and Peter Garrett

Introduction

The native title process is an arena in which, among other things, the sovereignty of a colonising society over its colonised subjects is enacted. As Julie Lahn (Chapter 7) points out, native title is based on a 'radical assumption of sovereignty' and the legislation and the growing body of native title case law 'can be said to continue to exercise the power that defines sovereignty…[a]nd in this sense, it is certainly possible to contend that native title is as implicated in ongoing processes of colonisation, as providing a remedy to aspects of it'.

The Yolngu response to the native title process in the Blue Mud Bay case was in continuity with a long-term tradition of political interaction with the colonising society and its institutions.[1] It is a response that declares, in essence, 'we know we are encapsulated, but we are not colonised'. Yolngu have never fully acceded to the proposition that their sovereignty has been eclipsed by the process of colonisation. When sovereignty was asserted over their region by the colonial power—in abstract and at a distance—their ancestors knew nothing of it. Although the colonial frontier encroached upon the fringes of their region many years later, in the early years of the 20th century, there was no significant permanent Euro-Australian presence in the Yolngu heartlands until the establishment of the first missions in the 1930s. At the time Yolngu did not perceive the coming of the missionaries as an act of colonisation nor did they view their own response as a ceding of sovereignty. Nancy Williams writes that: 'From a Yolngu perspective it was Mawalan, as head of the land-owning Rirratjingu clan, who granted permission to Chaseling, as agent of the "mission" to establish the station at Yirrkala [in 1935]' (Williams 1987: 20).

---

[1] The initial determination of the Blue Mud Bay case can be found at *Gawirrin Gumana v Northern Territory of Australia (No. 2)* [2005] FCA 1425. The determination of the Full Federal Court hearing may be found at *Gumana v Northern Territory of Australia* [2007] FCAFC 23. Links to the two determinations may be found on the website of the National Native Title tribunal at <http://www.nntt.gov.au/ntdetermination/1136779170_3832.html> (accessed 4 September 2007).

Yolngu were brought face to face with colonial power in the 1960s in what became known popularly as the Gove Land Rights case, when the clans of the Yirrkala area took the bauxite mining company Nabalco and the Commonwealth of Australia to court over mineral leases that had been granted to the mining company by the government.[2] The Yolngu view of the encounter and its aftermath is that although they lost that battle they won a longer war, in that the *Aboriginal Land Rights Act (Northern Territory) 1976* (ALRA), which granted the Traditional Owners rights in fee simple over the rest of the Yolngu clan estates (to the low water mark), is seen as a direct result of that earlier loss.

Manuhia Barcham, in his presentation to the workshop *Effects of native title* from which the present volume originated, drew attention to the 'politicised nature of the [native title] recognition space'. The politicisation of the space can come from more than one direction. Today's Yolngu are not naïve, nor are they in a state of false consciousness about the nature of the political situation in which they find themselves. They see and understand the power relations that allow the Australian state to assert its sovereignty over them. But they also consider that this sovereignty was imposed without their consent, and that there never was an act of conquest. They see the ALRA as an acknowledgement of that fact by the state, and to that extent they question the legitimacy of the state's assertion of sovereignty over their estates. In their view the native title process was as much about the issue of sovereignty—at least in the sense of the recognition of the jurisdiction of Yolngu 'law'—as about 'rights', and their participation in the process must partly be understood as a political act.

This much was clear in discussions with their representing barrister during preparations for the case. The view they put to him rhetorically was, in paraphrase: 'We know that we own our sea country under our law. Why is it not sufficient for us simply to state this to the court? Why do we have to prove our law under *ngapaki* [white] law?'[3] The barrister's response was, in effect, that as citizens of Australia they were subject to what they were calling *ngapaki* law, that *ngapaki* law was not just for *ngapaki* but for all Australians. He acknowledged that this situation had come about through a prior act of colonisation, but, to paraphrase again, 'that's just the way it is, and that's what we have to work with'.

For the late Mr Justice Selway, who heard the Blue Mud Bay native title case, sovereignty was naturally not at issue. The very existence of the Federal Court, and of the Native Title Act presupposes the sovereignty of the state, and, moreover, '[f]ollowing *Mabo (No 2)* the High Court rejected attempts to use native title as a vehicle to claim indigenous legal and political sovereignty'

---

[2] For a detailed account of this case (*Milirrpum vs Nabalco and the Commonwealth of Australia*) and the Yolngu response see Williams (1986).
[3] David Claudie (Chapter 5, see p. 89, 101 and fn. 15) takes a similar view.

(Mantziaris & Martin 2000: 28). But the judge did recognise explicitly that the applicants considered this case as: 'merely the latest aspect of a more protracted campaign. For my part it is difficult to imagine what more the Yolngu people, including the claim groups, could or should have done lawfully to enforce their rights' (Selway J 2005 [213]).

From the anthropologist's point of view then, the Blue Mud Bay hearing can be seen as Yolngu discourse about the sovereignty of *rom* (Yolngu 'laws and customs') embedded in a native title discourse about rights under European law. In analysing this discourse within a discourse, the paper looks first at the constraints created by the form and structure of the court, and then at the strategies Yolngu applied to insert their discourse about sovereignty. Their political agenda was rarely explicitly stated, but rather manifested in the strategies that they adopted in their responses to questioning and in their deliberate placement, at two carefully selected points in the proceedings, of performances of *rom*. The paper concludes with some thoughts about the more long-term effects of the case on the Yolngu view of their position as encapsulated but not colonised subjects.

A brief ethnography of the court: performance and enactment

The term 'arena' in the opening sentence to this paper is used quite deliberately. A native title court is an arena for the enactment of law—European law. *Rom* is present, and it may under certain circumstances be performed, but it is not enacted in the sense of having any legal force in this arena. This distinction between performance and enactment is central to the analysis presented here, for sovereignty is asserted through enactment. In the court, European law is sovereign in that it is simultaneously performed and enacted—or is enacted through its performance, whereas *rom* is the object of discourse; it is explicated through the mediating discourse of examination and cross-examination. If performances of *rom* are inserted into the proceedings, these do not count—from the court's point of view—as enactments of *rom*. They do not even count as evidence about *rom*, unless they are also explicated in oral or written evidence.[4]

But from the Yolngu point of view (for reasons that will be elaborated later), any performance of *rom*, in whatever context, simultaneously constitutes an enactment of *rom*, and performance in the context of the court it is therefore, among other things an enactment that demonstrates the sovereignty of *rom*.

---

[4] Sturt Glacken (pers. comm. 9 November 2005) notes that there is legal provision for evidence by performance. 'If it is used', Glacken notes, 'there would then need to follow conventional evidence explaining its symbols'. In this case, bark paintings made by the claimants that depicted their land and sea country were used as evidence in precisely this way.

The arena

The forms and rituals of the court come as second nature to those who are expert practitioners, but they are as exotic and potentially impenetrable to Yolngu claimants in a native title case as Yolngu ritual forms are to non-Yolngu.

The performance space—the courtroom—is a constructed ritual space. This much was obvious to Yolngu because the court was held in a building at Yirrkala to which everyone normally has access—the adult education centre. Fig. 2.1 shows how the main teaching/meeting room became a courtroom. The space was transformed symbolically by the placing of the symbol of the court—the Australian coat of arms bearing the figure of the kangaroo and the emu—at the front of the room, and then this symbolic space was divided into clear zones.[5] In front of the kangaroo and emu stood a table—the 'bench'—at which sat the judge and his associate. The court recorders sat to one side and the witness and the interpreter sat opposite them, to the other side of the judge.

Fig. 2.1 The ritual space of the court

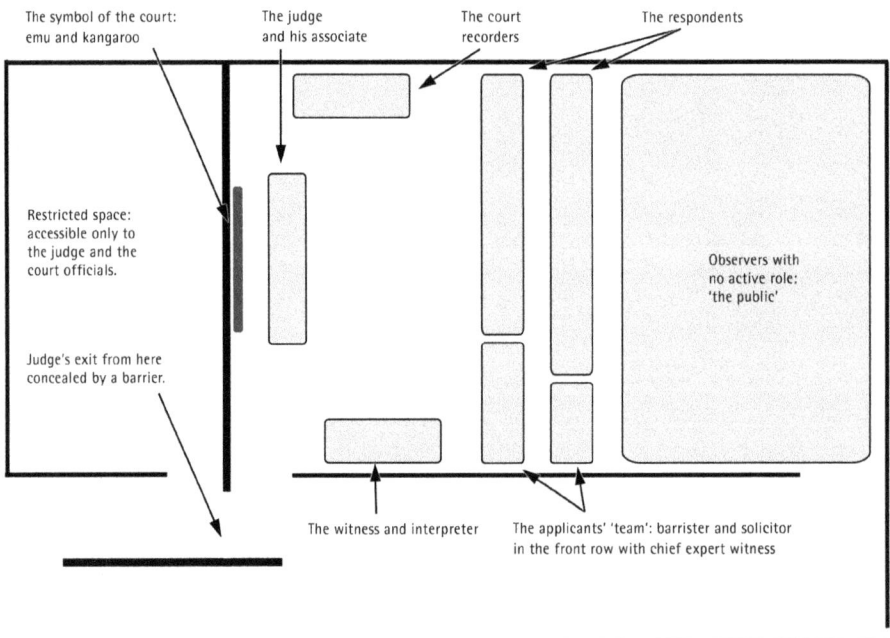

The space between these two flanking tables was empty. Facing the judge across this space were two lines of tables and chairs. The first row was occupied by the teams for the applicants and the most active respondents (the Northern

---

[5] Ironically, the emu is one of the main ancestral beings for one of the Yirritja moiety clans involved in the case, and the wallaby has the same status for one of the Dhuwa moiety clans involved.

Territory and Commonwealth governments), including the expert witnesses, and the second by the less active respondents and me (an expert witness with a non-speaking part). This completed the arena in which action took place. In the back half of the room, again separated by an empty space from the actors in the proceedings, was the space for the 'public' to sit.

Adjoining the public court there was a restricted space to which only the judge and the court officials had access.[6] The entry of the judge from the restricted space into the public space took place through a door at the front of the court. Everyone else entered through the door at the rear of the court.[7]

Who gets to speak, and how

The Australian court system has an elaborate set of rules for proper discourse, in which different actors have different roles according to their status and function. Certain categories of persons can speak publicly; others—solicitors and expert witnesses who are not on the stand—can give written advice to their colleagues with speaking parts, but may not themselves speak. The discourse rules are well understood and are manipulated (with varying degrees of subtlety) by the actors in the court who have legal training, but they are not transparent to, nor are they explicitly laid out for, the 'lay' actors—the witnesses—who must attempt to learn the rules as they go along. The system is also hierarchical, and that hierarchy is made manifest in the degree of constraint to which different actors must submit themselves. At the top of the hierarchy is the judge, who is the least constrained. It would appear that he or she can speak at any time, freely interrupting the speech of others.

The hierarchy of constraints is ostensibly designed to control the flow of information into the official record of the court, in such a way as to maximise the production of objective 'facts' that are relevant in law to the particular case, according to a particular set of 'rules of evidence'. It is a highly positivist enterprise. In native title cases it has a paradoxical effect, when viewed from the perspective of the applicants—the purported 'native title holders'. They, who are the most knowledgeable about their own system of 'laws and customs', have the most severely curtailed rights to speak in the body of the court. They may only speak when spoken to. Their barrister, who has spent time with them preparing the case and is likely to have more knowledge of their 'laws and customs' than any of the other counsel present, is bound by the rules of evidence to act 'as if' he knew nothing, because he may not ask leading questions—that

---

[6] Yolngu witnesses saw a parallelism between the public and restricted spaces of the court and the public and restricted grounds of Yolngu ceremonial performance. That only the judge (and his court officials) had access to the restricted space was seen (correctly) as an indication of his pre-eminent status in the proceedings.

[7] An exception was made for the witnesses and interpreters when it was realised that entry through the back door was impossible once all the barristers and others were seated.

is, he may not ask questions that contain knowledge that he and the applicants know that they all hold in common.[8]

Prior to the court hearing, a set of detailed witness statements had been prepared. The witnesses had understood that these were to form the basis of questioning that they would be facing in the court hearing. There had been some discussion at the directions hearings preceding the court hearing about how these statements were to be used. The respondents had wanted full statements in writing, and to have the portions to which they raised no objections accepted as the witnesses' evidence in chief. In the case of objections, the relevant paragraphs were to be lead orally from the witnesses. Counsel for the applicants had objected to this process. He favoured providing summaries of the evidence and otherwise leading evidence orally. The judge noted his objection to the process advocated by the respondents.

The judge was concerned to make the proceedings as short as possible. Accordingly, at the beginning of the court proceedings large portions of the witness statements were indeed accepted into evidence, with no objection from the respondents. But there remained certain paragraphs or sentences that the respondents did not allow into evidence, and insisted should be the subject of oral examination in the court. Although the counsel for the applicants was not explicitly confined to leading only the evidence in these excised portions of the witness statements, in practice the timetable set by the judge made it impracticable to do anything else.[9] As a result, the witnesses found themselves being asked a very narrow range of questions.[10] Towards the end, the last witness (X) obliquely voiced his frustration with this state of affairs:

> Counsel for the applicants (CA): Now, I'll move on to [paragraph] 66 [of X's witness statement]. Just – this deals with, X, this deals with the idea of catching a turtle or a big animal on a person's country. Can you tell us what happens when if you catch a turtle or a big animal on somebody else's country?

---

[8] This was not true in the original version of the *Native Title Act*, which was similar to the ALRA in terms of its attitude to evidence. The Act was amended in 1998, so that 'normal' rules of evidence now apply. The Blue Mud Bay case was run under both Acts, but before a Federal Court Judge rather than in a Land Rights Commissioner. Thus Federal Court rules of evidence prevailed.

[9] I am grateful to Tom Keely (pers. comm. 3 April 2007) for explaining the finer points of the leading of the evidence to me. Any remaining errors of fact and interpretation are mine.

[10] In the week immediately prior to the hearing, the young adult daughter of one of the main appellant witnesses died suddenly and unexpectedly. During the period of the hearing, her body was in Darwin for the coroner's inquest into the cause of death. One of the issues that the respondents' barristers wished evidence to be led on was the question of the closure of areas of the sea and shore following a death. So a side-effect of the strategy adopted by the court was that the witnesses (apart from the father), several of whom were also closely related to the young woman, were subjected to lengthy questioning on the topic of death and its consequences. While people found this emotionally difficult, they nevertheless saw that it strengthened their evidence to be able to show how they were acting in relation to this death.

> X: Yes, I think we are all aware about that. We had three – six people sitting down here telling the same stories. Now I'm going to do the same thing and tell the same stories. When we get turtle from – from another country…[11]

The counsel acting for the respondents are free to ask leading questions if they so wish, and are not confined to leading evidence from the witness statements. They may even, as a tactic, pose questions that are deliberately founded on ignorance or wilful misunderstanding of the facts. The latter were sometimes deliberately deployed to attempt to confuse the witness, or to lead them towards a conclusion that they would not freely subscribe to.

From the point of view of the non-initiate—Indigenous or non-Indigenous—the structure of the discourse imposed by the court seemed designed, whether intentionally or not, to emphasise the power of the European law by systematically constraining the ability of the knowledgeable practitioners of *rom* to express *rom* clearly in its own terms and in its fullness.

This was a paradoxical effect, because the judge's intention had been quite different. He was proceeding from the premise that he only needed to know from the witnesses that which was relevant to native title law—it was not his role, as he said, to become an anthropologist or an expert in Yolngu law. He was also clearly concerned to minimise the adversarial aspects of the judiciary process on the witnesses: he enjoined the respondents not to attack their credit, and he clearly wished to set limits on the number of witnesses, and on the length of their appearances on the stand, not simply to expedite the hearing and confine proceedings to what he saw as the relevant facts, but also to minimise the potential for adverse impacts on the Yolngu claimants.

To some extent, then, the judge and the claimants were at cross purposes. While the judge was concerned to minimise the impact of the proceedings on the claimants, the claimants were concerned to produce as much of an impact on the court as they could. They saw the court as a platform for demonstrating the power of *rom* and the depth of their knowledge about it—as a site for persuasion.[12] This is in continuity with earlier Yolngu views of the court in the Gove case, as described by Nancy Williams:

> The Yolngu leaders perceived the court less in adversary terms than as a setting where their role was to assist the court to learn about their ownership of land, They saw an opportunity 'to explain', and *explanation in their terms involved 'to demonstrate'* … *For the Yolngu the situation was marked by explanation that would result in understanding*. They found it difficult to accommodate defence counsel's mode of questioning, and of

---

[11] Court transcript (henceforth T) 815.26–35.
[12] On Yolngu and the concept of persuasion, see also Morphy (1983).

attempting to elicit from them inconsistent or contradictory responses ... the Yolngu leaders were unprepared for a situation in which Europeans explain only enough to 'win' (1986: 159; emphasis added).

During the proofing stage of the Gove land rights case W. E. H. Stanner and the claimants' solicitor Frank Purcell were taken to a place where they were shown sacred objects. Stanner recalled: 'One of the men said to me: "Now you understand". He meant that I had seen the holy *rangga* which in a sense is the clan's title deeds to its land, and heard what they stood for: so I could not but "understand"'(1979: 278).

In the Blue Mud Bay case, the claimants were more conversant with the conventions of court hearings than their forebears had been, having had more direct or indirect experience of the adversarial system in the intervening years. However the connections between explanation, demonstration and understanding, as detailed by Williams and Stanner, hold equally strongly for Yolngu today.

The witness statement—neither fish nor fowl?

From a sociolinguistic point of view, the 'witness statement' is an interesting and problematic document. The judge in this case considered it to be a valuable tool. In his judgment (Selway J 2005) he said in part:

> 182 ... in many cases it is convenient to have evidence in chief given wholly or largely by means of a prepared statement. This not only reduces the time involved in the hearing – it also assists in ensuring that the applicant's case is prepared well in advance of trial and that the respondent(s) is not taken by surprise ...

> 183 I accept that this may need to be qualified in relation to some witnesses who may be disadvantaged by this course, which may include some Aboriginal witnesses ... However, I do not think that those disadvantages arose in this case. The Yolngu witnesses were all obviously intelligent. Most of them seemed relatively sophisticated as to the ways of European society ... All the witnesses were senior law men in relation to a legal system of considerable complexity. These are not simple and naïve people. *Subject to potential issues arising from translation between Yolngu language and English* I do not think that the Yolngu witnesses were disadvantaged by the procedure adopted (emphasis added).

I would not quarrel with his Honour's concluding sentence, in this particular case. However, I want to pick up on the phrase that has been italicised. For the process involved in the construction of a witness statement is much more complex than this, and it is not, strictly speaking, translation (Fig. 2.2).

If it were possible to translate word for word between Yolngu-matha and English, and if we were only dealing with 'layman's' English, then maybe the process would be straightforward. Once the lawyers had written up the statements in English, it would simply be a matter of reading the statement back to the witness (or translating it word for word into Yolngu-matha and reading it back), or getting the witness to read the statement over for themselves. The Yolngu witness might find the formal style of the statement unfamiliar, but that would not be a barrier to comprehension. However, neither of these 'ifs' hold.

Fig. 2.2 The 'translation' steps in a witness statement

Yolngu-matha concept, e.g. *gurruṯu*, with no direct translation equivalent in English.

→ A statement by a Yolngu witness, in English, about 'permission': For example, my mother's mother came from X... yeah, I still have permit, or permission which is, that's *balanda dhäruk* [English word], our *dhäruk* is *gurruṯu*. I always know in my mind that I always call that country is my *märi* [mother's mother]...

↓

A statement about permission as written up by the NLC lawyers as part of a witness's affidavit: I can go hunting, camping or travelling across W, X, Y or Z countries, without first having to ask **permission** of the owning clan. This is because I have **close relationships** with these clans and because I know the countries.

← Statement is read to the witness by the NLC lawyer, with an interpreter present to assist, amended if necessary, and then **sworn** by the witness.

Firstly, there are very few words that can be translated literally from one language to the other. There is, for example, no English equivalent of the word *gurruṯu*, and no Yolngu-matha equivalent of the English word 'permission'. For an English speaker to understand what *gurruṯu* means, it is necessary for them to be familiar with the operation of the Yolngu kinship system, and for a Yolngu person to understand what 'permission' means (in the context of native title) it is necessary for them to be familiar with Anglo-Australian notions of property.

Secondly, and this is something the Yolngu witnesses are not privy to, many of the words that appear in witness statements—words like 'permission', 'speak for', 'resource', 'sing for' and 'connection'—have come to have particular meanings for lawyers who work in native title. Some are defined in the *Native Title Act 1993* itself, which gives them status as legalese; others are quasi-legalese—terms that have commonly been used by lawyers in native title cases, and which are in the process of definition as legal terms, with very particular meanings. The trouble is that they sound like ordinary English words. So a phrase like 'without first having to ask *permission*' could conceivably mean something very different to the Yolngu witness to whom it is read from what it means to the lawyer who reads it to him—even if that witness has reflected at length on what 'permission' might be equivalent to in the Yolngu system (as at least one witness had done). To a Yolngu who has not reflected on the meaning of the word, the phrase is, quite possibly, meaningless.[13]

With a moment's reflection, it is possible to see that the 'translation' of a witness statement 'back' into Yolngu-matha so that it can be verified as his own by a Yolngu witness with poor English, is a near impossible task, and one that would be extremely time consuming. For such a document is a hybrid.[14] It purports to be the statement by the witness about 'laws and customs' (*rom*), but it is to some degree actually a lawyer's statement about native title. It belongs fully to neither of its authors, and its meaning is inherently indeterminate.

The witness statement is a particular instance of what Mantziaris and Martin have in mind when they write: that 'native title involves a process of translation from indigenous "relations" defined by traditional law and custom to native title rights and interests enforceable within the Australian legal system. This process of translation becomes difficult, or impossible, when the terms of the translation are incommensurable' (2000: 29). I do not take the strong position that incommensurability is inevitable and always uncircumventable. However, I do take the witness statement to be an instance of 'enforced commensurability' in the context of an unequal power relation.

These statements are long documents. The one being discussed in the extract below from the court record is 89 paragraphs long. This in itself makes it unlikely that the witness has a full recall of its contents. Does this matter? Yes, because these documents are treated, according to an unstated convention 'as if' they were the *actual words* of the witness, when everyone in the court knows they are not. Hence the programmatic nature of their adoption into evidence, where much less attention is paid to the witness's response that the statement is 'true and correct'—this is a formulaic ritual exchange—than to its status as a legal document: which 'matter' it relates to, and which bits have not been accepted 'by consent' into the evidence before the court:

---

[13] The noun 'permit' is certainly in the everyday lexicon of most Yolngu people because of the permit system that applies on ALRA land in the Northern Territory. However, its meaning has been extended in Yolngu contexts in a way that makes the Yolngu lexical item 'permit' different from the Standard Australian English lexical item. For example it is possible for a Yolngu to say 'he is my permit for this country', referring to the *gurruṯu* relationship with another person that gives the individual 'standing permission' to access the resources of their relative's country.
[14] By this I mean hybrid in the third sense listed by the *Macquarie Dictionary*: 'anything derived from heterogeneous sources, or composed of elements of different or incongruous kind'.

Counsel for the Applicants (CA): Your Honour, there are two affidavits and also a supplementary witness statement in respect of X.
His Honour (HH): Yes.
CA: I wonder if X can first be shown the affidavit filed 18 June 2004.
HH: This is the affidavit in the - - -
BA: Judiciary Act matter, yes, your Honour.
HH: Judiciary Act matter, yes
CA: X, would you just have a look at that affidavit there, please? Do you remember some time in June swearing that affidavit? You might like to have a look at it, just to make sure you know what it is. I'm not asking you to read it all, unless you need to do that.
X: Mm.
CA: All I'm wanting to know at the moment is, is that your affidavit that you made in - - -
X: Yes.
BA: - - - June of this year? And what do you say as to the - whether the – what's in that affidavit, is it true and correct?
X: True and correct.
CA: Well, your Honour, I tender the affidavit as follows: excluding paragraphs 14, 18, 20, 36, 40, 50 the eighth and ninth sentences - - -
HH: Just - eighth and ninth sentence of 50?
BA: They're to be excluded. Paragraph 66 the last two sentences, paragraph 71 the last sentence, 73 the last sentence, 74, 87, 88, and 89. I tender the balance of the affidavit, your Honour.[15]

The trouble is that the respondents can, as a tactical manoeuvre, when it suits them, violate the unspoken convention. They can do this because it has no official status in the court. They can question the witness minutely about the precise meaning of a word that 'they' have used in 'paragraph n' of their statement. In his determination Justice Selway (2005) drew attention to the one instance of this tactic that came to his notice where, in his opinion, misunderstanding was evident (emphasis added):

> 185 Some mention should be made of the only clear example of a potential misunderstanding of the meaning of words within the written statements. In par 40 of his written statement Mr Y *said* 'As the river crosses X country, the bed, banks, waters and resources of the river belong to the X.' I would normally have understood the word 'resources' to mean physical resources, such as fish. However, *in his oral evidence Mr Y said that he had used the word, or at least understood it, to mean 'stories'*. Given the evidence as to the spiritual and traditional significance of 'stories' the use of the word 'stories' in that context is understandable. It seems

---

[15] T748.36–749.35.

> to me that this is an example of what is probably obvious – *some care needs to be taken in ensuring that a witness's evidence is not misunderstood by reason of a difference in understanding the meaning of words.* In the event this misunderstanding did not have any effect in this case. It was identified during cross examination. It also did not matter. It was clear from Mr Y's evidence that he did understand that physical resources, such as fish, within the river were 'owned' by or 'belong to' the clan over whose land the river (including the fish) was situated …

In this comment Justice Selway is treating paragraph 40 of the witness statement 'as if' Y had actually said or written the precise words quoted. However, 'resources' is one of those quasi-legal words that had been introduced in the writing up of the statement—a word that has a precise meaning for the lawyers in the court. It had been introduced to gloss what the witness had actually said originally, as a kind of shorthand, linking the statement efficiently to a particular point of native title law. The witness had no appreciation of this. In the context of the cross examination in which the contents of paragraph 40 were raised, the witness's concern was to try and make sense of the word in that more immediate context. The context 'paragraph 40 of a long document which is based on words I once spoke but was not written by me' was basically inaccessible to him. Since the place being talked about in that exchange happened to be a major sacred site, his fixing on the abstract meaning of resource as 'spiritual resource ('stories')' was unsurprising. Discourse mediated through witness statements is full of such moments, although often this is only fully evident to the linguist sitting uncomfortably in the second row.

At the end of his cross-examination, counsel for one of the respondent parties attempted to cast doubt on the status of the witness statements by putting the 'as if' convention on the record. He questioned X as follows:

> Counsel for the Respondent (CR): I just wanted to ask you about your affidavit: did somebody help you prepare your affidavit? Affidavit, that's your main statement; it's all your information in it. Did somebody help you prepare that?
> X: My statement?
> CR: Yes.
> X: I mean, do – somebody was writing it, or - - -
> CR: Yes
> [Discussion in language between X and the interpreter]
> X: Yes. There was – Howard, is it?
> CR: Professor Morphy was it? … Okay. Somebody else? Ms Hetherton, the lawyer?
> X: Yes [more in this vein] …

CR: ... And so some of the words in those statements perhaps are not your words, maybe they're words that somebody else has put in? For example, that word 'right' ... That's not your word, I gather, that's more - - -

X: What you mean 'right'? Rights?

CR: Yes, there was a bit in your statement that [one of the other counsel for the respondents] was reading to you and it talked about you having a right to do something, and ... all I'm asking you is, was that part of the statement written by you, or maybe that was written by, with the help of other people?

X: Oh, it was my language - - -

CR: Yes.

X: - - - because it is new to me to speak English. I have – this is my second language.

CR: Yes, and you're very good at it too, I must say. I wish I was as good at English as you are.

X: I wish I was going to speak proper English and I'm read or write - - -

CR: No, you're very, very good.

X: - - - then I can do it myself.[16]

It is fair to say, bearing in mind the judge's comments in his judgment, that this ploy was unsuccessful, and his Honour appreciated X's sardonic response at the time. But it is by no means clear that the ploy *ought to have been* unsuccessful. In native title proceedings a great deal of time and thought has gone into the precise evidential status of expert reports—particularly anthropologist's reports. But the evidential peculiarities of the witness statement have gone largely unexamined, and while they remain so they are potentially a source of disadvantage to the witness. They expose the witness to the possibility of hostile cross examination, in which they are asked to defend or reproduce statements—said to be theirs—that are not couched in the language nor in terms of concepts that they themselves would have used.[17] Moreover, in this case of 'enforced commensurability' the witnesses, in acceding to the proposition that the witness statements are their statements, are also, perforce, acceding to this particular representation of 'their' laws and customs.

---

[16] T905.16–905.43.

[17] Sturt Glacken (pers. comm. 9 November 2005) points out that scrutiny of experts comes for different reasons because they must be shown to be independent, and the factual basis and methodology for their opinion must be laid bare. While acknowledging this to be true, I would say, nevertheless, that there are also good reasons to scrutinise the status of the 'facts' as they are laid out in witness statements.

The Yolngu response

I now turn to a consideration of how the Yolngu witnesses viewed this arena, how they chose to act in it, and to what end. I use the word 'choice' because although the role of the witness is the most constrained of any of the actors in the court, there is still scope for alternative ways of acting in that role. It is fair to say that the Yolngu witnesses had a very precise appreciation of the ritual nature of the court and of the power relations that obtained within it. The second point on which most witnesses were pretty clear was the nature of the hierarchical relationship between customary law and native title, within the context of the court. But it is one thing to acknowledge differential power, and quite another to acquiesce to the legitimacy of the relationships so constituted, or to view them as just.

I will discuss two kinds of action that the Yolngu took within the constraints placed upon them, and their reasons for those actions. The first is the insertion of performances of *rom*. The second is the Yolngu commentary on difference, and insistence on difference, and on the need for *rom* to be seen in its own terms—the insistence on incommensurability. Through both these kinds of actions, I will argue, Yolngu were making statements about sovereignty, not simply about 'rights'.

The insertion of performance: sacred power made manifest

The Yolngu announced to the court that they wished to perform a short ceremony before the court started in order to 'welcome' the judge and the court. This wish was granted. A group of men, followed by women, all wearing white paint on their foreheads, processed into the court chanting loudly and calling out ceremonial names of country to the accompaniment of clapsticks (Fig. 2.3). They bore with them two very large public ceremonial objects representing the ceremonial walking sticks of Yirritja moiety ancestral beings associated with a place within the claim area called Gänganbuy, richly adorned with feather-string (Fig. 2.4). The choice to represent this place and its law was very deliberate. For the Yolngu clans of the Blue Mud Bay area it is the place from which the *rom* of the Yirritja moiety originates.

Fig. 2.3 The opening ceremony: approach to the court

Photo: Courtesy of Sonia Brownhill

In order to accommodate the performance inside the courtroom it was necessary to disrupt the spatial ordering of the native title court by moving aside the tables and chairs facing the judge's 'bench', where the judge sat. The performance in the confined space of the court was visually and aurally extremely powerful—the lawyers and other court officials were displaced to the periphery of the arena. The judge, significantly, was not; he sat at his 'bench' throughout the performance, which ended with the ceremonial objects being laid against the bench, and the Yolngu leaving the court. The court space was reconstituted, the ceremonial objects were moved out of the courtroom, and the court then got down to its business. But for a moment, it must have seemed to the non-Yolngu present, as it certainly did to the Yolngu, that *rom* had momentarily displaced Australian law in its own space.

Fig. 2.4 The opening ceremony: in the court

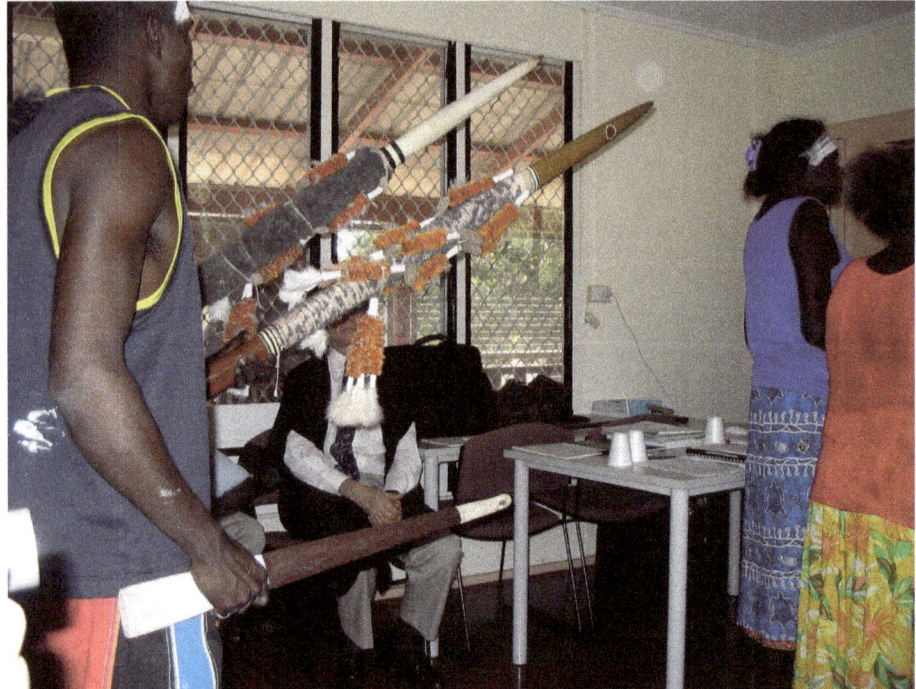

Photo: Courtesy of Sonia Brownhill

The second insertion of a performance of *rom* took place on the first site visit to the homeland settlement of Yilpara on Blue Mud Bay itself. The Yolngu had chosen this time very carefully, situating it near the beginning of the proceedings, and had been preparing for it for months. The male members of the court were taken to the men's ceremonial ground (Fig 2.5). Female members of the court, by consent, and including the female counsel for one of the respondent groups, were led to the edge of the ceremonial space, but then were led back (by me under instruction from the ceremonial leaders) to sit with the women in the main settlement while the men went to the restricted ground. As the men returned the women (including the non-Yolngu women) sat with their backs to them, only turning under instruction when the men were close (Fig. 2.6). This was not just a performance of *rom* in its own ritual space, but an enactment that incorporated the members of the Federal Court as actors, under the terms of *rom*.

Fig. 2.5 The court at the edge of the Yolngu law space

Photo: Courtesy of Daniel Lavery

Fig. 2.6 The return from the Yolngu law space

Photo: Courtesy of Daniel Lavery

The advantages of giving 'non-evidence'

These two ritual performances could have been admitted as evidence, had the ground to do so been prepared.[18] But before the welcoming performance, no-one had suggested to counsel for the applicants that it should be regarded as having evidential content. In the case of the performance on the ceremonial ground, there was an issue about procedural fairness, because the other parties had had no opportunity to ask questions, at the time of the performance, about what was happening. The judge was concerned about what an appeal court would make of the event in the absence of a transcript or other recording of it. His decision in the end was to treat it as a 'view', 'to be understood by me as a background or context to understand later evidence'.[19] He considered it to have been a 'wonderful experience',[20] and went further when counsel for the applicants tried to persuade him that at least the explanatory statements made by one of the witnesses in the 'restricted session' could be regarded as evidence:

> CA: ... I appreciate – I accept fully that my learned friends haven't any or any adequate opportunity to cross-examine, but that - - -
> HH: But they didn't have any capacity to object. It was – the Federal Court of Australia was not in session. I can't see how anyone could think we were in session. It wasn't –
> CA: Well, I'm in your Honour's hands.
> HH: *It would have been completely inappropriate, completely rude, completely out of the question for that to be the Federal Court of Australia having a session.*
> CA: I hear what your Honour says.
> HH: It simply was not that. That's not what it was.[21]

Although the judge did not then elaborate as to 'what it was', the implication was clear. The men's ceremonial ground—or perhaps the nature of the performance that took place there—was not within the jurisdiction of the Federal Court. Had the Yolngu submitted these performances as evidence, this arguably would have lessened their force, because once situated within the frame of the court as 'evidence', they would have been deemed by the court to be performances but not enactments.

These Yolngu performances were deployed in a politics of persuasion, as part of their embedded discourse about sovereignty. Although not evidence, the power of these performances, in their enactment, inevitably became part of the wider context in which their evidence in court was then heard.

---

[18] This section of the paper has benefited greatly from comments by Tom Keely (pers. comm. 3 April 2007).
[19] T221.46-7.
[20] T221.38.
[21] T222.28–43, emphasis added

The Yolngu were not necessarily fully aware of the court's distinction between performance as 'evidence' and performance as 'view', nor of its legal implications. Nor was it relevant to them, in that, to borrow Nancy Williams' terminology, demonstration is *in and of itself* explanation, in the Yolngu view. Indeed, the informal space of the 'view' is arguably the most effective space for a discourse about sovereignty precisely because it is not subject to the adversarial discourse of cross-examination. Thus the Yolngu had achieved exactly what they had set out to do in their two ritual performances. They had estimated, correctly, that the person whose opinion really mattered was the judge's, and they had asserted that *rom* had its own jurisdiction, by enacting it through performance.[22]

What happens to the discourse about sovereignty when it becomes overt in the context of the court is demonstrated by the following passage from the court transcript—an exchange between the counsel for one of the respondent parties and witness W:

> CR: ... Now, in that paragraph you say that Yolngu law applies to everyone on Yolngu country whether they are Yolngu or Aboriginals from other parts of Australia or even non-Aboriginal people; is that right? Does Yolngu law apply to non-Aboriginal people just because they're on Yolngu country?
> W: Yes.
> CR: So you really expect non-Aboriginal people who are on Yolngu country to follow all of Yolngu law?
> W: Yes.
> CR: Okay. Now, under Yolngu law people are either Dhuwa or Yirritja, is that right?
> W: Yes.
> CR: But non-Aboriginal people like the ones living at Nhulunbuy, they're living on Yolngu country, aren't they?
> W: Yes.
> CR: But they're not either Dhuwa or Yirritja, are they?
> W: No.[23]

The same question and answer routine was then deployed to extract a 'no' answer about clan membership, initiation ceremonies, and correct behaviour with kin, and the passage ended thus:

---

[22] It may be that the Yolngu actually wanted to achieve more through the enactment of *rom*—namely to force the recognition of its sovereignty in relation to Yolngu land and sea. However, although the judge was explicit in his recognition that this was a separate system of law with its own jurisdiction, he was not thereby making a statement about sovereignty. As noted before, like all the other non-Yolngu involved in the case he was working from the premise that the Australian legal system and the Australian law is, unequivocally, an expression of the sovereignty of the Australian state over all its citizens. I am grateful to Sturt Glacken (pers. comm. 9 November 2005) for comments that helped me to clarify my thinking on this point.

[23] T643.04–28.

CR: So really Yolngu law doesn't apply to non-Yolngu people, does it, just because they're on Yolngu country?
W: Yes, it does.[24]

It is hard to know what counsel for the respondent was trying to achieve here, apart from the undermining of the witness's confidence, to soften him up for subsequent questions. It was notable that he did not touch on those aspects of 'Yolngu law' relevant to native title—aspects relating to permission—until after this exchange. W's final response is interesting, since it seems at face value to be merely defiant, and to be unsupported by his answers to the previous questions.[25] It is, however, supported by a deeper logic concerning the nature of sovereignty.

Ancestral forces insert their own performance

On the second site visit it seemed that the sea itself had decided to make manifest its ancestral forces. In the preceding days it had been like a millpond (Fig. 2.7). Indeed this time of year had been chosen for the hearings because it was usually a time when Mungurru, this named body of deep saltwater, was calm.[26] But when the court arrived at Blue Mud Bay on the day appointed for the view by boat, it was anything but (Fig. 2.8). The party set off in two big boats and an aluminium dinghy, but once out in the bay, in big seas, it became clear that the view would have to be aborted. The dinghy turned back first. The judge, fortunately, was in the biggest and best protected boat, and he and the witnesses and barristers who were with him suffered only a bit of a buffeting. Those of us in the second boat, pictured in Fig. 2.8, returned somewhat battered, shivering and soaked to the skin.

---

[24] T644.26–29.
[25] It should be noted, however, that in cases where Yolngu forge friendships with non-Yolngu people those people are, invariably, incorporated into the Yolngu kinship system, and thus into a moiety and a clan. In many cases they are also given a Yolngu name.
[26] For a detailed discussion of the sea country of the Yolngu and their relationship to it see Morphy and Morphy (2006).

Fig. 2.7 Mungurru on a calm day

Photo: Frances Morphy

Fig. 2.8 Mungurru on the day of the 'view'

Photo: Courtesy of Daniel Lavery

In the boat, at the height of the battering, one of the interpreters had said to me, sotto voce, 'they won't forget the name of Mungurru now.' Later on the same day I heard Yolngu saying to one another that Mungurru had been offended by the presence of so many strangers. At least some of the non-Yolngu who experienced the power of Mungurru on that day were prepared to acknowledge the believability of the belief, or at least to acknowledge the strength of the Yolngu belief. In court the next day, the following exchange took place between one of the respondents' barristers and the witness who was then in the box:

> CR: ... Mr X, a last question from me: yesterday when we went out to sea, it was very rough; do you have a belief or an explanation as to why it was rough yesterday?
> X: I felt it myself too. Yes, I felt it; maybe the country didn't want us, or the sea didn't want us.
> CR: Was that that Mungurru you think?
> X: That's the Mungurru I'm talking about.
> CR: So was that the reaction you think he may have had?
> X: Yes.
> CR: Thanks very much, Mr X.
> X: Thank you.[27]

The Mungurru episode and its interpretation holds the key to understanding W's final assertion in the passage quoted above, and to the Yolngu insistence on incommensurability discussed below. For the basis of *rom*, in the Yolngu view, is not something that they as human agents have the power to determine. It is determined—always was and always will be—by the ancestral creator beings of the Yolngu world, and such forces are not something over which humans—any humans—have sovereignty. In that sense then, Euro-Australian law can never have sovereignty over *rom*, no matter what mundane power relations hold, in a political sense, between the two communities.

The insistence on difference

Technically speaking, Yolngu are Australian citizens and Australian law is 'their' law as much as it is any other Australian's. But their way of modelling the relationship between the two laws shows clearly that they view the matter rather differently. As one witness put it:

> We're living in the two worlds today, for example. Your world is change every day or every month or every year. My law and my story, it can't change.[28]

---

[27] T904.33–905.03.
[28] T284.02–04; the witness did not mean by this that *rom* cannot accommodate new circumstances, but that its basic and underlying principles are eternal and immutable.

It is not simply that Yolngu value their difference and assert their 'right' to be different. From their point of view it is not a matter of choice. They feel themselves to be fundamentally and intrinsically different from 'white' people because of their relationship to their country and its ancestral forces. As the same witness put it, succinctly, 'You stand for power, white people, but we stand for our land and the sea'.[29]

In the context of the court hearing, Yolngu constantly asserted difference. They pointed out the non-equivalence of concepts, and the problems of translation between the two systems, and in particular they asserted the permanence of *rom* (as opposed to 'law'). Here is just one example of several, in which a witness's evidence is being led by the counsel for the applicants. There are many things going on in this dialogue. One is an assertion of the difference between Yolngu *rom* and Euro-Australian 'law', but there is also, in effect, a debate about the nature of the translation process, in which Yolngu are compelled to use English terms such as 'law' when talking about their own institutions:

> CA: ... you mentioned your law, or 'our law' I think you said. Well, what do you mean by that? What do you mean by your 'law'?
> X: My law.
> CA: Yes.
> X: Well, what's that 'law' mean?
> CA: That's right.
> X: What in your - - -
> CA: That's the question I'm asking you.
> X: I'm asking too: what is 'the law' means?
> CA: Well, you - - -
> X: In balanda [English/white person's] way, what youse call it?
> CA: You – you said, 'Under our law, we line the turtle shells up', as I understood you.
> X: Okay, exactly - - -
> CA: That's part of your law. What did you - - -
> X: Well, exactly what I'm talking now. When I'm using Balanda English, well, you should know better than me, you know, because I'm – I'm talking in Yolngu way too you know? My – my tongues are turning around, like, Yolngu way I'm talking, and if I'm using your English now, you should understand this is new to me ... my really language is Yolngu language ... And I cannot – you know, when you talk to me, you know – what is Yolngu story, what this 'law' means, you know, well, I just pick up the English, 'law'. My ngarraku rom, my ngarraku rom is different. I call it rom.[30]

---

[29] T295.47–296.01.
[30] T126.41–127.39

CA: And what does that word mean?

X: Well, I'm telling you it – the law been there forever. It was given from our ancestors to our grandfathers to our father to me. This is what I call rom and law. I'm just putting that English into my – in my way of using of – using or thinking, you know, law. You call it law; I call it rom.[31]

This insistence on incommensurability might not necessarily have been to the applicants' advantage in the context of a native title hearing. And it is notable that X introduced it in a dialogue with his *own counsel*. He was, in effect, restating the Yolngu position as summarised in the introduction. Yolngu *rom* has been encapsulated by *ngapaki* law, but it has not been colonised by it. It cannot be—it remains distinct, it is everlasting, and it is incommensurable with *ngapaki* law. In this witness's view, stated in another context, so long as Yolngu hold fast to their own *rom* they will be Yolngu. If they abandon *rom*, the *rom* will remain in the country, but Yolngu will no longer be Yolngu—they will just be 'Aborigines'. Yolngu identity is thus deeply bound to the fundamental underlying principles of governance generated by *rom*. It is, as they say, the 'foundation' of their existence and identity. Native title as a process seeks to impose commensurability between *rom* and law in order to make the former legible to the latter, and so potentially 'recognisable'.

Yolngu thus find themselves in a complex double bind. To submit *rom* to commensurability is in itself impossible in the Yolngu view, whatever the pretensions of the *ngapaki* native title law. To submit their own conceptualisation of *rom* to a process of enforced commensurability risks alienation from *rom*, and from their identity as Yolngu. Yet in resisting commensurability they potentially deny themselves advantages that might accrue from recognition of 'their' native title. Their response to this double bind—seeking to maintain a discourse about sovereignty within the dominant discourse of native title—was equally complex.

Conclusion

At the time of writing, the Blue Mud Bay case is still in the court system. It is a complex case involving both native title and the ALRA—the latter with respect to the waters above the intertidal zone, which is Aboriginal land under ALRA. Both matters were run simultaneously, under native title conditions, that is, as a hearing before a Judge of the Federal Court. The determination (as finalised by Justice Mansfield following the untimely death of Justice Selway) found that Yolngu have exclusive native title to their land country, and while Justice Selway felt himself bound by the *Yarmirr* decision in the High Court to say that exclusive native title rights and land rights under the ALRA do not extend to the waters

---

[31] T127.45–128.05.

over the intertidal zone, this does not, in his opinion, reflect the situation under customary law which is no different to that on the land proper:

> The Northern Territory also submitted that the evidence did not establish a right to exclusive occupation of the sea. In this regard the Northern Territory referred me to the factual findings of Olney J in Yarmirr TJ. In that case his Honour was not satisfied that the relevant Aboriginal tradition involved a right of exclusive possession. I can only assume that his Honour was faced with different evidence to that which is before me (Selway J 2005 [214]).[32]

This initial finding can be seen as a partial victory—the most that could realistically be expected under the native title regime. It states, in effect, that prior to colonisation *rom* was sovereign both on the land and in the sea. But the Yolngu did not see this as a victory, and nor indeed was it, in terms of Realpolitik, since it did not give them the control that they were seeking over their sea country. For his part, Mr Justice Selway regarded his conclusions as problematic for reasons to do with the relative status of various kinds of European law, particularly the status of the common law 'right to fish' as against the status of fee simple under the ALRA, thus giving possible grounds for appeal. In the appeal to the Federal Court, three Federal Court Judges overturned the part of his determination relating to the operation of the ALRA in the intertidal zone, so that the waters over the intertidal zone now come under the ALRA (at least for the moment), and Yolngu (and all other traditional owners with coastal estates on ALRA land) have the right to exclude others from their intertidal waters. The case will now go to the High Court.

In the 'recognition space' of the native title arena the Yolngu, despite convincing the Judge that under their customary law they had the right to exclude others from their sea country, failed to get that exclusive right recognised in Australian law. Their interim victory on first appeal relies on the ALRA rather than native title, so has no implications for others outside the ALRA lands. From the perspective of the applicants if not from those raised to view the rules of Euro-Australian legal procedure as normative, irony has now taken centre stage. The only protagonists in the appeals process are judges and other lawyers—practitioners of Australian law. If Yolngu attend it is only as 'the

---

[32] Nicholas Evans, in a paper on the linguistic evidence in the Croker (Yarmirr) case, points out that 'much of the evidence that led Justice Olney to this conclusion [that the permission system applied only to Aboriginal people] turns on modal verbs [e.g. 'can', 'must', 'should] in the witness' evidence' (2002: 87). He goes on to show that Justice Olney misinterpreted a key witness's non-standard use of modal verbs, deriving a meaning from the witness's statement that was precisely the opposite of what the witness had intended by his evidence. There is a strong case for saying, then, that Justice Olney did not in fact hear evidence that was substantially different from that heard in the Blue Mud Bay case, but rather that the judgement in the Yarmirr case was based on flawed analysis of the evidence, with potential repercussions down the line for the Blue Mud Bay case and, indeed, all subsequent native title cases that concern the sea.

public', although it is the fate of their sea country and of their relationship to it that is in the balance.

The Yolngu experience of the native title process has thus far been relatively benign, certainly by comparison with the experiences of some other claimant groups detailed in this volume (see e.g. Redmond, Chapter 4). They started from a position of strength. They already held their land country under ALRA, and they had never been alienated from or forced off their land estates, so that many of the issues about identity that other claimant groups face did not arise. As a collectivity they were able to show a united front, and to put forward a coherent, consistent and convincing account of their system of 'laws and customs'. There were no competing claims. They brought to the arena a strong view of themselves as uncolonised subjects. The fact that part of the case related to ALRA rather than to native title was also an advantage, since there was the prospect of gaining delimited exclusive rights under that regime, whereas, because of *Yarmirr*, there was really no prospect of gaining exclusive native title rights to the sea. They also encountered a judge with whom they were able to forge a relationship of mutual respect, even if neither party fully understood the other's agenda. Justice Selway's clear insistence on the limits of his interests in the case, legally speaking, combined with his evident respect for their system of 'laws and customs', provided a space for Yolngu to reaffirm their sense of sovereignty—at least to themselves, and for the time being.

The Yolngu of Blue Mud Bay have not as yet been exposed to the full weight of codification, as described by Glaskin in this volume (Chapter 3), since there has been no move, as yet, to set up a prescribed body corporate for the claim area. For the moment, through resisting commensurability in the court, they have been able also to cleave to the 'two worlds' model, in which the state's particular objectification of 'their' native title is seen by them as essentially irrelevant to *rom* and the social field that is founded in it.

However, in the court's terms the dialogue could be perceived at most as being about jurisdiction, and 'rights'. In the longer term the Yolngu view of themselves as encapsulated but not colonised—as 'living in two worlds'—will come under increasing pressure. They have been able to sustain that view until now because ALRA, unlike most European law, appeared immutable. In reality, like any other piece of Euro-Australian law, it can be changed and its effects substantially undermined by a government with the will to do so operating in particular political circumstances. Those changes—which may be viewed as the final act of colonisation—are beginning to happen now.

Acknowledgments

I thank the participants in the 'Effects of Native Title' workshop for their comments on the version of this paper that was presented there, and Sturt

Glacken for his thoughtful and perspicacious comments on the first draft of the paper, and for saving me from solecisms that were the product of my unfamiliarity with matters of the law. I would like to have addressed all his comments, but that would have turned this into a different—and longer—paper. The second draft benefited greatly from Tom Keely's detailed comments, and I hope that I have gone some way towards taking them properly into account. I also thank Daniel Lavery, David Martin, Howard Morphy and Rebecca Morphy for their comments on the second draft. Needless to say, all remaining solecisms and errors of fact or interpretation are my responsibility alone.

References

Evans, N. 2002. 'Country and the word: linguistic evidence in the Croker sea claim', in J. Henderson and D. Nash (eds), *Language in Native Title*, Native Title Research Series, Aboriginal Studies Press, Canberra.

Gawirrin Gumana & Ors vs Northern Territory of Australia & Ors 2004. Federal Court Transcript.

Mantziaris, C. and Martin, D. 2000. *Native Title Corporations: A Legal and Anthropological Analysis*, The Federation Press, Sydney, in co-operation with National Native Title Tribunal, Perth.

Morphy, H. 1983. '"Now you understand": an analysis of the way Yolngu have used sacred knowledge to retain their autonomy, in N. Peterson and M. Langton (eds), Aborigines, Land and Land Rights, Australian Institute of Aboriginal Studies Press, Canberra.

Morphy, H. and Morphy, F. 2006. 'Tasting the waters: discriminating identities in the waters of Blue Mud Bay', *Journal of Material Culture*, 11 (1/2): 67–85.

Selway, J 2005. The 'Blue Mud Decision' *Gumana v Northern Territory of Australia* [2005] FCA 50.

Stanner, W. E. H. 1979. 'The Yirrkala case: dress-rehearsal', in W. E. H. Stanner, *White Man Got No Dreaming: Essays by W. E. H. Stanner*, Australian National University Press, Canberra.

Williams, N. 1986. *The Yolngu and Their Land: A System of Land Tenure and the Fight for Its Recognition*, Australian Institue of Aboriginal Studies, Canberra.

Williams, N. 1987. *Two Laws: Managing Disputes in a Contemporary Aboriginal Community*, Australian Institute of Aboriginal Studies, Canberra.

3. Claim, culture and effect: property relations and the native title process

Katie Glaskin

> Because the subjective necessity and self-evidence of the commonsense world are validated by the objective consensus of that world, what is *essential goes without saying because it comes without saying*: the tradition is silent, not least about itself as tradition; customary law is content to enumerate specific applications of principles which remain implicit and unformulated, because unquestioned …
>
> (Bourdieu (1977: 167), original emphasis).

Since the advent of the *Native Title Act 1993* (Cwlth) (NTA), Indigenous Australians have been able to make claims to their traditional lands. Patton (2000: 28) describes Aboriginal or native title as representing 'an attempt to translate indigenous peoples' spiritual and economic relation to their land into a form of property right recognisable by the common law'. One could argue that native title represents more a codification of some Aboriginal property rights than it does an attempted translation, given that native title is limited to only certain rights in lands and waters, and has not thus far included the recognition of incorporeal property rights (Glaskin 2003). Notwithstanding the limitations of native title and its capacity to recognise only certain Indigenous property rights, one consequence of the attempted 'translation' and subsequent codification of native title rights and interests through the native title process is a legal interrogation of certain aspects of Indigenous Australians' relations to land. To gain recognition of their native title, Indigenous claimants are required to demonstrate continuity with the 'traditional laws and customs'—those practiced by their antecedents at the time of the acquisition of sovereignty by the British Crown—from which their native title rights and interests are derived.

Property is inherently relational: it involves a person owning something as against other people, that is, in relation to them; or exercising rights and obligations with respect to the thing owned, as against others (Hallowell 1955: 238–9). A condition of demonstrating native title is that Indigenous claimants must articulate and objectify aspects of their property relations in response to the legislative requirements of the NTA. This objectification of relations to country occurs not only at a level that is in some sense external to Indigenous groups, in terms of a determination of native title (where a determination is ultimately made: not all claims result in determinations), but also occurs amongst and by Indigenous people themselves in response to various *processes* associated with making claims. These objectifications, I argue, have the potential to affect social relations within Indigenous groups, and hence their property relations.

This chapter examines some of the effects of participating in native title processes amongst Bardi and Jawi people, who live in the northwest Kimberley region of Western Australia. My focus here is on the native title processes they engaged in prior to the determination of their native title. Work on their combined native title claim first began in 1994, when the *Native Title Act* was quite new. The case was heard at various times between the years 2001 and 2004. In 2005, French J, the second trial judge to hear the case, made a determination,[1] and in February 2007 this determination was appealed before the Full Federal Court. At the time of writing the outcome from this appeal was pending. For Bardi and Jawi, the prolonged (and often onerous) process of claiming country has had a number of impacts, effects and consequences, apart from those arising from this determination and the appeal process. As they engaged with native title, some of the 'compelling but largely implicit premises of [their] cultural practice' (Scott 1993: 322) have been brought into the realm of discourse, objectifying aspects of their 'traditional laws and customs' and relations to country. Based on fieldwork carried out between 1994 and 2003, I argue that these objectifications, in turn, have had implications for the articulation and enactment of property relations amongst Bardi and Jawi peoples. By objectification, I follow Strathern (1999: 13) to mean 'the way in which entities are made into objects through the relations which people have with one another'.

Thomason (1982: 124,126) describes objectification as 'necessarily' involving a '"distancing" of man from his products', where these products become 'objects' or 'things', and 'are taken to be, in some sense, "external", "factual", "independent of how we might think about them ..."'. In the native title context, aspects of Indigenous culture such as 'laws and customs' and 'rights and interests' are made visible and conceptually divisible (sometimes extinguishable) by the political, economic and legislative circumstances in which such claims are and can be made. The articulation of native title rights and interests is an example of the way in which objectification can go, deriving from a set of relations to land a set of rights that may be apprehended as 'things', in some sense external from those relations from which they are sourced (Glaskin 2003).

In Wagner's (1981 [1975]: 34) view, 'when culture is assumed self-consciously', identity must always be involved, although 'identity by no means exhausts or explains the usage'. Roosens (1989: 150) argues that 'in order to see and use one's own culture as a right, one must first have gained distance from that culture'. Where indigenous claims are tested within legal contexts, the kinds of cultural characteristics indigenous groups are likely to ascribe to themselves and consider

---

[1] *Sampi v State of Western Australia* [2005] FCA 777.

relevant highlight those aspects of their cultures that are elicited (and indeed required to prove their claims) within those contexts. As writers such as Barth (1970: 38) and Roosens (1989: 12) suggest, only some features of a particular culture become diacritic markers of social or cultural boundaries, and this phenomenon of cultural differentiation reflects on intercultural communication and social action across these 'boundaries'. Objectification of certain cultural features over others becomes especially evident where indigenous peoples assert rights and the state seeks to recognise these, as in claims to native title. As I argue, the effects of these responses within indigenous groups is to foster self-conscious definitions of their culture at the least, and may also have an important role in internal group definition and reproduction, especially where such objectification becomes reified or codified in some form.

Law and culture

Like many Australian Indigenous peoples, Bardi and Jawi have long objectified certain facets of their culture, like the ancestral figures whose deeds and authority are inscribed in landscape and in ritual. The English word they typically use to encompass the kinds of notions that are embedded in the English word 'Dreaming' is 'the Law'.[2] 'The Law' is distinct from 'Law business'; the latter specifically refers to ritual activity which certain ancestral beings 'gave' them to follow, while implicit in the former is the totality of the ancestral beings' activities and precepts; it encodes the entirety of their religious belief and mythopoeia.

Most Bardi and Jawi view 'Law business' (male ritual) as the foundation of other aspects of 'culture'. The status accorded to male ritual in their society makes it one of the most significant and potent of the objectifications of the ancestral creative deeds. Most Bardi and Jawi who live in their country are involved in the practice of Law, which is a religious obligation of utmost importance to them. Many others who are resident in Broome or Derby travel up the peninsula to take part in ritual with those who are resident at communities in the peninsula. Young boys are 'put through' the Law every year. Women participate in many aspects of Law too, such as *Anggwuy*, the public ceremony before the boys are secluded for initiation, in *Nguril*, the public ceremony to welcome the boys out from the bush following *Irrganj*; and in a restricted way, in *Ululung* (Bagshaw 1999: 29). Men participate in all facets of Law business, and much of the Law is restricted and secret male-only business.

Bardi and Jawi consider their Law to be integral to their being-in-the-world, and consider it inalienable in the sense that, as one senior Jawi man described it, 'we can't stand, we belong to Law'.[3] Myers' observations regarding 'the

---

[2] Bardi do not have a single, collectively espoused term to encompass the concept of 'Dreaming' or 'Dreamtime'; see Glaskin (2005) for further discussion of this.
[3] Khaki Stumpagee Video Transcript 2001, p. 32. Interview with Geoffrey Bagshaw at Nillargoon outstation, Iwanyi, Sunday Island 16th July 1997, transcribed by Katie Glaskin. Tendered in the Federal

Dreaming' (which he equates with 'the Law') among the Pintupi are equally applicable to Bardi Law:

> The Dreaming—'the Law'—provides a moral authority lying outside the individual and outside human creation. It is not his idea or his will. Thus, although the Dreaming as an ordering of the cosmos is presumably a product of historical events, such an origin is denied. These human creations are objectified—thrust out—into principles or precedents for the immediate world (1986: 69).

As Myers suggests, Indigenous Australians have long possessed their own techniques of objectification, whereby their 'culture' has been revealed to them. Like other Australian Indigenous groups such as the Pintupi and Walbiri, Bardi and Jawi participate in these 'objectifications already created by the ancestors, and are [consider themselves] bound to them' (Munn 1970: 157). Thus their Law—the equivalent of Munn's (1970: 157–8) 'mode of orientation'—'mystifies human agency in the construction of forms of sociality' assimilating events 'to a pre-existing order which is objectified in features of the local landscape' (Rumsey 1994: 121; and see Merlan 1998: 215–16; Myers 1986: 286–8).

For Bardi and Jawi, like numerous other Kimberley peoples, the phrase 'Law and culture' is a shorthand way to emphasise the distinctiveness of their indigenous life-world.[4] Strathern's (1999: 128) comments on 'culture' are appropriate to Kimberley Aboriginal usage of the term: 'in borrowing the concept of "culture", people appear to be doing what is done everywhere, fastening on to certain "customs" as diagnostic of their way of life … culture/*kastom* is also used to signify difference'. The 'Law and culture' linkage and word order emphasises that Law, in a primordial sense, comes before 'culture'; Aborigines who have 'no Law' (who have ceased to practice Law) are often characterised by Bardi (at least) as having 'no culture'. Conversely, Aborigines who practice Law are 'culture people'. For Bardi and Jawi, humans are not the only beings with 'Law and culture'; dugongs especially, but turtles and other marine species are conceptualised as possessing ('they got') 'culture', because they have 'their own Law' (and see Rouja 1998: 244). This characterisation of these species as having their 'own Law' is based on their observable traits, their interactions with other members of their species and their behaviour (seasonality, mobility and foraging habits) within their marine environment. The predictability and immutability of their conduct gives rise to these creatures as being considered Law-like, and hence possessing 'culture'.

Court of Australia, Western Australia District Registry General Division, *Paul Sampi v State of Western Australia*, WAG 49/1998.

[4] For example, KALACC, the Kimberley Aboriginal Law and Culture Centre located in Fitzroy Crossing, specifically promotes indigenous 'Law and culture'.

Bardi and Jawi are proud of their culture, and many people assiduously collect objects reflective of it. Traditionally, they traded objects such as boomerangs (*irrgil*), hairbelts (*arnala*), engraved pearlshells (*riji*), hairbelts attached to plain pearl shells (*baali-guwarn*) and mangrove log rafts (*galwa* in Bardi; *biel-biel* in Jawi). Natural resources like red ochre (*bidimarr*) and white ochre (*maanga*) were also traded. Such trade or exchange occurred amongst Bardi and Jawi, and with other neighbouring and more distant Aborigines. Some of these traditional objects of exchange appear in contemporary Bardi personal collections today.

Along with various artifacts, most Bardi houses contain prominent photographic displays of their kin painted up and dressed for ceremony, as well as photographs of the 'old people' from previous generations. Many people also collect taped recordings (both amateur and professional) of traditional songs, and published and unpublished material on Bardi and Jawi culture and history. Several people have told me of their desire to set up a cultural centre, either at One Arm Point, or smaller displays at their outstations, with a view to engaging in cultural tourism. This is one of the few avenues for developing Indigenous business enterprise in the area. Some Bardi people already engaged in small-scale tourism ventures see tourist interest as also providing some cultural recognition, given the evident expertise in their own culture that they can readily display in these contexts. Since the early 1990s, some Bardi have been making home videos of traditional methods of cutting up dugong and turtle, identification and use of bush foods, and public aspects of ritual, including preparations like the painting and adorning of initiates, hairbelt spinning, and boomerang and shield production. These videos have proved to be popular with other members of the Bardi and Jawi community, among whom they are widely disseminated. Many of the videos are used in classrooms at One Arm Point and Lombadina; both schools have Bardi language programs as well.[5]

Bardi collection and recording of cultural material reflects considerable pride in their culture. Such practices are also illustrative of a concern for cultural preservation and reproduction, as against an implicit—and frequently explicit—acknowledgment that the terms in which their culture is expressed is changing with increasing engagement with a modernising world. In this respect, native title is the latest in a series of legislative regimes which they have encountered, but is distinct from them, both because it is legislation aimed at recognising their traditional property entitlements, and correspondingly because of its emphasis on the 'traditional laws and customs' that give rise to these. Consequently, engagement with native title has quite different *effects* amongst Bardi and Jawi than those produced through previous historical and legislative encounters (which are more fully explored in Glaskin 2002). As I demonstrate briefly below, while certain aspects of their culture have been objects of interest

---

[5] Although some Jawi words are still used, the language itself is no longer spoken.

historically, these are distinct from those aspects of their culture (in particular, of their property relations) that are central to their engagement with the native title process.

A historical view

Sunday Island mission was established on the Jawi island of Iwanyi (Sunday Island) in 1899. Originally established as a non-denominational mission by the pearler Sydney Hadley, it was taken over by the United Aborigines Mission in 1923, and, with the exception of an unsuccessful relocation attempt to Wotjulum on the eastern side of the King Sound (1934–5), remained operational at the island until 1962. Following its closure, most of the Jawi and Bardi people who had lived at the island moved to Derby, where their children had been relocated in order to attend school. In 1972, without government assistance, they returned to the Dampier Peninsula where they established the community of One Arm Point on the Bardi mainland. Also on the mainland, the Pallottine order of the Catholic Church set up Lombadina mission in 1910, which is today a secular Aboriginal community. (Djarindjin Aboriginal community, established in the 1980s, is situated immediately adjacent to Lombadina). Prior to the establishment of the missions in Bardi and Jawi country, the discovery of rich pearling grounds had brought pearling fleets into the area from the early 1880s, and interactions with the pearlers constitutes the beginning of sustained contact with Europeans in this region.

From the earliest days of colonial contact, missionaries and other Europeans who lived in close proximity to Bardi and Jawi peoples made distinctions between some cultural practices (which were considered acceptable) as against others (which were not). During the early period of the United Aborigines Mission at Sunday Island, for example, the missionaries opposed overtly different cultural practices (various initiatory rites, tooth evulsion, cicatrisation, junior levirate marriage, traditional burial practices and so on) and sought to transform indigenous belief as well as practice (Glaskin 2002: 92–6).

Some aspects of Bardi culture also became *objects* of interest and attention during the early days of missionary operations in this region. Father Nicholas Emo, who began a short-lived mission at Disaster Bay and later worked at Lombadina mission, was 'a keen collector of native weapons and other tribal artefacts ... and the Dampierlanders, warming to his interest, had gladly bartered their handiwork for tobacco, sugar and tea' (Durack 1997: 220). Emo took notes on the 'customs' of both Nyul Nyul in the Beagle Bay area and Bard[6] at Lombadina, and sought to identify marriage rules and kinship terms.[7] Father Worms, a

---

[6] Bard and Bardi are dialects of one language; Bard speakers are mainly associated with Lombadina and Djarindjin communities.
[7] Copies of these workbooks are located in Records of Daisy M. Bates [MS 365] in the manuscript section of the National Library of Australia, Canberra. These workbooks were compiled by Daisy Bates on

missionary at Lombadina between 1931 and 1955, wrote numerous articles on various aspects of Bard society and culture, showing that he had an active interest in these matters.[8]

The Western Australian government also had an interest in certain aspects of Aboriginal culture. In 1904, they produced a blank workbook[9] and distributed it to those working with Indigenous people in Western Australia. Most of the workbook, entitled 'Native Vocabulary etc., compiled by [blank to be filled out]', calls for vocabulary, but at the back of the workbook there is some space (pp. 87–97) for 'questions'. Among the questions in the back of the workbooks were the following:

Question 5: *Native modes of burial in the district?*

Question 8: *Game traps (kangaroo, emu, etc.), other methods of capture, description of?*

Question 14: *Legends, songs, and folklore (if any); legend of 'Bunnyar'?*

Question 16: *Extent of tribal country, and approximate number of natives in the district?*

Question 17: *Native names of tribes in the district?*

Question 20: *Do the tribes meet at any distant places for exchange or barter?*

Question 23: *Is cannibalism known to exist in the district?*

Question 26: *Any idea of a deity?*

Question 27: *Native beliefs in ghosts, or a future state?*

Question 28: *What beliefs have the natives in witchcraft, sorcery; and is there a 'boyl-ya' or sorcerer among the tribes in the district?*

Both Sydney Hadley and W. H. Bird filled out these workbooks[10] with respect to 'the natives' at Sunday Island mission. Bird's published accounts of Jawi language and 'customs' were based on the information in these books.[11] The production and distribution of the workbook by the Western Australian government indicates that they were, in some fashion, interested in collating material that could be potentially useful in their governance of Aboriginal people.

---

behalf of the Western Australian Government, and 'despatched to all the postmasters, police officers, station owners and settlers in the State' (Bates 1985: 10).

[8] See e.g. Worms (1940, 1942, 1944, 1949, 1950, 1957, 1959); this is not an exhaustive list.

[9] Copies of these workbooks are located in Records of Daisy M. Bates [MS 365] in the manuscript section of the National Library of Australia, Canberra. Bates evidently used these books during a certain period of her ethnographic investigations, although she is not the only one to have done so.

[10] These are located in Records of Daisy M. Bates, MS 365, Box 27, Item Numbers 53/110, 53/111, and 53/116. Canberra: National Library of Australia.

[11] See Bird (1910, 1911, 1915).

Various objects and practices were also imbued with a commercial dimension following colonisation and engagement with the capitalist state. In the early days of the pearling industry, Bardi and Jawi traded artefacts (as they had done traditionally with other Aborigines) and resources (such as water and knowledge of where to find water) with pearling crews in exchange for introduced objects (like tobacco, flour, tea and alcohol). Sunday Island missionaries used Bardi and Jawi labour to harvest pearl shell, trepang, tortoise shell and trochus shell in order to sustain the mission economically. In this respect they were reliant not just on labour but on Bardi and Jawi knowledge of the marine environment, and on their navigational and sea-faring skills. Lombadina missionaries sought to capitalise on 'traditional' skills evident in artefact manufacture, teaching handicrafts at the mission for some years prior to World War II. When servicemen were stationed at Cape Leveque during the war, Lombadina residents traded wood-carvings and pearl shell ornaments with them (Robinson 1973: 173). In the 1960s, under the direction of the missionaries, Lombadina residents manufactured boomerangs for sale to boost the mission economy.[12]

The focused attention upon certain aspects of their society, in connection with various legislation, economic, technological and other changes arising from colonial encounters, are significant components of the conjunctural field in which Bardi and Jawi objectifications of some cultural elements have emerged post-colonisation. These objectifications have typically concentrated on outward, observable cultural forms, not on the 'inner workings' of a system of land and sea ownership. Indeed, in Australia as in other colonised countries, European powers justified their colonisation of indigenous peoples and the appropriation of their lands on a basis that was directly antithetical to such investigations: namely, that indigenous peoples were considered too 'primitive' to have had property laws or institutions of governance (Culhane 1998: 31). Hence Aboriginal property relations, while of research interest to some, have not been subjected to the kind of wholesale elucidation that engagement with native title processes has elicited, in which principles of inheritance, succession, rights and interests, boundaries, genealogies, and so on, are objectified for the purposes of interrogating whether native title can be recognised, and to what degree.[13]

Among Bardi and Jawi, it is the case that certain missionaries and anthropologists in the region have been interested in some less overt aspects of their 'culture'. The effects of these interventions, however, are distinct from those engendered by engagement with the native title process. In the latter, the communal emphasis

---

[12] Father Kreiner, pers. comm., 15/12/94.
[13] Of course, it may be the case that under the Aboriginal Land Rights (Northern Territory) Act 1976 (Cwlth), Aboriginal groups bringing claims under the legislation were required to similarly objectify their property relations. In Western Australia though, native title represents the first legislative opportunity for Indigenous Australians to have their traditional property rights recognised in legal form.

of native title means that a broader socio-territorial group (not the individual) has been required to objectify their property relations in terms of 'traditional laws and customs': to articulate the 'rules' by which people are connected to country, by which they may succeed to it, and to elaborate on the kinds of rights and obligations that flow from their connection to country. While the elaboration of laws and customs that give rise to rights and interests in land is somewhat analogous to describing the external authority of 'the Law', these objectifications differ from those regarding 'the Law', both in *kind*—through stimulating explicit claims concerning individual or family group affiliations to publicly be made—and in terms of the *conditions* under which such objectifications occur—in response to the requirements of the NTA and in contexts where non-Indigenous people will test and adjudicate these claims regarding relations to country.

Objectifying culture in the context of native title

The outcomes of native title cases are finally determined through mediation or litigation. Both result in a legal determination of the extent to which native title rights and interests can be recognised at law, although in some cases, of course, determinations are made that native title cannot be recognised. The time between when work on a native title claim begins and its resolution can be quite substantial. In the Bardi and Jawi case, work on the claim formally began in 1994. Following litigation, a determination was made in 2005, and an appeal to the full Federal Court was heard in early 2007. During the years since work on the claim began, Bardi and Jawi have constantly been involved in various processes associated with their claim, including claim research, meetings to give legal instructions, to make communal decisions about land use in the area under claim in response to various developments, in mediations and negotiations, giving evidence in the Federal Court (in 2001 and again in 2003), attending other court evidence including the Federal Court appeal in this case in 2007, and more.

While some Aboriginal groups claiming native title may achieve consent determinations without facing litigation, all groups holding native title are required to form a prescribed body corporate (PBC) to hold and manage their native title rights and interests. My exploration of the effects of engaging with native title processes here focuses on discussions concerning the development of a PBC, which, amongst Bardi and Jawi, began long before the determination of their case in June 2005. The discussions I refer to here principally took place between 1996 and 1998. Further discussions have no doubt taken place since then, and it should be emphasised that my observations here are limited to those negotiations, and that these occurred pre-determination.

The *Native Title Act* requires an incorporated native-title holding body, a PBC, to hold the native title rights and interests that form the 'title' once the case has been determined. Like other corporations, a PBC requires a constitution outlining the rules and objectives by which the corporation will operate. Long before their native title claim had been heard in the Federal Court, the Kimberley Land Council—concerned about formalising land-use decisions in the area under claim—convened meetings with Bardi and Jawi claimants to discuss issues related to the development of a constitution for their PBC (this began in 1996; the claim was first heard in 2001). However, claimant discussions over these issues were not confined to larger public meetings, but spilled over into every-day talk among members of the claimant group. The issues were considered to be of much consequence, and most claimants saw themselves as vital stakeholders in the outcomes.

As members of the claimant group discussed the constitution for their PBC, one aspect they felt had to be incorporated within the constitution concerned the role of the *madjamadjin* ('Law bosses' or senior ritual experts) within their society. The *madjamadjin* became defined in the draft constitution as 'those Common Law Holders who are recognised in accordance with Aboriginal Law, as having authority to speak about Aboriginal Law, in relation to Traditional Country'. Clause 11.3 of the draft constitution of the Bardi and Jawi PBC defined the role of the *madjamadjin* as including:

> The Majamajin [sic] shall provide advice to the Governing Committee about membership application, assist in resolving disputes between members and advise the Corporation on all matters involving questions of Aboriginal Law.

During the course of their engagement with native title, as various internal disputes have arisen, Bardi have called upon the *madjamadjin* or 'bosses' to arbitrate matters having to do with their 'culture'. This has not provided straightforward solutions, for as one *madja* or 'boss' described it to me—this is my paraphrase—while the roles and responsibilities of the *madjamadjin* within the ritual context are circumscribed, outside of the ritual sphere, no such circumscription exists, and bosses do not necessarily hold uniform opinions or interpretations in relation to cultural matters (and see Keen 1997: 62). This was evident in a number of situations I witnessed and discussed with various people, and the reflection regarding the *madjamadjin* just described was derived from one of these conversations.[14] Authority is often contested between *madja*, and resolution of non-ritual issues in which *madja* intervene is rarely the direct outcome of their actions alone.

Notwithstanding this, the bosses themselves as well as the majority of the claimant group held the view that where a contentious issue concerning land ownership arose, it was the bosses who needed to be called upon to arbitrate the issue. The codification of the role of the *madjamadjin* within the draft constitution represents the Bardi and Jawi attempt to translate and transpose

---

[14] Kolig (1981: 83) describes a similar situation with respect to Fitzroy Crossing.

traditional cultural principles into the context of a draft constitution for a PBC, reflecting what Sullivan (1997: 139) described in another context as being 'nothing less than an attempt at a self-governing structure reflecting customary Aboriginal Law.'

The incorporation of the role of the *madjamadjin* within the draft constitution, like other matters there that I will come to, stemmed from the public discussions concerning the reasons that Bardi and Jawi sought a determination of native title in the first instance. At the time of these discussions, most middle-aged and older Bardi saw native title as inseparable from aspects of their traditional laws and customs that underlay their claim to native title and provided its content. The formation of a PBC was, in their view, closely linked with the development of a particular kind of constitution—one they believed should adequately reflect the basis of their native title, that is to say, their 'culture'. Thus, the 1998 draft constitution of their PBC sought to uphold Bardi and Jawi 'Law, language and culture'. While PBC constitutions do not require this kind of reflection of a group's law and custom, claimant perceptions that native title concerned their culture meant that they approached the development of the constitution from this basis. For example, one claimant expressed the view that 'seeing that this land claim is a countryman thing, *it's about our culture*, it's [the constitution] gotta be Aboriginal more than whiteman'.[15] Another claimant expressed it this way:

> Native title means getting our land back to use it traditionally, so we need to put [into the constitution] those traditional things first, they have to be implemented, but we have to put whiteman's side to protect us from pearlers, miners etc. *But tradition needs to be foremost, our own culture.*[16]

In the context of these public discussions, one claimant[17] pointed out that prescribed rules within a constitution could not ensure cultural reproduction. He said, 'can I strongly talk about this? I'm not against what's been said here, but culture should be taught from home. Sit down with *jawul* [ritual godparent/s] tell stories, who is related to who ...'. This man's observation indicated his reflexivity about the ways in which 'culture' is reproduced, stressing 'the home' as the place where this should occur; an apparently more organic and kin-based form of cultural reproduction than that represented by the codification of certain aspects of 'culture' within a PBC's constitution. His comment goes to the essence of one of the issues I wish to identify here: the effect of the native title process on cultural reproduction, which becomes potentially splintered between dynamism and codification, caught between 'tradition' and the objectification

---

[15] Author's notes from claim meeting, 4 April 1997, emphasis added.
[16] Author's notes from claim meeting, 4 April 1997, emphasis added.
[17] Author's notes from claim meeting, 4 April 1997.

of 'tradition', whether that occurs through PBC 'rules' or indeed through native title determinations. The coexistence of dynamism and objectification also means that, regardless of the extent to which 'rules' reflecting 'tradition' are written into a constitution, 'tradition' will remain open to negotiation and contestation, and therefore the PBC's fidelity to 'tradition' will remain so too. And while dynamism and a codification of sorts (as exemplified in 'the Law') has long been a feature of Aboriginal societies (Glaskin 2005), and are not, in that sense, antithetical to each other, the question of how such dynamism might interact with the written legally enforceable rules of the constitution remains.

As these issues were debated among members of the claimant group, opinions emerged regarding the notion of 'traditional' and whether the use of such concepts by members of the claimant group actually represented a fidelity to tradition. A true understanding and application of 'tradition' was seen as an issue of considerable importance, for the rationale was that if traditional cultural principles ('rules') were sufficiently specified within the constitution, they would provide a base-line for determining process and authority through which internal conflicts over land could be resolved. In this sense, an expectation was placed on the constitution that it would act as an impersonal external authority on these matters (perhaps a bit like 'the Law'). The claimants maintained that the constitution of a PBC should reflect their culture, and therefore saw it as a matter of paramount importance to get the rules 'right'.

'Tradition', property relations, and the constitution

The talk concerning 'tradition' and the authority of the *madjamadjin* within a PBC constitution engendered diverse and shifting reactions among members and sectors of the claimant group. A consequence of this shifting political ground was that some members of the claimant group tended to view the recognition of 'traditional ownership' and systems of attachment to country by Australian law (within the native title context) as leverage through which they could protect their own interests in country. That is, prior to the determination of native title made in 2005, native title for them presented itself as a democratic outside enforcement of 'tradition', such that their rights and interests would be *as* recognised and protected as those of others in their own society. Throughout the native title process, a number of claimants maintained that they would not be involved in the claim unless they had secure undertakings that their specific rights in country would be recognised and respected by the rest of the claimant group, following a native title determination. Accordingly, they maintained a position that principles of land ownership (recognising specific interests in country, with reference to estates or *bur(u)* should be enunciated within the constitution for the PBC. Given that most Bardi and Jawi share this ideal, the principle became enshrined within clause 12.1 the draft constitution of the Bardi and Jawi PBC:

> In so far as it lies within the power of the Corporation to make a decision about a proposal affecting a particular *Bur* [estate], the Corporation shall, before carrying out or authorising or permitting the carrying out of any such proposal… have regard to the interests of, and consult with the common law holders of that *Bur*, or otherwise affected by a proposal, and take all reasonable steps to ensure that those Common Law Holders: (a) are informed; (b) understand the nature of the proposal; (c) have had the opportunity of expressing their views to the Corporation; and (d) consent to the proposal.

That is, the principle they frequently articulate, that the *gamelid* (often equated with patrifiliate or 'traditional owner') of the *buru* (estate) should have the 'top hand' or the 'final say' over what happens in their *buru*, was given an imprimatur of sorts within the draft constitution. The principle of who has 'final say' over country was stated; but the question of who specifically will have authority over particular *buru* will be contested in some cases. Some *buru* too will become deceased estates as their members die out; others are in the midst of processes of succession in the present (Bagshaw 2001: 41–2). There is plenty of scope then for contention over the elaboration of specifics within these principles. Clause 12.2. addresses this issue, again placing the *madjamadjin* in the role of arbitrating disputes and as the authorities on culture: 'Any disputes concerning a *Bur*, including a dispute as to the holder of an interest in that *Bur*, is to be resolved by the Governing Committee on advice from the *Majamajin* [sic], in accordance with Clause 13.'

The constitution thus not only prescribes general principles, but also processes (who is to be consulted; at what time, in what circumstances and contexts). The codification of principles and processes within portions of the draft constitution represents a transition from informal negotiations that may have occurred among the wider jural public over the same issues, and is an articulation elicited through engagement with native title. Such textual codification may transform 'social values and practices' by freezing these at a given point in time and thereby encouraging stasis in the system, and the system itself may dialectically evolve with reference to these representations (Mantziaris and Martin 2000: 43). Perhaps more consequentially, Mantziaris and Martin (ibid.) point to the possibility that such textualisation can 'result in the loss of control by the relevant indigenous people over the interpretation and content of their traditional laws and customs', which could fall to outside specialists such as lawyers and anthropologists. Contexts where this could occur is in 'litigation between indigenous people or between indigenous people and the native title corporation regarding the nature of their entitlements as against one another (their rights *inter se*)' (Mantziaris and Martin 2000: 66).

Conclusion

In this chapter I have argued that the ways in which Bardi and Jawi have articulated and objectified aspects of their culture and identity through engagement with native title processes represents a different kind of objectification of their 'culture' than has previously arisen through colonial encounters. Further, I have suggested that codification arises in part through the native title process itself and in part through the claimants' dialectic engagement with native title, following such objectification. Weiner's description of the effects of codification amongst the Foi of Papua New Guinea is apposite to this discussion:

> Although I have argued elsewhere that for the Foi, what we call law and the quality of being law- or rule-governed is not something that was consciously articulated, the coming of the government administration and Missionaries provided them with exposure to the idea that social law and customary action ... were something that could be objectified, codified and altered by human effort, rather than as phenomena that were only revealed in the course of humans reacting to otherwise situational and contingent social engagements and encounters (1998: 2).

Unlike other contexts in which the imposition of the colonial order, whether through the arrival of missionaries or otherwise, resulted in the codification of Indigenous customary law (Weiner and Glaskin 2006), my view is that this process has only begun to be realised among Bardi and Jawi as they engage communally with the processes of the *Native Title Act*. Through their engagement with the native title process, their principles of customary law are becoming explicit and formulated, and this reflects the formal elicitation of these (through various aspects of the native title process) and the informal elicitation of these that emerges dialectically among the group in response to the former.

While the state is able to circumscribe indigenous claims to country, and this may have an effect on the terms in which Aboriginal claims to country are articulated, this process should not be seen only in these terms. Elsewhere I have demonstrated something of the ways Bardi and Jawi have altered their own conditions of existence, using various strategies to negotiate their relationship with the state, its agents and its policies (Glaskin 2002: 80–105; 107–37). Like other historically constituted actions (such as their return from Derby to Sunday Island), their attempts to draft a constitution for their prescribed body corporate reflecting their 'culture' is an index of their agency, a strategy aimed at ensuring their survival and cultural reproduction.

The circumscription both explicit and immanent within native title (as legislation and as process) should not therefore be limited to being read as having the outcomes of objectification and incorporation of Indigenous groups, even though these are significant effects. Bardi and Jawi reactions to the native title process are manifold, and have resulted in much negotiation over aspects of 'tradition', 'culture', and 'authority' (to take a few examples) amongst them. These internal negotiations within the group were elicited through engagement with the native title process and are reflective of historical engagement with the state. They reveal an articulatory dialectic emerging within what Weiner, following Sahlins, calls 'the culture of the conjuncture, a relational moment that has particular historical and temporal as well as semiotic properties' (2000: 262). The boundaries between the 'internal' and the 'external' are constructed through this process, constituting the claimant group both to members of the group and to the state with which they are engaged.

But amongst Bardi and Jawi too, important 'dialectics of articulation' have been occurring, impacting social and political relations within the group. During the latter part of their Federal Court evidence in 2003, many of the claimants referred to themselves as 'Bardi–Jawi', a term which in 1994 had been primarily used self-referentially by those persons having one Bardi and one Jawi parent, not by Bardi and Jawi people *per se*. This was seemingly consequential for the judge's assessment of the nature of their contemporary society and how this related to Bardi and Jawi socio-linguistic identities in the pre-colonial context. While this is not the place for further discussion of this, it does demonstrate something of the effects of participating in native title processes on the ways that people articulate their identities in response to legal requirements, and signals something about how these articulations might transform over a short period of time. In litigation, much is read into these kinds of objectifications of identity, which might otherwise appear as the kind of shifting ground of articulation occurring commonly in societies in relation to various social processes, and which may indeed reflect temporary responses rather than real ontological or societal transformations.

Quite apart from the form of legal recognition finally made in native title determinations, one of the consequences of engaging in the native title process is the effect this may have on a group's own property relations, on how these relations are articulated and objectified, and perhaps, subsequently codified (and see Glaskin 2007). Amongst Bardi and Jawi, during the PBC discussions preceding their determination, significant questions were raised; not just about their relationship with the state (historically and contemporarily), but also with respect to how they conceptualised and constituted themselves. These questions alone are significant, but they also have important consequences for the descendants of the current generations and for the ongoing reproduction of their culture and property relations over time.

Acknowledgements

This paper is substantially drawn from my PhD research (Glaskin 2002), which would not have been possible without the assistance of the Kimberley Land Council and The Australian National University. I particularly wish to thank my supervisors, Francesca Merlan, Ian Keen and Tim Rowse, for their comments and advice along the long thesis road. I wish also to thank the Berndt Foundation at the University of Western Australia for the postdoctoral fellowship that allowed me to continue writing and thinking about these things. James Weiner and David Trigger provided comments on an earlier draft of the paper on which this chapter is based, and I am grateful to them. I am especially grateful to Geoffrey Bagshaw (my long-term anthropological colleague in this case), and to the many Bardi and Jawi people (including those now deceased) who have generously shared their lives and struggles with me over many years.

References

Bagshaw, G. C. 1999. Native Title Claim WAG 49/98 (Bardi and Jawi) Anthropologist's Report, a report prepared for the Kimberley Land Council on behalf of the native title claimants, February, 1999, Kimberley Land Council, Derby.

Bagshaw, G. C. 2001. 'Applicants' additional anthropological report concerning distribution and spatial extent of local estates (bur[u]) within the Bardi and Jawi native title claim area', filed in the Federal Court of Australia, Western Australia District Registry, General Division, in *Paul Sampi & Ors vs The Premier and State of Western Australia & The Commonwealth of Australia*, WAG 49/1998, 8 February 2001.

Barth, F. 1970. 'Introduction', in F. Barth (ed.), *Ethnic Groups and Boundaries: the Social Organization of Culture Difference*, George Allen & Unwin, London.

Bates, D. M. 1966 [1938]. *The Passing of the Aborigines*. William Heinemann, Melbourne.

Bates, D. M. 1985. *The Native Tribes of Western Australia* (I. White ed.), National Library of Australia, Canberra.

Bates, D. M. n.d. Box 27, Items 53/110, 53/111, 53/116, Records of Daisy M. Bates, MS 365, Manuscript Section, National Library of Australia, Canberra.

Bates, D. M. n.d. Box 50, Items 97/439–458, Records of Daisy M. Bates, MS 365, Manuscript Section, National Library of Australia, Canberra.

Bird, W. H. 1910. 'Some remarks on the grammatical construction of the Chowie-language, as spoken by the Buccaneer Islanders, North-Western Australia', *Anthropos*, 5: 454–6.

Bird, W. H. 1911. 'Ethnographical notes about the Buccaneer Islanders, North Western Australia', *Anthropos*, 6: 174–8.

Bird, W. H. 1915. 'A short vocabulary of the Chowie-language of the Buccaneer Islanders (Sunday Islanders), North Western Australia', *Anthropos*, 10: 180–6.

Bourdieu, P. 1977. *Outline of a Theory of Practice*, Cambridge University Press, Cambridge.

Culhane, D. 1998. *The Pleasure of the Crown: Anthropology, Law and First Nations*, Talon Books, Burnaby, Vancouver.

Durack, M. 1997 [1969]. *The Rock and the Sand*, Corgi, London.

Federal Court Transcript WAG 49/98, *Paul Sampi & Ors v State of Western Australia & Ors* [2001], prepared by Transcript Australia.

Glaskin, K. 2002. Claiming Country: a Case Study of Historical Legacy and Transition in the Native Title Context, PhD Thesis, The Australian National University, Canberra.

Glaskin, K. 2003. 'Native title and the "bundle of rights" model: implications for the recognition of Aboriginal relations to country', *Anthropological Forum*, 13 (1): 67–88.

Glaskin, K. 2005. 'Innovation and ancestral revelation: the case of dreams', *Journal of the Royal Anthropological Institute*, 11 (2): 297–314.

Glaskin, K. (2007). 'Outstation incorporation as precursor to a prescribed body corporate', in J. F. Weiner and K. Glaskin (eds), *Customary Land Tenure and Registration in Indigenous Australia and Papua New Guinea: Anthropological Perspectives*, Asia-Pacific Environment Monograph 3, ANU E Press, Canberra.

Hallowell, A. I. 1955. *Culture and Experience*, University of Pennsylvania Press, Philadelphia.

Keen, I. 1997 [1994]. *Knowledge and Secrecy in an Aboriginal Religion*, Oxford University Press, Melbourne.

Kimberley Land Council 1998. Draft Constitution for the Bardi and Jawi Prescribed Body Corporate 1998, unpublished typescript, Kimberley Land Council, Derby.

Kolig, E. 1981. *The Silent Revolution: the Effects of Modernization on Australian Aboriginal Religion*, Institute for the Study of Human Issues, Philadelphia.

Mantziaris, C. and Martin, D. 2000. *Native Title Corporations: a Legal and Anthropological Analysis*, The Federation Press, Sydney.

Merlan, F. 1998. *Caging the Rainbow: Places, Politics and Aborigines in a North Australian Town*, University of Hawai'i Press, Honolulu.

Myers, F. 1986. *Pintupi Country, Pintupi Self: Sentiment, Place, and Politics among Western Desert Aborigines*, Smithsonian Institute, Washington.

Munn, N. 1970. 'The transformation of subjects into objects in Walbiri and Pitjantjatjara myth', in R. M. Berndt (ed.), *Australian Aboriginal Anthropology*, University of Western Australia Press, Perth.

Patton, P. 2000. 'The translation of indigenous land into property: the mere analogy of English jurisprudence', *Parallex*, 6 (1): 25–38.

Robinson, M. V. 1973. Change and Adjustment among the Bardi of Sunday Island, North-Western Australia, MA Thesis, University of Western Australia, Perth.

Roosens, E. 1989. *Creating Ethnicity: the Process of Ethnogenesis*, Frontiers of Anthropology, Vol. 5, Sage Publications, Newbury Park.

Rouja, P. M. 1998. Fishing for Culture: Toward an Aboriginal Theory of Marine Resource Use among the Bardi Aborigines of One Arm Point, Western Australia, PhD Thesis, University of Durham, Durham.

Rumsey, A. 1994. 'The Dreaming, human agency and inscriptive practice', *Oceania*, 65 (2): 116–30.

Scott, C. H. 1993. 'Custom, tradition, and the politics of culture: Aboriginal self-government in Canada', in N. Dyck and J. B. Waldram (eds), *Anthropology, Public Policy, and Native Peoples in Canada*, McGill-Queen's University Press, Montreal and Kingston.

Strathern, M. 1999. *Property Substance and Effect: Anthropological Essays on Persons and Things*, The Athlone Press, London.

Sullivan, P. 1997. 'Dealing with native title conflicts by recognising Aboriginal political authority', in D. E. Smith and J. Finlayson (eds), *Fighting over Country: Anthropological Perspectives*, CAEPR Research Monograph No. 12, Centre for Aboriginal and Economic Policy Research, The Australian National University, Canberra.

Thomason, B. C. 1982. *Making Sense of Reification: Alfred Schutz and Constructionist Theory*, Humanities Press, Atlantic Highlands, New Jersey.

Wagner, R. 1981 [1975]. *The Invention of Culture*, University of Chicago Press, Chicago.

Weiner, J. F. 1998. 'The incorporated ground: the contemporary work of distribution in the Kutubu oil project area, Papua New Guinea', *Resource Management in Asia-Pacific Working Paper No. 17*, Division of Pacific and Asian History, Research School for Pacific and Asian Studies, The Australian National University, Canberra. Available from: http://coombs.anu.edu.au/Depts/RSPAS/RMAP/weiner.htm, accessed 9 July 2007.

Weiner, J. F. 2000. 'The epistemological foundations of contemporary Aboriginal religion: some remarks on the Ngarrindjeri', *Aboriginal History*, 24: 260–3.

Weiner, J. F. and Glaskin, K. 2006. 'Introduction: the (re-) invention of Indigenous laws and customs', *The Asia Pacific Journal of Anthropology*, 7 (1): 1–13.

Worms, E. A. 1940. 'Religiöse Vorstellungen und Kultur einiger Nord-Westaustralischer Stämme in fünfzig Legenden', *Annali Lateranensi*, 4: 230–82.

Worms, E. A. 1942. 'Die Gonara-Feier im Australischen Kimberley', *Annali Lateranensi*, 6: 207–35.

Worms, E. A. 1944. 'Aboriginal place names in the Kimberley, Western Australia: an etymological and mythological study', *Oceania*, 14 (4): 284–310.

Worms, E. A. 1949. 'An Australian migratory myth', *Primitive Man*, 22 (1–2): 33–8.

Worms, E. A. 1950. 'Feuer und Feuerzeuge in Sage und Brach der Nordwest-Australier', *Anthropos*, 45: 145–64.

Worms, E. A. 1957. 'Australian mythological terms, their etymology and dispersion', *Anthropos*, 52: 732–68.

Worms, E. A. 1959. 'Verbannungslied eines Australischen Wildbeuters: ein Beitrag zur Lyrik der Bad', *Anthropos*, 54: 154–68.

4. Some initial effects of pursuing and achieving native title recognition in the northern Kimberley

Anthony Redmond

This paper is an exploration of some shifts in regional socio-political dynamics brought about by native title litigation between Ngarinyin people and European pastoralist families in the northern Kimberley. Many of the visible signs of violence, mutual antagonism and clear conflicts of interest between the Indigenous and non-Indigenous groups who have co-existed on pastoral leases in the region have often been submerged in the course of everyday interactions between them which seek to highlight shared interests (Redmond 2005; Smith 2002, 2003). The inevitably adversarial process of pursuing native title, however, laid bare many of these conflicts of interest by presenting in the public forum of the Federal Court the moving personal testimonies of those who have lived through an era which arcs across the polarities of initial pastoral settlement (between the two World Wars) and the achievements of Ngarinyin native title holders in the courts (in 2004). Despite the painful revelations produced in court of the underlying power imbalances which have characterised their relationships, both parties are now required to, and indeed often espouse a desire to, continue to co-exist on this same country. Here I attempt to describe and analyse the shaken but persistently preservative nature of some of these relationships.

Some initial effects of the judgement on local lives

In August 2004, Justice Ross Sundberg of the Federal Court delivered to Ngarinyin people the final determination of their native title which recognised their exclusive possession of nearly 30 000 square kilometres of their country in conjunction with the co-existent use and occupation of another 38 000 square kilometres of non-Indigenous owned pastoral leases. The ceremony to present this determination was held at Anbada (Mt Barnett station, an Aboriginal owned pastoral lease), in Gubungarri clan country, 300 kilometres up the Gibb River Road from the service town of Derby. As one might expect, the event was something of a field-day for plying moral capital.

In attendance over three days were about 200 Ngarinyin people, Kimberley Land Council staff and consultants, various station owners and other interested parties, local politicians and a large contingent of lawyers including those acting for the applicants, those acting for the various respondents (e.g. the State, the Western Australian Pastoralists' and Graziers' Association (PGA), individual station owners, the Western Australian Fishing Industry Council, and others), the National Native Title Tribunal, and, of course, the whole Federal Court retinue.

In my view, by far the most frank appraisal of the recent relationship between the applicants and the respondents was given by the judge himself who declared that the legal battle had been a bitterly fought one in which 'no quarter' was given by either side. This statement was in stark contrast to the rather fulsome expressions of sentiments about peaceful co-existence and 'sharing country' emanating from some other parties including the local MP, officials from the Land Council and from the State. The PGA, which had maintained an extremely uncompromising stance throughout the proceedings, pushing the concept of adversarial litigation to its limits, later sent a letter to the National Native Title Tribunal complaining that they had not been invited to speak at the determination ceremony. Fred Chaney, the most senior member of the Tribunal in Western Australia, made a speech in which he frankly admitted his total failure in negotiating an outcome outside of the court. Chaney's admission of the failure of his strong overtures to the claimants to accept a negotiated outcome resonated strongly with the applicants and their legal counsel because the State's out-of-court offer, although only made after the whole of the case had been presented, apparently came nowhere near what the applicants hoped to, and as it turned out, did achieve in court. This result confirmed the applicants' suspicions that mediation may only succeed when the respondents are staring down the barrel of a certain and expensive failure in court, and perhaps not even then.[1]

Amongst the pastoralists attending the ceremony under the Kimberley Land Council's marquee was Susan Bradley, the manageress of two of the larger white-owned leases in the region. This socially prominent woman, once a local shire president and former owner of two iconic properties in the region (originally founded by the Duracks), accompanied by a female British colleague, took up her accustomed position at centre court. Mrs. Bradley is a member of what could be called, without exaggeration, the elite pastoralist contingent. In recent years she has hitched her wagon to the ever-rising fortunes of a Melbourne based QC, Alan Myers, who is now a major lease holder in this region. Although, as far as I am aware, she is not presently an owner of leases here in her own right, her status as something of a rural aristocrat has been preserved through this vicarious association and accompanied her rise to a prominent position on the Pastoral Lands Board. The owner himself seldom visited his remote properties and even his manageress resided part of the year in Broome, some 500 kilometres to the

---

[1] I do not have the space to go into this issue here, but the increasing (and understandable) reluctance of resource starved Representative Bodies to litigate native title claims might be seen as undermining applicants' capacity to achieve a reasonable outcome in negotiated settlements. Talking quietly, as Teddy Roosevelt famously observed, is most effective when 'carrying a big stick'.

west. The day to day management of the station seemed to be designated to various underlings.

The presence of this particular manager at the determination ceremony was something of a provocation to some of the claimants. Over the course of the two years just prior to the instigation of the court proceedings, she and her husband had wooed the claimants with offers of joint economic enterprise initiatives. Although some senior Ngarinyin people always maintained serious reservations about such an involvement they were in no position to reject out of hand any potential economic development opportunities. Thus had begun an informal patronage relationship which saw a number of prominent business and legal people, including some top Sydney silks and company directors, visiting the outstation at Maranbabdidi and discussing their proposals for enterprise development, including purchasing cattle leases in the area in conjunction with Ngarinyin people. A charitable trust called the Wanjina Foundation was established partly for these purposes. However, the senior Ngarinyin people's misgivings about their benefactors began to increase when they were reportedly refused any positions on the board of that foundation. By now, these wealthy patrons had begun to be locally referred to as the 'million thousand mob'.

By the time the Ngarinyin were in the first stages of native title court hearings their alienation from the erstwhile philanthropists was complete. Some members of the 'million thousand mob' appeared to have tired of the joint-enterprise idea, and having accurately assessed the economic possibilities in the region through the auspices of the small office operated by Ngarinyin people in Derby, sought to buy privately the very stations for which the Ngarinyin had recently gained purchase approval from the board of the Indigenous Land Corporation (ILC). Not surprisingly, some members of the 'million thousand mob' were able to secure finances to make an offer which the ILC could come nowhere near matching. In a rather sad irony, the valuation of the stations was enhanced by the potential value of the Aboriginal rock art on those properties (Redmond 2002). The manageress for the Melbourne QC was one of these people and she was later to block station access to the small cultural tourism enterprise run by Ngarinyin people on adjacent Crown Land. During the subsequent court hearings on the station lands which she managed, she assisted the PGA's barristers in opposing the Ngarinyin claim. These barristers attempted to damage the credibility of a senior Aboriginal witness under-cross-examination by utilising Mrs. Bradley's rather jaundiced account of events which had occurred at a time when she had had privileged access to the claimants as a friend and mentor:

> PGA BARRISTER: When you came to this place on the bush university, do you remember telling Susan Bradley and people there that you don't know anything about this site?
> PADDY NEOWARRA: No.

> PGA B: You don't remember that?
> PN: No.
> PGA B: I put it to you didn't know those stories?
> PN: No, I knew it. I knew it. They used to tell us about the story when I was just little boy about this country and the Wanjina, where it came from, yes.
> PGA B: Yes. And you remembered that story right up 'til then, did you?
> PN: Yes, that's right, 'til today.
> PGA B: Okay. And you didn't tell anyone - - -
> PN: No.
> PGA B: - - - in that bush university – just wait 'til I ask the question.
> PN: Yes.
> PGA B: You didn't tell anyone at that bush university time that you didn't know the story for here?
> PN: No, I know the story but I didn't want to say 'til I get the permission from the people.

And then later again:

> PGA B: you don't actually know where your country is any more do you?
> PN: I know where it is.
> PGA B: Do you?
> PN: Yes.
> PGA B: Well, do you remember a time in about 1996 or 1997 when you were on the bush university with Susan Bradley here?
> PN: Yes. Well, I couldn't take the chopper right in; pretty rough.
> PGA B: Well, you went — just a minute. Remember that? You went out looking for it and you told her you got lost and you didn't know where your country was. Remember that?
> PN: I know I didn't say anything about that.
> PGA B: You didn't say that?
> PN: No.
> PGA B: Well, I put it to you that you did say that at that time?
> PN: No.
> PGA B: So you didn't say to her that you didn't know where it was?
> PN: I know where it is.[2]

These attempts to damage the reputation of the witness were, in the end, an abject failure, the judge summing up Neowarra's credibility as a witness in the most glowing terms.

---

[2] *Neowarra v Western Australia and Ors* 2002, Federal Court Transcript (henceforth T), pp. 3305–06.

Also in the elite pastoralist contingent at the ceremony was the owner–manager of a pastoral property adjacent to Anbada. This woman is the daughter of an eminent Sydney silk, and reportedly came into possession of the million-acre-plus property as a twenty-first birthday present from her father. Somewhat in contrast to her elite peers, she enjoys a reputation for roughing it and eschews the pearls and jodhpur look in favour of the more common white boss's uniform of Akubra, moleskins, and RM Williams boots.

Another group of pastoralists in the region is more of the 'battler' type, or at least perceive themselves this way. There are some very evident differences in the approaches to the cattle business between the 'battlers' and the more elite group. Most pertinently for the native title holders, the battler-type pastoralists have long supplemented their income by running home-stay and cultural tourism enterprises on their stations (often without the required licenses). Only at the far eastern end of the claim area, on El Questro Station, a multimillion dollar tourism operation in the Cockburn Ranges, have corporate pastoralists engaged in these lucrative activities in a sustained manner in addition to running cattle.

Many of the elite pastoralists seemed to regard cultural tourism aimed at the general public as somewhat déclassé and invest a great deal of their self-image in the fact that they make their money from beef, something which has not been particularly difficult over the last decade when prices have remained relatively high and labour costs remain low. Nevertheless, as I have shown in another paper (Redmond 2002), at least two of the corporate-owned leases have been running exclusive tours to local rock art sites for small groups of wealthy visitors. These tours are presented as exclusive glimpses into the 'mysterious world of the Bradshaw paintings' and attract patronage from elite charitable foundations, such as one run by Dame Elizabeth Murdoch, which has funded rock-art research into the *guyon guyon* (or so-called Bradshaw Paintings) and *wanjina* sites by the controversial archaeologist, Graeme Walsh. In this respect the wealthy visitors are buying a form of cultural distinction, in Bourdieu's (1984) terms, rather than the wilderness or 'real live cattle ranch' experience offered on the battler stations. As Bourdieu pointed out, this cultural capital is readily convertible into actual capital.

My impression of the recent effects of having had native title recognised in the region is that there has been a considerable hardening of the position of the pastoralists, both of the elite and the battler variety. When I recently asked the senior Ngarinyin man, Paddy Neowarra, how the white pastoralists have reacted since the judgment came down, he replied (with his characteristic good grace):

> I think they was a bit worried. That's what I can see. They was all worried. They think we are going to kick them off, or take over the whole country or this sort of thing. But we can't. If he's sitting on his own pastoral lease, well that's okay. Just not going over the line. You

know, over his pastoral lease. Say you've got Crown Land over there, or reserve over there, he's not allowed to go over it because he's got to look after his own business, his own money what he can make, so we all, we help one another you know? We don't know what they want. [People are saying] that they are still locking all the gates.

During this visit in 2005, I received many reports of pastoralists locking gates to exclude local Aboriginal people. Though this was not uncommon before the judgment was delivered, there now seems to be a more systematic and coordinated attempt to exclude Ngarinyin people from some of these leases. It has been suggested that some of these pastoralists have received advice from the PGA that Aboriginal people are required to seek permission from them to enter their lease, something which is directly contrary to the terms of the judgement. Some lease-holders have informed the Representative Body for the area that all the native title holders need do is come up to the station-house and ask for the key, well aware that the majority of Aboriginal people in the area would be most disinclined to do so as a result the relative power imbalances which have prevailed for so long throughout the region and long set the tone of black and whitefella engagements. Some pastoralists have also claimed that they only lock the gates to keep out unauthorised tourists and to prevent disturbance of their stock. This campaign of locked gates suggests a renewed solidarity amongst the various pastoralists in the face of the newly recognised Aboriginal rights in the area. While, as Neowarra's statement indicates, none of the European leaseholder's material rights have been diminished by a native title judgement which grants primacy to their rights as pastoralists over native title rights, there appears to be a very real sense of a loss of political and moral supremacy on the part of the whitefella pastoralist class as a whole. This loss in itself may be a harbinger of cultural change in the area from which new power alignments may emerge over time.

The Indigenous Land Corporation as a new pastoral boss

The other major leaseholder in the region is the ILC, which purchased three large but nearly derelict properties 'on behalf of the traditional owners' in 1998 but which, in keeping with its current national policy, shows no inclination to divest these titles even to a well-organised Aboriginal corporate body with stringent business plans in place. Though not actually excluding their supposed beneficiaries from the properties, the ILC continues to conduct its business in such a way that the native title holders, all ex-cattle station workers, have at most a very peripheral role in decision making, despite the fact that they now legally hold exclusive possession of these stations 'as against the rest of the world'. Nevertheless, their most active involvement to date has been as CDEP-financed 'trainees' in menial station work.

By way of contrast to the pastoralists' sense of drastic change in the wake of the judgement none of the Ngarinyin people I spoke to in 2005 could pinpoint any noticeable changes in their day to day lives 12 months on from determination, other than this increased resistance to their presence by many of the pastoralists. The native title holders have only recently established the Prescribed Body Corporate which is required to manage their rights in land. I expect that when this is in place more concrete economic and political gains may be achieved.

The effects of the court process itself

Perhaps one of the most intriguing aspects of the native title litigation process for me has been in observing how the claimants managed their relationships in court with the pastoralists on whose properties they reside and for whom they have worked, in many instances, for several generations. In this part of the paper, I discuss some of these engagements in the interests of showing how various Aboriginal people attempted to sustain the established tone of those relationships at the same time as frankly putting on record their own views of the power relationships involved. Many Ngarinyin people were all too aware that the court room drama presented a once in a lifetime opportunity to put their stories 'on the paper' (i.e. on the public record). As an ethnographer who has generally tip-toed around the deeply ambivalent and politically sensitive worker–boss relationships in the region for years (mainly for the self-serving purpose of retaining access to these settlements), I was sometimes startled by the frankness of the claimants' narratives (see also Merlan 1994, which challenged some earlier assumptions about the 'nostalgia' of Aboriginal workers for the pastoral era).

In one of the earliest court sessions at the Mowanjum community hall the local non-Indigenous pastoralists were present in force as their past and present workers prepared to take the stand. Indeed, one senior witness, now deceased, prefaced his evidence with a declaration of how his boss, sitting two rows behind him, 'been minding me very well'. The fact that he felt moved to offer this character reference for the same people who were opposing his rights and interests in land suggests that, on the one hand, he remained acutely aware of his own dependent situation, and secondly that this kind of contestation over land was not simply to be avoided. His character reference for his boss was made very much in the local Aboriginal rhetorical style in which denials of ill-intent and hostility frequently open up dispute proceedings.

Later, a former head stockman for the same pastoral lease (and who still resides there) took the stand. This man is also a renowned composer of traditional dreamt songs known as *jurnba* and carries his reputation as a *barnman* (healer/composer) with considerable gravitas through the local life-world. His evidence revealed that he had come to live at the station from a young age when his step-parents and extended family, who had been living a hunting and gathering life along the Drysdale River until the end of World War II, were captured by a police party, before which time, as the witness put it, they 'never work or anything like that, only just walking backward and forward'.[3] When they returned to their 'special camp' on the Drysdale River the police arrived, put his parents and the other adults, male and female, on neck chains and took them to Mt Elizabeth.[4] At Mt Elizabeth, his parents were tied to trees at night to prevent them running away. The young boy spent his time by himself down by the river.[5] After about 10 days at Mt Elizabeth, his parents were taken in chains by the police from Mt Elizabeth west to Munja, leaving the boy behind at the station. His parents were being used by the police to find other people living in the bush. The police chained up the people living in the bush in order to, in the witness's words, 'make them civilised'.[6] Months later, at the beginning of the Wet, his step-parents returned to Mt Elizabeth and they were released from their chains.[7] Meanwhile the witness had been cared for by another step-mother. His parents stopped there then and worked at the station for many years. The witness never attended school and began working as a boy at 'old Mt Elizabeth'.[8] When he was 17, he began adult stock work: mustering, branding, droving cattle to Wyndham through Karunjie, and breaking horses.[9] The witness lived and worked with a large group of older people[10] in humpies about 100 yards from the boss's house.[11] When the people living at Mt Elizabeth decided to set up their own community away from the station-house in 1982, the owner eventually agreed to give his work-force, in the witness's words again, 'a little bit of matchbox on a bit of side of road'.[12] They lived in tents there for five years before the first permanent shelters were built.[13]

It was clear during the witness's evidence concerning the circumstances under which he came to live on Mt Elizabeth that a wave of annoyance was running through the pastoralist contingent. He was after all a 'favoured son', formerly head-stockman, and brought up from a child on the same beef, if maybe not the same cut, as the heir to the lease. After a short recess, the barrister for the PGA put it to the witness that the reason he and his family had been apprehended in their camp along the Drysdale River was that this was part of a benevolent campaign to control leprosy amongst the indigenous population. Here I cite the transcript of the cross-examination by the barrister for the PGA.

[3] T2137 00–05.
[4] T2137.15–45.
[5] T2138. 00–46.
[6] T2138.30–2139.40.
[7] T2138.35–2139.15, 2140.00–25.
[8] T2146.35–2147.30, T2264.15–40.
[9] T2148–2149.
[10] T2214.25–45.
[11] T2206.05–30.
[12] T2250.00–10.
[13] T2252.35–40.

PGA Barrister: And I think you told the story about how they were - your mother and your father, and I think it was just you - you didn't have any brother and sister - picked up by the Police; is that right?
WITNESS: Yes.
PGA B: And you were taken to Mount Elizabeth Station?
W: Yes.
PGA B: Has anyone ever told you that that was what used to be called a leprosy patrol?
W: Yes, just had a bit of sore on.
PGA B: Yes.
W: Just – just wanted to take them for bit of treatment.
PGA B: That's right. So your mum and dad, the Police collected them to take them for some treatment; is that right?
W: No.
PGA B: No?
W: No, they didn't have those sores. They just took them for – show those Police where the other people, what was living out in the bush.
PGA B: Yes.
W: That's all they took him for.
PGA B: So just so that I understand that. Has anyone ever told you that when the Police found people wandering in the bush, they would take them to be checked to see if they had leprosy?
W: Yes.
PGA B: And is that what you understood happened to your parents and to you?
W: Not that I know.
PGA B: Not that you know. Has anyone ever told you that when you got taken to Mount Elizabeth Station that you and your mum and dad were going to be taken off to the Leprosarium to be checked; did anyone ever tell you that?
W: No.
PGA B: No. Has anyone ever told you that [the lease-holder] who was the manager at the station, he asked the Police if you could stay there and you'd be checked out by the Flying Doctor when they came next time?
W: No.
PGA B: No one's ever told you that?
W: No.
PGA B: But you stayed at Mount Elizabeth Station, didn't you?
W: Yes.[14]

[14] T2267.43–2269.45.

The witness's revelations about his capture and subsequent life of work on the station was stated as a set of fairly unproblematised biographical facts and without any evident sense of malice towards the boss's family. Indeed, it is not at all uncommon for Ngarinyin people to express sympathy but also to laugh and joke about the humiliations and punishments inflicted on their older relatives, though whether this was a means of concealing their embarrassment at such subordination was never entirely clear to me. Othering one's own subordinate position is a common means of projection and denial. Though by no means naïve, simple, or compliant, the witness was also eager to 'do the right thing' by his employers and was probably dismayed at their annoyance. After all, in his terms he had just told his story as he had been asked to do.

Later in the proceedings, the witness was punished for his revelations when the barrister for the PGA asked him on the stand, in front of a roomful of his countrymen, whether or not it was true his current marriage was *murlal* or 'wrong way', a question which could have occurred to the barrister to ask only if he had been informed by those intimately acquainted with social life in the settlement. This use of shaming techniques continued throughout the proceedings through constant suggestions under cross-examination that individuals had either 'lost their culture', 'didn't know where their country was', were 'lying about their connections', 'didn't follow the law' or only danced or painted 'for money'.[15]

I was surprised how robustly these individuals responded to such suggestions despite the formal and intimidating context of a courtroom, which for most of them had only ever been experienced as a place of punishment. That reservoirs of resilient self-appraisal underlay the usually very circumspect interpersonal styles of dealing with whitefellas came as even more of a shock I think to their employers and managers than it did to me. After all, a number of these pastoralists enjoyed a fairly jocular relationship with these same witnesses and made a show of this during the lunch breaks when they intermingled with the witnesses to show that they were, at heart, one of the boys.

Conclusion

In the aftermath of the judgement, the pastoralist contingent shows signs of having begun to splinter again, reverting to its constituent social classes, while maintaining solidarity in regards to the control of keys to locked gates. Some of the battler pastoralists have also begun to rekindle relationships with select groups of 'good blackfellas'.

The response of the European pastoralists suggests that they are undergoing a process of schismogenesis (Bateson 1935) both complementary (in regard to the

---

[15] This last suggestion was a bit rich in a context in which not one of us whitefellas was earning less per day than a month's welfare payments for the witness being accused of venal intentions.

claimants, and to their class counterparts) and symmetrical (in regard to each other). This movement parallels a similar trajectory which has long been emergent in the Ngarinyin community (Redmond 2006). For short periods of time, the two ethnic communities drew their various divergent interests together to partake in the adversarial litigation process. To sustain this unity of interests between their strongly autonomous fragments, two distinct notions of shared kinship, law and interests in land were pitted against each other, even to the extent that previous long-standing ideologies of some of the pastoralists being 'family' to Ngarinyin people (Redmond 2005) were put to a test—which they were seen to dismally fail by Ngarinyin people's standards.

Post-determination, indications exist that both of these cultural or ethnic blocs are now beginning to seek out new alliances as well as implementing further internal differentiations and distinctions which may well open up pathways out of the almost hegemonic relationships of the past. I expect that as a result of the litigation process, change in the political culture of the Gibb River Road pastoral region will be accelerated at the same time as resistance to such change sporadically intensifies over issues such as locked gates. The ILC cattle properties have the potential to significantly shape the direction of this change by bridging black and whitefella interests within an expanded beef (and possibly tourist) economy of scale. The native title stakeholders with rights in these S.47 type tracts of land,[16] now the most robust form of land tenure in the Kimberley, need to take a place at the centre of that process to create any possibility for future economic and political developments.

References

Bateson, G. 1935. 'Culture contact and schismogenesis', *Man* (n.s.), 35: 178–83.

Bourdieu, P. 1984. *Distinction: A Social Critique of the Judgement of Taste*, Routledge, London.

Merlan, F. 1994. 'Narratives of survival in the post-colonial north,' *Oceania*, 65 (2): 155–74.

Neowarra vs. Western Australia and Ors 2002. Federal Court Transcript.

Redmond, A. 2002. '"Alien abductions", Kimberley Aboriginal cave paintings, and the speculation about human origins: on some investments in cultural tourism in the northern Kimberley, Western Australia', *Australian Aboriginal Studies*, 2002 (2):54–64.

---

[16] Section 47 of the Act states that if a group of native title claimants held a pastoral lease at the time they lodged their claim, and are subsequently able to prove their native title claim, then all prior extinguishing acts are disregarded, yielding full beneficial ownership of the portion of the application area covered by the pastoral lease.

Redmond, A. 2005. 'Strange relatives: mutualities and dependencies between Aborigines and pastoralists in the Northern Kimberley', *Oceania* (Special Issue), 75 (3): 234–46.

Redmond, A. 2006. 'Further on up the road: community trucks and the moving settlement', in G. Cowlishaw, T. Lea and E. Kowal (eds), *Moving on: Critical Indigenous Studies*, Charles Darwin University Press, Darwin.

Smith, B. R. 2002. 'Pastoralism, land and Aboriginal existence in central Cape York Peninsula', *Anthropology in Action*, 9: 21–30.

Smith, B. R. 2003. 'Whither "certainty"? Coexistence, change and land rights in northern Queensland', *Anthropological Forum*, 13: 27–8.

5. 'We're tired from talking': The native title process from the perspective of Kaanju People living on homelands, Wenlock and Pascoe Rivers, Cape York Peninsula

David Claudie

This paper investigates the native title process from the perspective of Kaanju families living on our traditional homelands at Chuulangun on the upper Wenlock River in central Cape York Peninsula, Northern Australia. Our experiences reinforce our view that the native title process and the structures it upholds are at odds with Indigenous land tenure and governance systems, that they create and maintain obstacles for the carrying out of on-ground Indigenous land and resource management aspirations and obligations, and that they work against the homelands development and economic development aspirations of Kaanju Traditional Owners living on homelands. This paper draws particularly on the experiences of core Kaanju families with a native title claim to some 241 000 hectares of our homelands centred on the Wenlock River in central Cape York, locally known as the Batavia Claim. This claim was lodged with the National Native Title Tribunal in 1997 and eight years on 'we're tired from talking'[1] and engaging in a process that works on the assumption that we have to justify and prove our ownership of homelands, while government and other 'stakeholders' presume control over our traditional lands.

This paper stresses three main points. First, our frustration with a native title process that has:

- accommodated the 'interests' of the State government and other 'stakeholders' to the detriment of our rights as Traditional Owners of our lands under claim, and

---

[1] This paper is dedicated to my Aunty, a Kaanju woman (my father's father's younger brother's daughter), who sadly passed away in December 2003. I often heard her, along with a number of other Senior Aboriginal people bemoan 'we're tired from talking' when not seeing any progress for their considerable and protracted effort and engagement in meetings and dealings to do with land. I stress at the outset that the issues discussed in this paper are personal as they directly affect myself and my family and our futures. This paper is written from the perspective of Kaanju people living on homelands—my family and myself. We are local families and descendants of key Kaanju ancestors, therefore focal families in the claim to Batavia Downs. The views I express here in this paper are, of course, necessarily my own.

- led to proceedings being dominated by claimants whose connection to the area under claim is questionable.

It also documents our serious concerns about the ability of the *Native Title Act 1993* (Cwlth) (NTA) and the system of prescribed bodies corporate (PBCs) contained in the NTA to adequately and effectively recognise 'proper' on-ground indigenous governance, primary Indigenous land and resource management and decision-making on homelands, and the right of Traditional Owners to use and develop their land and associated resources economically in order to sustain their people and land into the future.

Finally it makes the point that the NTA needs to recognise that Aboriginal people should be compensated for their sovereignty being taken out of the land.

The paper will first outline briefly Kaanju governance, which determines the system of land tenure for the Kaanju people and the formation of the Chuulangun Aboriginal Corporation. This brief summary will provide the necessary framework for the discussion that follows.

Kaanju Ngaachi: Kaanju Pama[2]

Kaanju (Kaanichi) Ngaachi (homelands) encompass some 840 000 hectares centred on the Wenlock and Pascoe Rivers in central Cape York Peninsula, Northern Australia (see Fig. 5.1). Our lands stretch westward from the Lockhart River valley and across the peninsula to and including Embley Range (meeting the Wik people and the Thanakwithi people of the west coast region). Our lands continue south to the Archer River (to meet the 'Southern' Kaanju) and north along the Wenlock as far as Schramm Creek (to meet the Atambaya and Angkamuthi people), then across to the southern bank of the upper Olive River (to meet the Wuthathi people).

Kaanju governance

Importantly, the Kaanju worldview, particularly Kaanju governance and cosmology, underlie all aspects of Kaanju relationships with homelands including land tenure and ownership, land management practices and regimes, and our rights and obligations in regard to the management of Ngaachi (see also Chuulangun Aboriginal Corporation 2005: 11–12). To Kaanju people living on homelands 'governance' refers to the system of territoriality found in the region's Aboriginal law. Our use of governance refers to the division of Kaanju country into different 'named Ngaachi' (or estates), each with their associated bloodline

---

[2] In this paper I mainly refer to the Kaanju people associated with Kaanju traditional homelands north of the Archer River in central Cape York (sometimes referred to as 'Northern' or 'Top' Kaanju); these are not to be confused with Kaanju people associated with traditional lands south of the Archer River ('Southern' or 'Bottom' Kaanju). When I use the term Kaanju I mean only the former category of people, unless otherwise stated.

or family. Thus bloodline ties people to particular country, language and resources, and to the species whose Stories lie in their Ngaachi (see Smith and Claudie 2003: 4). A number of these named Ngaachi are shown in Fig. 5.1 and include Chuulangun, Malandaji, Pa'un, Muula, Puul'u, Kathu Pathu, Nhanthanji and Iipajiko. Each estate and its associated bloodline(s) is associated with a particular Story. For example, Malandaji is the Story for 'Lightening and thunder, coming of wet season' and Chuulangun for the frilled-neck lizard (see also Chuulangun Aboriginal Corporation 2005: 12).

Fig. 5.1 Kaanju homelands showing clan estates

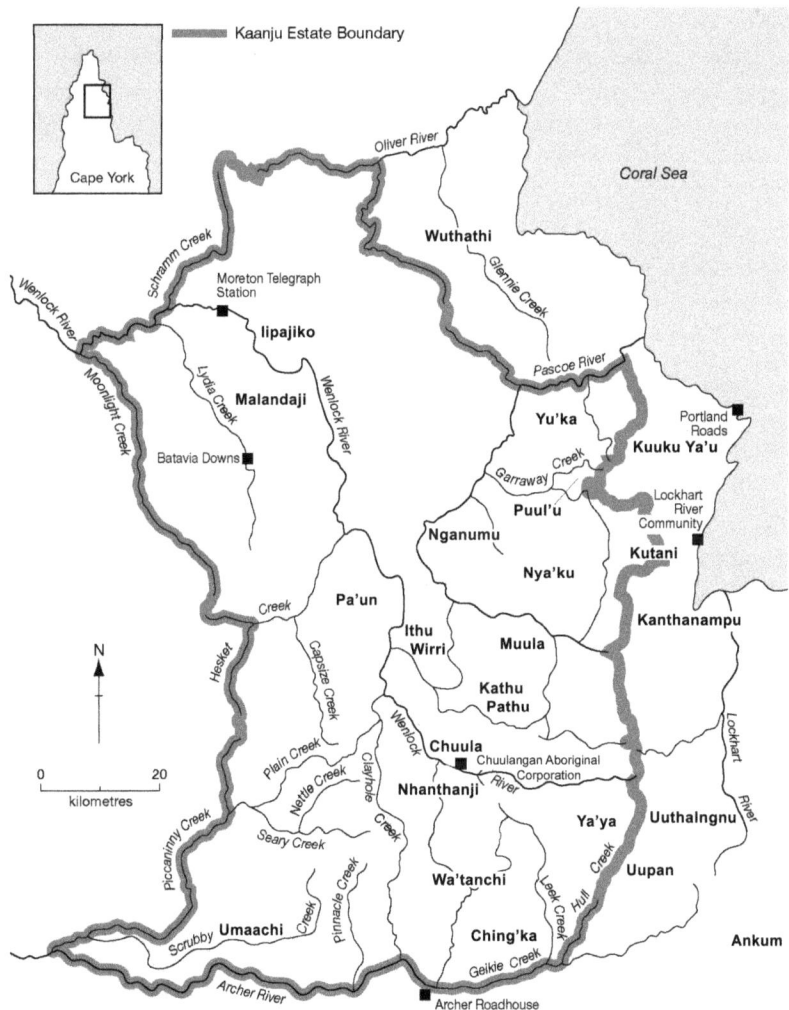

Thus particular families or bloodlines 'come from' or are connected to one or more particular clan estates. Kaanichi people determine their connection to particular country by way of their patrilineal descent from particular Kaanju ancestors. Thus according to Kaanju governance a person traces their bloodline through their father. It is understood by the majority of local families that while someone may be Kaanju due to their descent from a particular Kaanju ancestor connected to a particular clan estate, they do not necessarily have the right to 'speak for' the whole of the Kaanju homelands. Rather they have connection to a particular clan estate (or estates) within Kaanju homelands, and depending on their position (which is determined by the nature of their descent from a Kaanju ancestor and that particular ancestor's position) they may have a right to speak for that particular clan estate (or estates). At the same time it is recognised that there are particular families, and importantly, certain individuals within these families who, due to their descent from focal male Kaanju ancestors with authority, have greater authority and standing in terms of their right and obligation to speak for country and particularly to speak for the whole of Kaanju homelands. Essentially, there is a hierarchy of authority and connection to country that is determined by the nature of a person's descent and from whom they are descended. Thus a person descended from a focal male ancestor through the male line would have greater authority to speak for country and a greater area of country over which that authority is held.

Despite a significant period of disruption by colonialism, forced removals from homelands, and decades of centralisation in missions, reserves and later townships and communities, Kaanju people living at Chuulangun assert that this system of governance is as relevant today as in the pre-colonial past (see Claudie 2004). However, there are people, particularly those of the 'diaspora' living in southern cities and even people living in local communities on Cape York who operate on the assumption that this ancient system has been eroded and is no longer relevant. This dismissal of the ancient system of Kaanju governance and thereby dismissal of the authority of particular Kaanju families and individuals has enabled them to take advantage of the problems inherent in the native title process. The native title process has falsely legitimised them as traditional owners for the area under claim and legitimised what they see as their position to hold authority and make decisions in regard to the claim.[3] This will be discussed in more detail later in the paper.

Today, a number of 'local' Kaanju families continue to live in centralised communities and towns including at Lockhart River, Coen, and Napranum/Weipa

---

[3] The NTA shapes outcomes from the native title process, and the Land Council and anthropologists working on claims are bound to work within the requirements of the Act. This has lead to the inclusion, from our perspective, of the 'wrong people' in the claimant group for the Batavia Claim. People might be 'all one mob' for country in terms of a claim, but that does not mean that all native title holders necessarily have the same rights and interests as each other, even under the NTA.

on the west coast of Cape York. Some Kaanju families, including those whose forebears were removed to distant locations during the previous century, live in towns including Cairns, Yarrabah, Townsville and Palm Island. A number of these latter families are recognised as 'Kaanju people' and kin by local Kaanju families, and their ancestors are recognised as being Kaanju. While they may not be necessarily living on or near their homelands they do maintain close contact with kin living in communities on Cape York (see also Smith 2006: s. 5.2.6), and they visit and attend events such as funerals. There are however a number of people, members of the 'diaspora', who claim to be Kaanju, but whose connection is disputed by local Kaanju people, particularly by those living on homelands.

In the late 1980s a number of local Kaanju families began the permanent reoccupation of homelands and re-established a home at Chuulangun (or Chuula) on the upper Wenlock River. Chuula was a main meeting place for Kaanju people before they were forcibly removed from homelands so it is appropriate that Chuula now act as the hub for Kaanju homelands development, economic development, and land and resource management on Ngaachi. The Kaanju families living at and focused on Chuulangun have undertaken considerable planning to ensure the reoccupation of homelands is sustainable and consistent with Kaanju land and resource management principles. The reestablishment of a home at Chuulangun has demonstrated the commitment of particular local Kaanju families to Ngaachi. Importantly, these families trace their descent patrilineally through the male line from key Kaanju ancestors. In the case of the Moreton/Claudie/Nelson family of which I am a member, our key ancestor is recognised among a significant number of Kaanju people living on or near homelands and by Aboriginal people more widely as having been an important law man and holding important knowledge to do with the land, governance and cosmology. He is recognised as a key Kaanju ancestral figure (see also Smith and Claudie 2003: 6).

Chuulangun Aboriginal Corporation

In July 2002 our family-based community living at Chuulangun incorporated under the *Aboriginal Councils and Associations Act 1976* (Cwlth). Our organisation is localised and based on Kaanju governance structures. As for the Murray Lower Darling Rivers Indigenous Nations (MLDRIN) (Weir and Ross, Chapter 10), the Chuulangun Aboriginal Corporation is a modern-day extension of traditional governance structures. Our organisation's founding principle is:

> a person must live on their particular homeland in order to have a say in its management.

The main objectives of our organisation include:

- representing the Kaanju people associated with the Wenlock and Pascoe Rivers on land tenure, land and resource management, economic and homelands development issues;
- facilitating the practice and maintenance of the customary obligations of Kaanju people in regard to land and resource management for homelands;
- promoting the wider recognition and support, particularly by government, of primary Kaanju management and decision-making for our homelands;
- facilitating the reestablishment of permanent Kaanju communities on our homelands;
- establishing homelands-based economic enterprises that will sustain or people and our homelands into the future; and
- having greater access and control over the resources and funds available to help meet the above objectives.

Foremost, our incorporation was fuelled by our frustration at the inability of regional and sub-regional Aboriginal bodies (particularly our Native Title Representative Body) to help us meet our land and resource management, homelands development and economic development aspirations (see also Smith and Claudie 2003: 7–8). Incorporation was seen as a strategy for the wider recognition of Kaanju governance and assertion of the primacy of Indigenous land tenure and our authority as landowners and land and resource managers.

Chuulangun Aboriginal Corporation is undertaking a number of land and resource management, homelands and economic development activities on Ngaachi. Recently, focal Kaanju Traditional Owners living at Chuulangun (and native title claimants to Batavia Downs) have been investigating the establishment of an Indigenous Protected Area (IPA) over some 470 000 hectares of our homelands centred on the Wenlock and Pascoe Rivers. This area includes the Kaanju portion of the Batavia claim. Our aspiration is that the area be declared as an IPA and that it be managed in accordance with the International Union for the Conservation of Nature and Natural Resources' Protected Area Category V: 'Area of land and/or seascape protected mainly for conservation/recreation purposes'. It is not our intention to use the land for pastoral purposes as we are not pastoralists, and this land use would work against our conservation purposes for the land. It is however our intention to benefit from the land economically, mainly by way of the management of public use and access (e.g. establishment of designated campgrounds and low-key tourism), and other natural resource management based activities (e.g. feral animal control, sustainable use of plant products). These activities would generate opportunities for employment and training for our people on homelands as well as provide revenue to support the permanent reoccupation of homelands and help sustain viable homelands communities.[4]

Background to the claim

Malandaji is an important Kaanju Story Place on the upper Wenlock River. It has particular significance as the Story for 'Lightening, Thunder and the Coming of the Wet Season'. For a number of decades core Kaanju people associated with the area of Malandaji and living at Chuulangun have been concerned about prolific and unregulated public access to the area, which has resulted in damage to this significant site. We are concerned that abuse of the area will get in the way of the ability of Malandaji to carry out its role in the Kaanju cosmology. There is also concern that people who abuse the area and who are there without the authority of Traditional Owners will suffer severe consequences under Kaanju law and custom.

Malandaji, and some 635 000 hectares of the (Northern) Kaanju Homelands,[5] have been alienated from Traditional Owners by the imposition of a number of government land tenures including pastoral lease, National Park and timber reserve. Malandaji was imposed upon by the Batavia Downs Pastoral Holding, a former Experimental Farm Reserve now managed by the Queensland Department of Natural Resources and Mines (DNRM), and locally known as Batavia Downs. Our particular concern for Malandaji as well as our aspirations to regain control and management of our traditional homelands drove our claim to Batavia Downs.

In October 1997 a native title claim (Northern Kaanju People & Yianh People QC97/45)[6] was lodged to some 241 000 hectares of our homelands along the Wenlock River, an area that includes the former Batavia Downs Holding and Moreton Telegraph Station. Specifically, the area of the application includes the area known as PH 43-5371, Experimental Farm. Lot 2 Crown Plan DLH5, including an area previously known as Batavia Downs Pastoral Holding. The claim has become known as the 'Batavia Claim'. Due to amendments to the NTA the claim had to be relodged with the National Native Title Tribunal (NNTT) so it did not really get going until 2000. Under Kaanju law and custom, the Kaanju people living at Chuulangun as well as a number of families living at Coen, Weipa/Napranum, Lockhart River and at more distant locations are the particular Kaanju people from the particular area under claim.

---

[4] For more information on the Chuulangun Aboriginal Corporation and its activities visit <www.kaanjungaachi.com.au>.
[5] A further 204 150 hectares of the Northern Kaanju Homelands fall within the boundary of the former Lockhart Deed of Grant in Trust (DOGIT) that was transferred as inalienable Aboriginal Freehold under the *Aboriginal Land Act 1991* (Qld) to traditional owners as part of the Mangkuma Land Trust.
[6] In this paper I am speaking only for our Kaanju Homelands in the claim area, not also for the Yianh territory in the claim area.

The Government-appointed Native Title Representative Body for our claim is the Cape York Land Council (CYLC). Our claim is currently subject to negotiations towards an Indigenous Land Use Agreement (ILUA) with the Department of Natural Resources and Water the peak State government body for land tenure and management negotiations (formerly the Department of Natural Resources and Mines (DNRM)). Moreton Telegraph Station is currently subject to annual lease arrangements as a camping ground with Cook Shire as trustee.

The native title process

Kaanju traditional owners living at Chuulangun recognise three main impediments to the claim: the State, the Native Title Representative Body, and the nature of the claimant group and its representation. The native title process itself has been at the heart of and/or exacerbated these problems. The nature of the native title process is such that it has enabled our claim to be dragged out for eight long years while (1) the State takes its time to come to an agreement with us on land tenure, land use and management arrangements, (2) our Native Title Representative Body pauses then attempts to organise itself, and (3) claimants whose actual connection to the claim area is questionable continue to dominate proceedings to the detriment and exclusion of Kaanju families actually from the area under claim.

Native title and State land dealings

During 2001 the registered native title claimants were approached to prepare a negotiating position relevant to the tenure resolution of Batavia under the framework of the State Lands Dealing Project. We spent considerable time, money and energy, meeting and synthesising three years worth of planning material compiled by planners, environmental scientists, anthropologists, and other professionals who have worked with the Kaanju people. The resulting report, the *Batavia Downs Aspirations Planning Report* (BDAPR) (Kaanju People and Salmon 2000) set out in detail our plans and aspirations for the management of our homelands under claim. This report is based on Kaanju Indigenous governance and land and resource management principles and practices that have been passed down over many thousands of years through Kaanju bloodlines to the current generation of Kaanju land owners, land managers and law makers living on country. It also addresses major land management problems not of our making, including weed and feral animal infestation and the destruction of sensitive ecological areas and desecration of important cultural sites due to prolific and unregulated public access to and use of our homelands.

In September 2001 we presented our report to the State government. While the report suggested an extremely high probability for a successful tenure resolution, which would satisfy the needs of all stakeholders, we never received a response from the State. Instead, 12 months later in September 2002, when we were under the impression that our claim might be close to resolution, the State, under the guise of the State Land Dealings branch of the DNRM, announced that they had to produce a 'Land Evaluation' report on the claim area, a process that would take up to 18 months. The native title process was essentially captured by DNRM's 'Land Evaluation processes'.[7] Up until that point we had the impression that we had been dealing in good faith with a State framework aimed at the rapid resolution of a long-standing land issue of critical importance to us. However, with no formal notification or explanation regarding a change of process we were left guessing about the status of our land and the State government's intention in relation to it. We had no clear picture of departmental responsibility for an expedited dealing on Batavia. There was even some confusion amongst government officers as to the status of our dealings on Batavia. It was even suggested to us that Batavia was no longer 'on the table' for dealing'.[8] The sentiment of one senior Traditional Owner when the CYLC advised that claimants should question the State about the bureaucratic hold-up over Batavia was: 'I don't want to keep talking and wasting my voice.'[9]

Indeed, the land tenure history of Batavia Downs has been uncertain from the start. The whole area has been a pastoral lease at some stage so according to government, native title to most of the country has been extinguished due to previous interests. However, the CYLC advised claimants at a Steering Committee meeting held in September 2003 that the State was uncertain about extinguishment of native title on Batavia. We were advised that native title determination was still of value particularly as there were no current leaseholders.[10] We were further advised that based on the extinguishment of native title scenario if the claim went to court the best determination we could expect over Batavia Downs would be non-exclusive determination of native title. However, Aboriginal Freehold under the *Aboriginal Land Act* (ALA) was seen as a lot more valuable than non-exclusive native title, so we pursued the former option. Nevertheless, there was still (and still is) the question of whether native title has really been extinguished over the area.

We waited for the State's Land Use Evaluation Report. When we expected that the report would be finished we spent considerable time and energy making numerous inquiries to DNRM about the report. Our repeated requests to view the Land Evaluation report were ignored. Although at a National Native Title Tribunal Mediation Conference held in Cairns on 24 July 2003, the State's

---

[7] Letter to the Minister Hon. Steve Bredhauer RE: HoAIG Meeting held 20 September 2002 from Gerhardt Pearson, Executive Director, Balkanu Cape York Development Corporation, dated 24 September 2002.
[8] Letter to the Minister Hon. Steve Bredhauer re Batavia Downs (Formerly the Batavia Experimental Farm Reserve) Cape York, from David Claudie, dated 20 September 2002.
[9] M. Sellars, at Batavia Downs Steering Committee Meeting, Cairns, Friday 18 January 2002, CYLC minutes from meeting, p. 6.
[10] K. O'Rourke, at Batavia Steering Committee Meeting, CYLC Conference Room, Monday 1 September 2003, minutes from meeting, p. 1.

representative did state that he would seek Ministerial approval to release the report to parties to assist with the process of tenure resolution over Batavia Downs.[11] However this was to no avail. Finally, in late 2003 through our contacts within an Australian conservation organisation which accessed the report through Freedom of Information legislation we were finally able to access this report, albeit a very poor quality facsimiled copy. To date, the DNRM has not provided Kaanju Traditional Owners living at Chuulangun with a copy of this report.

My initial impression of the report was that it was merely a 'desktop study' and a very poor one considering the amount of time it took to produce it. The authors undertook a 'site inspection' over only four days, holding meetings with caretakers at Batavia and Moreton, and Bramwell Station (not even in the claim area). No attempt was made to meet with Kaanju people on homelands. The authors make assumptions and generalisations about the land and associated resources that indicate a very poor understanding of the area under claim. They also do not seem to have read very carefully the claimants' submission (BDAPR). My comments are centred on a number of issues as discussed below.[12]

Batavia Downs and cattle enterprise

Overall, the report makes a lot of assumptions and simplifies considerably and to our disadvantage, Kaanju people's aspirations with regard to the area under claim. For example, it notes that the Traditional Owners 'have a strong interest in seeing Batavia Downs return to a viable cattle enterprise'. This is completely false, and the Batavia Downs Planning Report (the submission we sent to DNRM for the purpose of informing the State of our aspirations) does not say this at all. The only mention our report makes about cattle is the need for management of land degradation caused by cattle and the maintenance of a 'killer' herd for local use. The assumption that Kaanju people want to run a viable cattle enterprise, along with the very strong support for pastoralism on Cape York (e.g. submissions from Agforce, Peninsula Cattleman's Association, Cape York Live Export Group, Cook Shire, Cape York Peninsula Development Association, as well as some pastoralists) only supports the State's plans for pastoralism in the region and

---

[11] J. Bednarek, at National Native Title Tribunal Mediation Conference, Meeting Summary, Native Title Determination Application QC97/44, Summary of Outcomes, 24 July 2003, p. 3.

[12] I have not attempted to discuss the views of those who wrote the Land Evaluation Report for a number of reasons (1) because I do not agree with these views, (2) because I do not understand how the authors of that Report came to their conclusions or how they justify them (not least because they did not consult with the Traditional Owners in reaching them), and (3) because including those views here would grant them a degree of legitimacy I do not consider appropriate. The views I express here are, of course, necessarily my own. It is important to note a possible difference here between the norms of academic practice—a (supposedly) 'objective' encapsulation of various viewpoints—and the ways many Indigenous people speak on similar issues. As suggested by Smith (2005: 9) the presumption of an 'objective overview' involves an idea that the commentator can view a situation 'from outer space'. Many Aboriginal people would view this as either impossible or meaningless. I can only speak from what I know is right from my own Indigenous governance, with my feet planted solidly on my homelands.

justifies (from their point of view) their discussion on and recommendations that the majority of the holding be pastoral.

For Batavia to return to a viable cattle enterprise would involve considerable financial resources, which would be provided by whom—the State? The report does mention the considerable distance of Batavia from markets and the poor nutritive value of native vegetation (Sinclair 2003), which are only two factors against pastoralism (there are many more), but it does not consider these when recommending that the majority of the holding return to pastoral use. This recommendation they base on the findings of only one document, which was produced by the Department of Primary Industries. Further, Aboriginal people do not 'belong to cattle'; it is an industry that was forced upon us. There is a widespread assumption that because a few of our old people were 'cattlemen', all Aboriginal people want to do with the land is run cattle. This is completely false.

The State's Land Evaluation Report seriously misinterprets and misrepresents core Traditional Owner aspirations with regard to the claim area. It is not our intention to return Batavia to a viable cattle enterprise. We intend to resume our customary management of this area, which is our obligation under Kaanju law. This management will involve, amongst other considerations, repairing the considerable damage caused by the cattle industry, as well as by the prolific access and use of our homelands by third parties, and weed and feral animal infestation, as part of the framework of the IPA.

Moreton Telegraph Station

The report also recommends that Moreton Telegraph Station remain under the management of Cook Shire. There is absolutely no consideration of the Kaanju people's aspirations with regard to the area (again detailed in our submission to the State). Our position in the case of Moreton is ignored or seen as irrelevant. Cook Shire's stake in the area of Moreton Telegraph Station is seen as more important than that of the Traditional Owners.

Conservation values

The report does not acknowledge that Indigenous rights and obligations with regard to land and resources extend beyond cultural considerations. The State's assumption is that our management is only relevant in the case of significant cultural sites, in this case Malandaji or what they call 'Wenlock Falls'. In the Report the State recommends transferring the area around the 'Wenlock Falls' to traditional owners under the ALA. Perhaps they think that this will satisfy our obligations to 'look after' our country.

Further, the State sees 'nature' conservation and sustainability as the domain of conservation groups and government themselves.[13] They recommend that any land transferred to Traditional Owners or taken up by Traditional Owners as pastoral lease be subject to conservation arrangements and restrictions on tree clearing. Under customary law, Kaanju people do not clear trees, and today we would only clear land if it was absolutely necessary for our homelands development, say for an airstrip for access to essential services. But even before clearing trees for an airstrip there is a process of customary obligations to be undertaken in order for that activity to be sanctioned under Kaanju law. Again the State assumes that Indigenous people cannot manage the land in a sustainable manner and that our land use and management regimes have no legitimacy in contemporary society. This equates with the view of some of the diaspora and even local Kaanju people who are of the opinion that traditional Kaanju governance should belong to the past.

The State needs to recognise that Kaanju people's obligations with regard to the management of our traditional lands and associated resources encompasses more than merely cultural aspects. Our BDAPR report outlines in detail the background and key principles of Traditional Owner land use and management responsibilities for Batavia. It states, 'the natural and cultural values of ... [Batavia] cannot be separated'. Further, 'how people want to use and manage land is often informed by their particular responsibility to and for places, as well as a responsibility to generally manage country responsibly' (BDAPR 2000:30).

After several years of guessing about the status of our land and the State government's intention in relation to it, the State finally put their position to us at the 24 July 2003 mediation. The State's position at the time of this meeting was that the acquisition of the former pastoral lease and also the Moreton Telegraph station had extinguished native title (being most of the claim), and that it would like to settle the claim in the following ways:

- a pastoral lease for native title holders of the area to the west of the Wenlock River;
- the area east of the Wenlock River to be ALA Freehold grant, and
- the northern part to be part pastoral lease and part National Park (the reason for this was so the government could do a deal for National Park around the Olive River Area).

[13] Chuulangun Aboriginal Corporation have recently entered into a Cooperation Agreement with an Australian conservation organisation with the aim to further core Kaanju Traditional Owner rights and interests in regard to our Ngaachi and to support our native title and land and resource management aspirations. Importantly, this agreement has been initiated by core Kaanju families living on homelands who are recognised by this conservation group as the core Traditional Owners for the Wenlock and Pascoe Rivers. To view the agreement visit <http://www.indig-enviro.asn.au/#kaanju>.

Further, the State wanted a conservation agreement to be made over certain areas and a common management regime over the rest of the area.[14]

It is my impression that the State had already made their decision on where they wanted Batavia to go and that the 'land evaluation process' and preparation of the Land Use Report was just a way of formally getting the support needed to justify the position they put to us at the 24 July 2003 mediation meeting. Further, there appear to have been only three players in this whole process: the government, the pastoral lobby and the conservation groups. Core Kaanju Traditional Owners have been pushed aside in this process and our case as major stakeholders and legitimate owners and managers of the land and associated resources has not been recognised from the start of the process. As Traditional Owners of the land under question, we are infuriated at the State's arrogance in presuming that our homelands are theirs to make deals over. Aboriginal people are repeatedly being asked to prove land ownership to government; what about government proving that they own the land?[15]

The CYLC outlined our two options regarding our claim at a Steering Committee meeting held on 1-2 September 2003:

- progress Native Title, the possible outcomes being a) non-exclusive determination of native title, b) no native title outcome and further mediation; or
- propose a deal with the State (as above).

The Native Title Claimants Proposal for Tenure Resolution over Batavia Downs was submitted to the then Minister for Natural Resource and Mines, Stephen Robertson, on 3 September 2003. We confirmed our desire for the State to move to a speedy resolution of tenure issues on Batavia and stated that we were prepared to negotiate an outcome with the State based on the following:

- that the area to the far north west of the claim area be set aside for a National Park;
- that the majority of the area be transferred to Traditional Owners as Aboriginal Freehold with conservation agreements over identified areas; and

---

[14] National Native Title Tribunal, Mediation Conference, Meeting Summary Native Title Determination Application QC97/44, Summary of Outcomes, 24 July 2003.
[15] Muir (1998: 4) notes that the 'approach to native title should reflect the fact that the Mabo decision recognised a system of laws, Indigenous laws, and that those laws allocated rights in land, albeit subject to the Crown's right of extinguishment. Where extinguishment did not occur then as a matter of logic native title or rights to land allocated through Indigenous laws must continue to exist'. In other words, where government cannot prove that they own the land through extinguishment, Traditional Owners for those particular tracts of land should not have to prove their ownership, as it still exists.

- that an area on the north west portion of the claim area be leased for pastoral purposes and that any such a pastoral lease be made available to Traditional Owners.[16]

Our overall position was that if it is the case that native title had been extinguished over much of the area, these areas should become Aboriginal Freehold under the ALA. From there conservation agreements and land management arrangements may be negotiated, with the bottom line being primary Kaanju management and decision-making regarding the land and associated resources. Further, our proposal to establish an IPA over the claim area would satisfy the State's proposal for conservation agreements over much of the claim area.

Cape York Land Council

Throughout almost the entire period of the claim the role of our Native Title Representative Body, CYLC, has been problematic. For example, during the whole process of the dealings with the State it was not able to access the State's report on Batavia Downs (or if it did access the report it did not make it known to the Traditional Owners). Numerous requests made by the author of this paper to the lawyer heading the claim that CYLC obtain a copy were all but ignored, or at least from our perspective it seemed they made little effort to obtain a copy. Throughout the whole process of the dealings with the State as described above the CYLC appears to have been taking a minor role, waiting for the government to call the cards rather than acting in the interests of the people they are supposed to represent.

In June 2004 the CYLC contacted native title claimants for the Batavia Claim explaining why they had not heard from the Land Council in such a long time and also to provide an update on what had been happening with the Batavia claim.[17] The letter explained that there had been a large turnover in staff and they were making a number of changes as action on decisions made by the Executive Council.[18] One of those changes was to develop a native title claims policy. In their words:

> This policy provides a way to manage the work of the Land Council. It is simply not possible for us to deal properly with more than two dozen claims, as we have at the moment. Everyone involved in native title and land work understands that we need to work out which matters need to

---

[16] CYLC, Letter to Stephen Robertson Minister of Queensland Department of Natural Resources and Mines from Traditional Owners of Batavia Downs. 2 September 2003.
[17] J. Brooks, Letter to Native Title applicants Northern Kaanju and Yianh People (Batavia) from the Cape York Land Council, 10 June 2004.
[18] It should be noted that during the history of the Batavia Claim there have been at least four changes in the Land Council lawyers heading the claim.

be given more attention now, so that all traditional owners groups across the Cape benefit in the long run.[19]

It was decided that the most complex matters—*Wik* and *Eastern Kuku Yalanji*—needed to be completed as soon as possible so that staff and resources could be freed up for pushing other claims along in the future. It was noted that finalising those claims should pave the way for sorting out other applications, 'for everyones' benefit'. They asserted, 'Based on that policy, we need to prioritise our work on applications and put the necessary resources against the matters which have the highest priority' (Brooks 2004).

The Land Council hence put Batavia on the back burner while they concentrated on more complex claims. Only recently have the Land Council contacted claimants about Batavia. This has come at the same time as negotiations over a proposed gas pipeline that will pass through Cape York Peninsula.[20]

The claimant group

As discussed earlier, under the Kaanju land tenure system particular families or clans are particularly associated with or 'come from' particular tracts of land or clan estates within the overall umbrella of the Kaanju homelands. Further, based on hierarchy particular individuals within these families have authority to speak for the land, while others do not. What this means is that not all people who identify as Kaanju come from the entire (Northern) Kaanju homelands. However, the native title process is such that, although the claim is only to part of the Kaanju homelands north of the Archer River and therefore covers only particular clan estates, people who identify as being Kaanju people from north of the Archer River are listed as claimants. This presents a number of questions for the core Kaanju families who are actually from the area under claim. How can people who are not even from the area under claim be listed as claimants on the native title claim? How is it that a number of these people speak for the land under claim at mediation and steering committee meetings when they have no right to do so under Kaanju law and custom? Further, in formal discussions and negotiations regarding development proposals concerning the area under claim, these people also speak for the country, as has been the case with negotiations over the gas pipeline.

What this translates to is that there are claimants on our claim who are not from the area under claim, and therefore people speaking for our land when they have no right to do so under Kaanju law and custom. This has been particularly

---

[19] J. Brooks (ibid.).
[20] The Cape York Land Council signed an agreement with the original proponents for this gas pipeline back in 1997. The proposal involves a 2500 kilometre pipeline to transport natural gas from the Papua New Guinea highlands, across Torres Strait, through Cape York, northern and central Queensland, to Townsville and Gladstone. The proposed route for the gas pipeline travels through some 60 kilometres of Kaanju homelands, some 45 kilometres of which is in the Batavia claim area.

evident at a number of the mediation meetings at which I have been present, where claimants who actually live on country have been obstructed in having a say by Tribunal staff who have given preference to claimants who do not live on the peninsula, who are not from the particular area under claim, and indeed whose claims to being Kaanju people, according to Kaanju people living on homelands, are questionable.[21] It is the inadequacy of the claims process that has allowed this to happen. 'The land does not belong to them' is the sentiment of the focal Kaanju people from the claim area.

Our understanding is that when the claim was first lodged with the National Native Title Tribunal it was rejected, due not only to amendments to the NTA, but also to there being a small claimant group. This original claimant group was a more accurate indication of the Kaanju people connected to the area under claim than the present claimant group that is made up of people who identify as Kaanju north of the Archer River, but not necessarily as Kaanju belonging to the actual area under claim. To reiterate, a number of the claimant families may identify as Kaanju, but they do not come from the actual area under claim. Herein lies another of the failings of the native title process, being that it does not recognise that Indigenous land tenure systems are very localised. The native title process, particularly the Native Title Representative Body in that process, takes a regional and sub-regional approach to land tenure systems that is inappropriate and non-Indigenous and thus inherently problematic and goes against the proper recognition of native (Indigenous) title and governance. As noted by Bauman and Williams, 'broadly defined regional native title systems can overlook specific localised and individualised rights and interests as representatives of the broader group are seen to have an equal say in making decisions about matters which may not be their primary concern' (2004: 11).

The Batavia Native Title Application identified the claimant group in the following terms:[22]

> The Northern Kaanju claimants identify themselves, and are identified by the other Aboriginal people of the Central Cape York Peninsula region, as the group of people whose native title rights and interests under Aboriginal law and custom, are to that area of land associated with the Kaanju language which lies north of the Archer River and extends north to the area of the Moreton Telegraph Station. (CYLC 1999: 1).

---

[21] I have been present at a number of Mediation meetings during the eight year long history of the claim. I recall in detail the events of one particular meeting where my Aunty (who has since passed away) began to talk about claim and raise an important issue but was rudely interrupted by Tribunal staff who gave preference to diaspora claimants who wanted to have their say. Despite attempts my Aunty was not given the opportunity to speak up later in the meeting. I noted that my Aunty's attempts to speak were not noted in the official minutes of the meeting.

[22] As noted above this paper concerns the Northen Kaanju people and Northern Kaanju portion of the Batavia claim, and not also the Yianh people and Yianh portion of the claim area.

The application outlines current membership of the group as being primarily through the principle of cognatic descent, that is, descent traced through both male and female ancestors. Further, members traced their descent from a limited set of persons recognised in the regional Aboriginal community as having been Kaanju occupants of the claim area (CYLC 1999: 1). Thus the current membership of the Northern Kaanju peoples, according to the application, comprises a number of cognatic descent groups or families who are identified by their main surnames together with the apical ancestors from whom they trace their descent cognatically (CYLC 1999:1). The application lists 21 Northern Kaanju families and their apical ancestors. Notably, the 'descendants of George Moreton Snr and his wife Mary Ann (both deceased), being members of the Moreton/Nelson Family' is the first listed cognatic descent group. However, the application does not indicate that not all the Kaanju families listed are from the actual area under claim, nor does it indicate that particular families and individuals within those families have the right to speak for particular tracts of land within the claim area, while others do not. It has been a 'boxed up' claim from the start which today is not necessarily the perspective of core Kaanju families living at Chuulangun for that area of their homelands.

This approach to the formation of the claimant group is supported in the draft Connection Report. As Smith notes:

> ... it is my conclusion with regard to the Batavia Downs native title claim that the proper 'social scale' at which the claim be determined is that of the 'macro-grouping' of one or more (in this case, three) contemporary language-named or place-based 'tribal' groups (despite the fact that a number of claimants might not regard this as the most significant social scale at which customary interests are articulated among the indigenous people of the region). *This conclusion is based on native title case law and the contemporary and continuing forms of local custom and law pertaining to the claim area,* both of which lead me to conclude that this is the most proper way in which the native title holding group for the Batavia Downs area can be recognised (2006: 8, 10, emphasis in original).

At the same time in the draft Connection Report Smith acknowledges the importance of the principle of patrilineal descent to a number of Kaanju families:

> [A]n emphasis remains among many members of the 'home population, on the 'proper' principle of patrifilial recruitment or 'patrilineal descent' ... whilst Northern Kaanju people recognise both descendants of Northern Kaanju men and women as Northern people, and as 'proper' Northern Kaanju claimants in Native Title claims ... there remain vestiges of the greater weight placed on patrifilial recruitment ... this remains a matter for decision and negotiation between and within Northern Kaanju families rather than a hard and fast rule (2006: s. 5.2.6).

Smith (in an earlier version of Chapter 6) notes the difficulties apparent in 'reified codifications of such groups that anthropologists, lawyers and others inevitably create in the production of "connection reports", prescribed bodies corporate and other statements of the relationship between Aboriginal people and their "traditional land".' Claimant groups are seen as 'categorically defined, bounded and non-negotiable' (Bauman and Williams 2004: 11). The problem with such groups is that what is presented on paper does not necessarily reflect what exists in reality on the ground where the action is taking place in terms of land management and Traditional Owners living and working on country. From our perspective as Traditional Owners living on homelands the claimant group is an artificial group, but has become legitimised by the native title process. Bauman and Williams (2004: 11) note that the 'need to define groups categorically does not account for differentiation within and across groups', which 'creates fertile climate for disputes concerning who has the greater claim or authority over the country and the appropriate grouping to which native title should be attributed.'

Foley (Chapter 7) alludes to the 'usurpers' who, through the power structures of specific land councils, are given legitimacy under New South Wales statute law and become custodians in European terms over issues of native title. Similarly for the Batavia claim, a number of claimants have had their position as Kaanju people, and in the case of named applicants on the claim, as people who hold authority to speak for the land under claim, legitimised by the native title process. Thus while under government law their identity as Kaanju people and authoritative people to speak for land is recognised, under proper Indigenous law they are not recognised. This situation of being recognised under government law but not under Indigenous law further fuels the view of local people that these claimants see government law as superior to Indigenous governance. This is reinforced by the NTA itself. As noted by Muir, 'the "determination process" established by the NTA takes us full circle to a situation that again supports the notion that the Australian law is the only legitimate law' (1998: 3).

As noted by Smith what comes across as problematic in land claims is the marked difference between how local people and diaspora people assert connections to country. 'Diaspora people often reject a distinction between their connection and those of local families, asserting that, regardless of location, they hold equal interests in (and connection to) the country of their forebears' ((2000: 2; see also Smith 2000: 4). However, in the case of Batavia Downs who their actual forebears are is also questioned by local people.

While for a significant number of local people ancient or 'classical' forms of governance and associated kinship and territoriality remain, for diaspora people, the shift towards a tribal identity has been far greater (see also Smith 2000: 4). Within such a model, 'diaspora people tend to presume that each tribe holds homogenous rights over a *"tribal area"* of language-associated country' (Smith 2000: 6).

Again as noted by Smith in the draft Connection Report:

> Given the existence among Northern Kaanju people of a widespread assertion of customary connections to the broader Northern Kaanju homelands area, and the requirement under Native Title law to recognise such wider connection, rather than delimiting the membership of claim groups to those asserting a particular or primary connection to a claim area within such broader assertions of connection, the description of the Northern Kaanju group for the purposes of this (and other) claims necessarily includes the wider set of 'Northern Kaanju' families (2006: 10).

This situation is made worse by the philosophy that can be summarised as: 'get your land back first and then sort through internal issues after that'. One of the justifications for this idea is that it is not the business of the government where the Aboriginal boundaries are within the claim area, only where the external property (government) land boundaries are. However, this creates problems for legitimate Traditional Owners (that is, the focal claimants) who have to 'pick up the pieces' and dismantle the obstacle of the imposed government-sanctioned prescribed body corporate (PBC) or land trust in order for the unobstructed carrying out of land management rights and obligations.

The prescribed body corporate

Under the NTA an incorporated native-title body, a PBC, is required to hold the native title rights and interests that form the 'title' once the claim is determined, or in the case of the Batavia Claim an ILUA is established (once tenure arrangements issues are resolved). Like other corporations the PBC (or land trust) requires a constitution outlining the rules and objectives by which the corporation will function. We anticipate problems when at the determination of the claim or tenure resolution a PBC or land trust is formed that includes all members of the current claimant group. How will a constitution be drawn up and how will the constitution, if at all, address issues concerning management and decision-making of the land? And particularly how will it deal with the issues of which members of the group hold the authority to speak for country? We anticipate serious problems in this regard.

It is useful here to refer to Glaskin's contribution to this volume (Chapter 3). Glaskin focuses on the discussions concerning the development of a PBC for the Bardi and Jawi native title claim in the north-west Kimberley region of Western Australia. She notes that as claimants discussed the constitution for their PBC, one aspect that they felt had to be incorporated within the rules concerned the role of the *madja-madjin* ('Law bosses' or senior ritual experts) within their society. While it might be useful to incorporate such a consideration in the constitution for the PBC or land trust for the Batavia claim determination, the problem of differing opinions on who are the proper people who hold authority will inevitably be hotly debated as the situation is now. Glaskin (Chapter 3) notes that from the view of the claimants the formation of the PBC was closely linked with the development of a particular kind of constitution that adequately upheld Bardi and Jawi 'Law, language and culture'. Glaskin cites Sullivan's (1997: 139) description in relation to the Rubibi constitution as being 'nothing less than an attempt at a self-governing structure reflecting customary Aboriginal law'. But what happens when different claimants have differing views on what that is, as is the case for the Batavia claim?

Again as Glaskin describes in Chapter 3, another group of claimants maintained a position that principles of land ownership (recognising specific interests in country, with reference to estates) should be made clear in the constitution for the PBC. Such a principle would be of considerable importance in the drawing up of the constitution for the native title holding body for the Batavia claim based on the current claimant group. However, the drawing up of a constitution that considers the existence of specific interests in country and the association of particular families with particular estates has been slowed down by decisions made at a March 2006 meeting organised by the CYLC. Agenda items for this meeting included the identification of 'all the Kaanichi Kaanju Elders' and confirmation of 'traditional laws and customs of the Kaanichi Kaanju People in relation to their tribal lands and decision-making processes'. Notwithstanding the seriously questionable process by which the meeting was organised and the process and context of the actual meeting itself, at the meeting, after the 'Elders' were identified, one of the decisions made by the Elders was that 'there are no special sub groups rights' in the consultation or decision making processes for the Kaanichi Kaanju People.[23]

Indigenous land management, sovereignty and compensation issues

We have concerns about the ability of native title to recognise that our sovereignty has been taken out of the land by the colonisation process and successive series of government policies and practices past and present, that saw

---

[23] The Kaanichi Kaanju Elders, in a letter addressed to David Claudie, 2 March 2006. Two weeks' notice was given for this meeting and it was held in Cairns, some 1000 kilometres from Kaanju Homelands, during the wet season. A number of people were unable to attend who should have, including myself. If native title is about recognising traditional law and custom the Land Council should be recognising Elders under traditional law and custom, and not by way of a meeting organised by them to identify Elders under non-Indigenous Land Council processes and the native title process. As for the claimant group for the Batavia claim, the processes of the Cape York Land Council and the native title process itself have given 'all the Kaanichi Kaanju Elders' legitimacy as the authority for the land. This is very problematic.

Kaanju people forcibly removed from homelands and centralised in towns and government orchestrated communities. When we were taken out of our land, the sustainable management of the land and associated resources were severely disrupted. Associated with taking the sovereignty out of the land is the prevailing assumption that the land is 'empty' and Indigenous land and resource management is no longer effectual, no longer exists or is not relevant in today's 'modern' society.

However, Kaanju land and resource management does exist and permanent Kaanju communities are being re-established on our homelands, including in the area subject to the Batavia claim. Focal Kaanju Traditional Owners have developed a comprehensive *Land and Resource Management Framework* and an *IPA Management Plan* that sets out in detail the management of our lands and associated resources. Like our BDAPR report these documents are based on Kaanju governance and land and resource management principles and practices that have been passed down over many thousands of years through Kaanju bloodlines to the current generation of Kaanju land managers and law makers living on homelands.

When we were forcibly absent from our homelands other management regimes had taken over (namely by government) in the form of pastoral and mining leases, National Parks and forest reserves. Due to the inappropriateness of these regimes we now face a myriad of land management problems not of our own making, including weed and feral animal infestation, land degradation, the destruction of important ecological environments, and the desecration of cultural sites by prolific and unregulated public access.

What the NTA needs to recognise and enforce is that our sovereignty is still in the land and that Traditional Owners need to be compensated, in the form of funding and resources, in order to carry out obligations as primary land managers and decision-makers and return the land to its sustainable state. This includes support for homelands and economic development. However, what will need to be reinforced is that any funding and resources that are forthcoming would have to be spent on country. During recent negotiations over the proposed gas pipeline the issue of compensation or royalties was discussed. From the perspective of Kaanju people living on homelands any royalties from the gas pipeline would have to go into a trust or incorporated body as described above and be spent on country for the benefit of the land through which the pipeline passes, for example, on land management projects such as weed and feral animal control, biodiversity conservation and fire management. The way that Kaanju people would benefit financially would include being actively engaged in these projects on homelands and be paid wages for their work.

Further, the legal system does not recognise commercial rights under the NTA, only traditional rights, therefore we often have to negotiate with government and other stakeholders to make agreements in order to get what we want. Apparently, 'Native Title is about rights and interests not ownership'[24] and as such does very little to accommodate Traditional Owner plans for homelands and economic development, and aspirations for the improvement of our health, social, spiritual, and economic well-being.[25]

Conclusion

The dealings with the State regarding tenure resolution and management arrangements over the area of Batavia were cause for considerable concern in the period from about 2001 to 2004. From our perspective the State was (and still is) taking its time on the issue and playing bureaucratic games over our traditional homelands. But while our own and the efforts of our Native Title Representative Body were engaged with this issue, dispute about who has the right to speak for country and questions about the nature of the claimant group itself were festering in the background. From the start of the claim the native title process has allowed claimants whose connections to the claim area are questionable to come forward, leading to proceedings being dominated by this group to the detriment of the rights and interests of the proper Traditional Owners for the area. Unfortunately, despite our considerable effort and dialogue with the Land Council concerning this issue, the claim is continuing along its current path. While greater weight is placed on the wider Northern Kaanju identity and the claim being 'boxed up', core Northern Kaanju families for the claim area will continue to be marginalised in decision making processes to do with the claim and development proposals concerning the claim area. Put simply, our Native Title Representative Body is not listening to us, the primary Traditional Owners for the claim area, and the very people whose extensive knowledge of Indigenous law and custom and continuing connection to and engagement on homelands is supporting the claim.

Further, while the claim continues along its current path we see only problems for the formation of the PBC and for negotiations over major developments concerning the land such as the gas pipeline. We are firm in our determination that this impasse be broken and are currently seeking advice from the National Native Title Tribunal and lawyers on the best way to proceed in order to achieve the best outcome for the land and justice for the proper native title holders.[26]

---

[24] M. Salmon, in Batavia Downs Steering Committee Meeting, Moreton Telegraph Station, 16 October 2001, CYLC minutes from meeting, p. 9.

[25] While it is possible to seek some 'economic' rights and interests through the native title process, such rights and interests appear—given previous native title cases—to be essentially limited and 'backwards-looking'. As such, even if such rights were recognised in our case, they would provide a very limited basis for the current and future aspirations of Kaanju people living on our homelands.

[26] There is not space in this paper to discuss these options. Our preference would be for the claim to be re-lodged with the Northern Kaanju claimant group comprising only those families actually from the area under claim. Otherwise we see the following alternative options: 1) withdraw from the current claim and lodge a rival claim to the same area; 2) as the claimant group in the current claim encompasses

Through the Chuulangun Aboriginal Corporation we have also engaged directly with the corporation overseeing the negotiations over the gas pipeline to inform them of the issues and to ensure that the views are sought from the appropriate Traditional Owners for the land through which it is proposed the pipeline will pass. Similarly for sovereignty and compensation issues, the NTA needs to recognise that native title claims are considered on a case-by-case basis and as such claimant groups need to also be considered as such. While for a number of native title claims regionally based native title holding groups may be appropriate, this may not necessarily be the case for all native title claims. The NTA and process needs to recognise that for some claims locally based land holding bodies are the most appropriate scale for proper decision-making and better reflect traditional governance structures, law, custom, and continuing connection and engagement with country.

I would like to conclude with a few comments made by legitimate senior claimants during the claims process. In one instance, continuing debate over the issue of whether to extend the claim group to include another language group with connections to the northern area of the claim was met with the following response from a senior Kaanju Traditional Owner: 'But all the answers are gotten now and we need to finish this talk and get on with it'.[27] This issue had been discussed in depth and resolved at a meeting held four months earlier. Another comment from the same Traditional Owner at the same meeting on the same issue was: 'Just make decision today—tired of talking all the time'.[28]

Finally, at a Steering Committee meeting held on country in 2001 a Kaanju Traditional Owner expressed his frustration over the NTA: 'All these Acts belong to the government but what about Aboriginal people. Can we produce a new Act that will combine everything?'[29] In response, an officer from the CYLC replied: 'We won't change the law but we can make progress through mediation and expedited native title process'.[30] Almost five years on we are still waiting to get our land back.

---

all the Northern Kaanju people from north of the Archer River, change the claim area to include the entire area of the Northern Kaanju homelands; 3) retain the existing claimant group, change the named applicants to include only people who are from the actual area under claim, and include a declaration in the application, and provide evidence for this in the Connection Report, that names the particular families that are actually from the area under claim and have the primary rights to the area in terms of decision making, land use, ownership and management, and notes that the other Northern Kaanju families are included as a courtesy, that is, that they are recognised but they do not necessarily have the primary rights to the area in terms of decision making, land use, ownership and management.

[27] M. Sellars, in Batavia Downs Steering Committee Meeting, Cairns, Friday 18 January 2002, CYLC minutes from meeting, p 3.

[28] M. Sellars, in Batavia Downs Steering Committee Meeting, Cairns, Friday 18 January 2002, CYLC minutes from meeting, p. 4.

[29] D. Claudie, in Batavia Downs Steering Committee Meeting, Moreton Telegraph Station, 16 October 2001, CYLC minutes from meeting, p. 4.

[30] P. Blackwood, in Batavia Downs Steering Committee Meeting, Moreton Telegraph Station, 16 October 2001, CYLC minutes from meeting, p. 4.

References

Bauman, T. and Williams, R. 2004. 'The business of process research issues in managing Indigenous decision-making and disputes in land', *Research Discussion Paper No. 13*, Native Title Research Unit, Australian Institute of Aboriginal and Torres Strait Islander Studies, Canberra.

Kaanju People and Salmon, M. 2000. Batavia Downs Aspirations Planning Report (BDAPR), Draft for Comment, unpublished report, November 2000, Balkanu Cape York Development Corporation, Cairns.

Cape York Land Council (CYLC) 1999. Batavia Native Title Application, Section A, CYLC, Cairns.

Chuulangun Aboriginal Corporation 2005. *Kaanju Homelands Wenlock and Pascoe Rivers Indigenous Protected Area Management Plan, March 2005*, Chuulangun Aboriginal Corporation, Chuulangun, Cape York Peninsula, Qld.

Claudie, D. 2004. '"Ancient but new": policy development from the ground up', Paper presented at the *Community Engagement Programs for Improved Collaborative Indigenous Policy Development* Conference, Cairns, 26–27 July.

Muir, K. 1998. '"This Earth has an Aboriginal culture inside": recognising the cultural value of country', *Land, Rights, Laws: Issues of Native Title*, Issues Paper No. 23: 2–9, Native Title Research Unit, Australian Institute of Aboriginal and Torres Strait Islander Studies, Canberra.

Sinclair, I. 2003. Batavia Downs Land Evaluation Report, unpublished report, Catchment and Regional Planning, North Region, Department of Natural Resources and Mines, Atherton.

Smith, B. R. 2000. '"Local" and "diaspora" connections to country and kin in central Cape York Peninsula', *Land, Rights, Laws: Issues of Native Title*, 2 (6): 1–12.

Smith, B. R. 2005. 'We got our own management: local knowledge, government and development in Cape York Peninsula', *Australian Aboriginal Studies*, 2005 (2): 4–15.

Smith, B. R. 2006. Connection Report, Batavia Downs Native Title Claim, confidential first draft prepared for the Cape York Land Council, 16 January 2006.

Smith, B. R. and Claudie, D. 2003. 'Developing a land and resource management framework for Kaanju homelands, central Cape York', *CAEPR Discussion Paper No. 256*, Centre for Aboriginal and Economic Policy Research, The Australian National University, Canberra.

Sullivan, P. 1997. 'Dealing with native title conflicts by recognising Aboriginal political authority', in D.E. Smith and J. Findlayson (eds), *Fighting Over Country: Anthropological Perspectives*, CAEPR Research Monograph No. 12, Centre for Aboriginal and Economic Policy Research, The Australian National University, Canberra.

6. Towards an uncertain community? The social effects of native title in central Cape York Peninsula

Benjamin R. Smith

Introduction

Aborigines in central Cape York Peninsula have lived alongside non-Indigenous pastoralists from the late-nineteenth century onwards. Despite a fraught and violent history, strong social ties developed between Aborigines and settlers during this period of coexistence. But in recent years these ties have become strained following a decline in Aboriginal employment on stations, the arrival of a number of new station owners and the passing of Queensland's *Aboriginal Land Act 1991* and the *Native Title Act 1993* (Cwlth). The success of the Wik and Wik Way People's native title claim—which determined that native title could coexist with pastoralists' rights on the central Peninsula's pastoral leases—has been particularly detrimental to social ties between Aboriginal people and settler pastoralists.[1]

In this paper I take up the theme of 'pathways out of the near-hegemonic relations of the past' (Redmond, Chapter 4), revisiting my earlier work on native title, certainty, and the coexistence of Aborigines and settler pastoralists in central Cape York Peninsula (Smith 2003). In considering such pathways, I also build on Patton's (1995) call for a more 'open' response to the possibilities offered by native title following the initial impetus of the Mabo No.2 decision and the *NTA*.

Writing shortly after the NTA's passage into law, Patton suggested that a more open response would be more likely to lead to progress towards social justice for Australia's Indigenous peoples. This progress would result from processual approaches to native title that would maximise rather than restrict:

> options for Aboriginal communities ... to take a stand against forms of closure, in favour of openness or the continuous play of possibilities ... [this] amounts to demanding alegally and politically open-ended space of possibilities for action, a space of becoming that allows for the non-self-identical character of individual and collective agents (Patton 1995: 161-2).

---

[1] In addition to settler pastoralists, a number of the region's Aboriginal people regard themselves as pastoralists. In recent years a number of these Aboriginal pastoralists have gained control of cattle properties, or have established their own herds on their homelands (see Smith 2000a, 2002, 2003).

Such approaches would seek to enable 'openness' in relation to the outcomes of native title and the resulting possibilities for social justice and Indigenous futures. However, such openness can only hope to exist 'on the basis of specific mechanisms for identifying and dealing with native title' (Patton 1995: 162).

In this paper I seek to extend Patton's arguments through an anthropological consideration of the relation between 'openness' and social justice in the context of native title claims in central Cape York Peninsula. But rather than focusing only on the ways in which native title affects Indigenous Australians, I instead recast Patton's approach, conceptualising social justice in relation to a broader local or regional community affected by native title. As a 'total social fact' (Weiner 2003), native title affects not only Indigenous Australians but also the broader local communities associated with any given area for which native title is claimed or determined. Anthropological consideration of these communities, and the social fields (Gluckman 1949; Sullivan 2005) through which they are constituted, can shed light on the social effects of native title within a given locale. An anthropological engagement of this kind both points towards the ways in which some measure of social justice might be achieved within such fields, and indicates what forms social justice might take. A useful starting point for such an engagement is to consider the ways in which recognition and coexistence already take place within a particular social field and may thus be extended from existing foundations.

The limits of recognition

The most concerted discussion of recognition in the context of native title stems from Noel Pearson's (1997) model of the recognition space, which presents legal recognition as being constituted in an overlap between distinct fields of Aboriginal law and Australian law.[2] Martin (2004: 68) rightly emphasises the particular character of the process of recognition represented by this model, arguing that it involves a fundamentally transformative mode of translation that is brought to bear on those aspects of Aboriginal law that are 'recognised'. This forceful translation is made possible by the dominance of the categories of Australian property law within the recognition space. But Martin also notes that the native title recognition space is 'only one dimension of the complex zone of social, cultural, political and economic interaction between Indigenous and non-Indigenous societies' (Martin 2004: 68).

Patton is similarly critical of the operation of recognition enabled by the Native Title Act, describing it as 'a secondary reterritorialisation [of "recognised" customary law] by legislative means' (Patton 2000: 126). The term

[2] Although Pearson has more recently resiled from this conceptualisation of native title (see Martin 2003: 2-3), the recognition space model has remained influential, not least in anthropological discussions of native title. Among those who have drawn on Pearson's model are Mantziaris and Martin (2000), Martin (2003, 2004), Sullivan (2001), and Weiner (n.d.).

'reterritorialisation' used by Patton suggests both that customary law is taken over or 'captured' by Australian law, and also that it becomes a mere object of the categories of the NTA and of Western legislative practice more generally.[3] But despite this, Patton is more equivocal than Martin in his account of the forms of translation that occur in the process of recognition:

> the recognition of native title involves a becoming-indigenous of the common law to the extent that it now protects a property right derived from indigenous law; and a becoming-common law of indigenous law to the extent that it now acquires the authority along with the jurisprudential limits of the common law doctrine of native title (Patton 2000: 129).

Like Martin, Patton's analysis is suggestive of the kinds of translation that occur in any act of recognition.[4] In the native title process, recognition means that the character of Aboriginal law is at least partly transformed as a result of its acquiring the jurisprudential limits of the common law's articulation of native title. But Patton also suggests that the process of transformation operates in both directions. The common law 'becomes indigenous' in its extension of protection, through recognition, to proprietary interests previously articulated only within the domain of Aboriginal law. On this basis, Patton suggests that the recognition of native title also involves 'a partial deterritorialisation of the legal apparatus of capture by means of refusal of its primary stage: the establishment of a uniform space of comparison and appropriation' (Patton 2000: 129). Rather than mere capture and objectification, then, the native title process might allow Aboriginal law to exert a transformative effect on the Australian legal apparatus. By maintaining substantial aspects of Aboriginal law in the space of 'mainstream' legal practice, this would radically undermine the uniform space of Australian law, 'opening' it through the introduction of cultural difference within that space.[5]

Of course, Patton was writing at a time in which the radical potential of native title seemed greater than has actually proved to be the case. The 1998 amendments to the NTA and the developing trajectory of native title case law have served to limit any deterritorialisation of Australian law. In retrospect it seems that Patton was being overly optimistic in his suggestion that Aboriginal law and custom would be able to avoid capture within a uniform space of comparison and appropriation in native title claims. Rather, history has supported Merlan's (1998: 175) suggestion that the NTA would assimilate customary rights

---

[3] Patton draws the terms 'reterritorialisation', 'deterritorialisation' and 'capture' from the work of Giles Deleuze, and in particular from Deleuze and Guattari (1987).
[4] On the problems of translation in the context of native title see also Morphy (Chapter 2); Glaskin (Chapter 3) and Lahn (Chapter 7).
[5] See Morphy (Chapter 2) for an example of the introduction of Aboriginal law within the native title process despite the best efforts of the court to maintain the uniform space of Australian law.

and interests into 'the existing class of property rights at common law' only so far as such rights and interests can be dealt with by Australia's legal system.[6]

The formal outcomes of native title claims have increasingly tended towards the radical translation of limited aspects of Aboriginal Law within the recognition space. Nonetheless, the wider social fields within which native title is enacted may yet bear out Patton's hope for the development of heterogeneous spaces of interaction between Aboriginal and non-indigenous life-worlds. What is lost in the formal aspects of determination may persist in other aspects of the complex zone of interaction between Aborigines and settlers. But rather than existing as a result of forms of 'social, cultural, political and economic interaction *between* Indigenous and non-Indigenous societies' (Martin 2004: 68, emphasis added), in central Cape York Peninsula such heterogeneity seems to be situated *within* shared social fields.

Indeed, despite its formal, legalistic emphasis, native title may yet prove to have contributed to meaningful coexistence by further intensifying social relationships between Aborigines and settlers in places like the central Peninsula.

Fundamental coexistence

Previous accounts of native title have tended to conceive of recognition as occurring in an overlap between different bodies of law, or as an interaction between substantially distinct Aboriginal and settler societies. Such accounts tend to conceive of native title relatively narrowly, in terms of a legal process focused on the articulation of systems rather than as an event taking place within the daily lives of claimants, respondents and other interested parties.

If we place native title within its broader social context, we are able to include within our analyses not only the formal aspects of recognition—those driven by the operation of the Native Title Act—but also other kinds of recognition. These other kinds of recognition occur elsewhere in the complex zone of interactions between Aborigines and settler Australians. Within this zone, the analysis of native title (and in particular its social effects) becomes centred on questions concerning coexistence. Indeed, viewed from within this zone, coexistence is revealed as existing *prior* to a native title claim, and as the foundation upon which any act of recognition, formal or otherwise, is able to occur.

This prior coexistence takes various forms. At its most diffuse it exists at the level of the Australian nation-state, which provides both the limit and the necessary social and legal framework for native title *per se*. But the coexistence that underpins native title as a total social fact also occurs in more limited and

---

[6] Merlan (1998: 176) also notes that, at the time of writing, other interpretations of native title were emerging 'that would allow some freedom from constraining … structures'.

socially substantial forms. Perhaps most importantly, this prior coexistence occurs in the form of the local social field or community that is concerned with a particular area subject to a native title claim.

In using the term 'community', I am mindful of the problems of its suggestion of a homogenous character or substantial identity to those Aboriginal people who live together in a particular locality.[7] Regarding the social effects of native title, however, it is useful to consider community in the sense identified by Wagner (1967: 186, 207-17, 1988: 44-45, 59). For Wagner, communities are not pre-existing social entities sharing a single identity. Rather, communities are continually *emergent* in the social interactions between those living alongside and interacting with one another. The 'concretivity' of such communities 'is that of locale and event rather than continuative substance or identity'. For this reason 'they are not so much the objects as the subjects' of ongoing local histories (Wagner 1988: 59).

In central Cape York Peninsula—and particularly in Coen, the region's main township—this usefulness of this notion of community is not limited to those Aboriginal people who live together in the town and in 'outstation' camps in the township's hinterland. Community of this kind also inheres amongst the wider regional population, both Aborigines and settlers, whose interactions continue to lie at the heart of regional sociality. In this region—as elsewhere in Northern Australia—the communities whose coexistence is the basis of the social effects of native title include many, if not all, of those Aborigines and 'whitefellas' who live within or close to the area subject to a native title claim.[8]

The work of the French philosopher Jean-Luc Nancy (e.g. 1997, 2000) clarifies the importance of the prior coexistence of such communities in relation to the social effects of native title. For Nancy, coexistence is the fundamental 'groundform' of all human life-worlds. What consociates have in common is not merely more or less specific ways of thinking, being and acting, possessions or property rights and the like which tie together a series of individuals. Coexistence—'being-with' others—is not merely a secondary aspect of human existence; rather, coexistence is the fundamental condition of existence in general. It names the way in which we can only meaningfully exist through our ongoing relations with others; the character of our existence depends on the community that we share with our consociates. This shared situation provides 'the capacity in and by which something, "some-things"' and "some-ones" come to "be"'

---

[7] See Peters-Little (2001) and Sullivan (1996) for critical accounts of the use of the term 'community' in relation to Aboriginal Australians.

[8] The arguments regarding coexistence made here might also be usefully expanded to include others who, despite not living locally, understand themselves as having an interest in a given area, and act in relation to that interest. This might include, for example, State or Federal agencies concerned with a particular tract of land, and members of the 'stolen generations' or Aboriginal 'diaspora' (Rigsby 1995; Smith 2000b), who are typically also involved in native title processes.

(Nancy and Ten Kate 2004). Within community the enactment of recognition, on the basis of coexistence, thus generates both particular social effects (e.g. 'rights and interests' and their 'enjoyment') as well as one's sense of selfhood, the latter being at least partly constituted in relation to the former. As such, coexistence might be understood as the 'groundform' of recognition where native title is understood as a total social fact.

Another name for this fundamental form of coexistence is 'the inter-' (Nancy and Ten Kate 2004). Given that Northern Australian life-worlds are now self-evidently constituted through 'the co-presence of people with different ideas and forms of action' (Merlan 2005: 169),[9] it is perhaps not surprising that anthropologists working in that region—as well as philosophers like Nancy—have placed the 'inter-' at the heart of their analyses. Merlan (2005: 169), for example, has drawn on various theories of intersubjectivity, which 'do not begin with a notion of a pre-existing "subject" … [but rather] from a notion of interrelationship and its specific moments of interaction' to model the character of coexistence in the Katherine region of Australia's Northern Territory. For Merlan, these accounts of intersubjectivity can usefully be the basis of understanding the 'intercultural' situations that now predominate across much of Northern Australia:

> In a similar fashion [to the way in which the 'inter-' operates in theories of intersubjectivity], I was looking for a formulation of the 'cultural' which recognizes difference but does not begin from an overspecified notion of 'culture'; as well as for a way of writing about relations 'between' people that focuses on the processual character of interrelationship … An 'intercultural' description needed to emphasize processes of reproduction as well as non-reproduction of socio-cultural patterns, interaction, and the varieties of reflexivity of participating subjects (Merlan 2005: 169).

Even where social life depends on sharply demarcated social boundaries—between Aborigines and whites in most North Australian towns for instance—one can nonetheless perceive such a substantive interrelationship 'of categories, understandings, modes of practical action' (Merlan 2005: 170). Moreover, rather than being pre-given, the character of such interrelationships necessarily means that Aboriginal categories, understandings and modes of action are reproduced and reshaped 'in interaction, interrelationship and

---

[9] This has, of course, always been the case; in small scale 'societies' like those extant in Australia at the 'threshold of colonization' (Keen 2004), the power of various understandings and actions to reshape both the social field and local cultural production is pronounced. However, only when anthropologists have been both methodologically and practically confronted with the co-presence of radically different ways of thinking and acting has the anthropology of Northern Australia begun to properly grapple with the question of the 'inter-'. (See the essays in Hinkson and Smith 2005 for a series of contributions on this theme).

event—sometimes in engagement with whites' (Merlan 2005: 170).[10] Here Merlan's account of the 'inter-' points towards the iterative character of all meanings, norms, and practices, which are continually reshaped in interactions between Aborigines and settlers as well as in interactions among Aborigines.

In Coen, for example, the interactions between Aborigines and local whites have been transformative of the life-world of the wider Coen community, despite ongoing social distinctions between Aborigines and whitefellas. Such transformations were particularly marked during the period of majority employment of Aboriginal people on the region's cattle stations. On these stations the formal distinctions between Aborigines and whites were often weakened, resulting in intense forms of consociality between them (see also Redmond 2005). The day-to-day patterns of station consociality and the mutual exposure of Aborigines and whites to each others' ways of dealing with the region's landscape resulted in the reshaping of whites' and Aborigines' forms of knowledge and practice relating to the landscape and to each other (Smith 2002, 2003). But a decline of Aboriginal employment on stations from the late 1960s and early 1970s onwards has since increased the sense of social distance between most Aborigines and settlers until recently, when the establishment of a local Aboriginal Corporation in Coen and advent of land claims and native title have led to more substantial interactions between Aboriginal people and the settler population in the central Peninsula (Smith 2000a).

On first glance, Merlan's 'inter-' is of a somewhat different order to Nancy's, dealing with particular instances of social and cultural life, rather than coexistence as a more abstract groundform of sociality. Nancy, however, argues that this 'groundform' only ever exists *within* the various enactments of social life. As such, Nancy's 'inter-', like Merlan's, inheres in the ongoing social articulation of categories, understandings and modes of practical action. If the 'inter-' is a groundform, it does not sit outside of everyday sociality; rather, it *is* that sociality, coexistence or community in each of its ongoing manifestations. The 'inter-' exists only in the interactions of consociates that ensure that there is a continually 'open' character to local life-worlds, even as they draw upon and reiterate established socio-cultural forms. This open character means that the possibility of change and creativity—Patton's 'deterritorialisation'—inheres continually in social life, providing it with its vitality.

Placing the 'inter-' at the heart of the socio-cultural field thus reveals all cultural production[11] as inherently intercultural. Whilst every social interaction depends on previously established meanings and norms, these are simultaneously

---

[10] Needless to say, the categories, understandings and modes of action of whites are also subject to transformations through interactions with Aborigines. However, the effects of local power relations, racism, and wider structural factors may mitigate the transformations produced through such interactions.

[11] Here I follow Merlan's (1998, 2005) use of the term to indicate the continuing iteration of particular cultural categories, understandings and modes of practical action within day-to-day social life.

reshaped—either subtly or radically—in the course of all interactions. This is not to say, of course, that meanings and norms are not maintained over time, nor that cultural differences and incommensurability are not more evident in some interactions than in others. Von Sturmer's (1984) discussion of the 'Aboriginal domain', for instance, makes it clear that distinctly Aboriginal styles of thought and action have persisted across Northern Australia despite the encapsulation and saturation of Aboriginal populations by 'mainstream' Australian society. The domains in which these styles of thought and action persist are maintained through intense, ongoing interactions among Aborigines at a remove from non-Indigenous consociates and local manifestations of the 'mainstream'. Further, even where long-term interactions between whites and Aborigines have taken place for generations, it is not uncommon for incommensurable understandings and actions to predominate. Despite a lifelong history of co-residence by Aborigines and whites in Coen, it is not uncommon for misinterpretation and incommensurability, rather than shared meanings and norms, to predominate in their interactions.

The ongoing misunderstandings and incommensurability between whites and Aborigines suggests that whilst the coexistence of local communities depends on particular perceptions or understandings about consociates—that is, on forms of recognition—such recognition is not necessarily either accurate or affirmative in character. Coexistence in central Cape York Peninsula has long involved 'recognition' in the form of racist stereotypes of local Aboriginal people. Local whites have variously seen Aborigines as savages, backwards, primitive, in need of supervision and guidance, as not owning land and as an available source of indentured labour for the region's cattle stations. At the same time, despite the continuing existence of such stereotypes, recognition has also taken more positive forms, for example in the ongoing close social bonds that have developed between local Aborigines and white pastoralists.[12] Even as coexistence depends on recognition, recognition—whether affirmative or negative in character—always falls short of the underlying 'openness' of coexistence. If the recognition enacted in the formal determination of native title is particularly ossifying and transformative of Aboriginal identities (Smith 2003; see also Glaskin, Chapter 3), its actions are nonetheless illustrative of the effects of recognition more generally.

Any act of recognition, legalistic or otherwise, reduces the potential of coexistence through an unavoidably reductive, particularistic framing of relationships and identities. Such acts are always regulative, in the sense that they bring a necessary definition to social interactions. Whilst they serve to

---

[12] Redmond (2005) usefully writes of these close social bonds, and the forms of misunderstanding and incommensurability that persist within and partly constitute them, in terms of R. D. Laing's notion of the 'family phantasy'.

enable sociality, they simultaneously limit it by foreclosing (at least temporarily) other potential forms of interaction. In identifying someone as a 'claimant', for example, all other possible relationships with that person are (temporarily, at least) subsumed by an interaction on the basis of that identity.

Given that the formal recognition offered by native title may be necessary to restore some wider meaning to Aboriginal customary interests, it is important to recognise that the ossifying effects of such recognition may be mitigated in other areas. The principal possibility for such mitigation inheres in the enactment of 'rights and interests' within the social life of local communities. If the formal recognition enacted within the 'recognition space' is necessarily dominated by a Western legal demand for certainty, based on a legalistic 'ontology of determinacy' (Smith 2003: 41, after Gaonkar 2002: 6), a more open style of recognition may nonetheless be maintained elsewhere in ongoing social interactions between Aborigines, local non-indigenes and others concerned with a particular area. This open style of recognition would not be overdetermined by fixed legal categories, but would rather subsume these categories within the complex field of ongoing social relations.

In this way the 'openness' required to achieve some measure of social justice for Aborigines may still be found in the context of native title, but only where the ongoing negotiation of the meaning of 'rights and interests' can take place in the interactions between native title holders and their consociates. This negotiation must therefore take place in the context of the wider community concerned with a particular area where native title has or will be determined, allowing for the establishment of relatively satisfactory coexistence between its members.

Social justice will thus never be brought about simply by a determination of native title. Instead, native title law can only impel an adjustment in the forms taken by local coexistence, which—in order to be both meaningful and relatively satisfactory for all members of a local community—must always exceed the 'letter of the law'. Legal processes, in and of themselves, will always be unsuccessful in their attempts to produce social justice. The 'thin simplifications' (Scott 1998) that such determinations represent can only ever be meaningful in the context of ongoing social interactions, although they may exert powerful leverage within these interactions. Here law and justice are both distinct yet inseparable; justice itself may remain incalculable, but any aspiration towards justice nonetheless requires an act of calculation, in particular through the application of law (Derrida 2002: 257). If the enactment of the law aspires to the achievement of just outcomes, social justice—situated in the 'open' exposure of consociates to one another—is nonetheless never simply achieved or arrived at. Social justice inheres in a sufficient potential for relatively satisfactory coexistence between members of a given community, not in the ossified articulation of rights and interests.

Beyond formalism, towards community?

One of the most important aspects of Martin's critique of the native title 'recognition space' is that the form of recognition that constitutes that space is dominated by the categories of Australian property law (see also Patton 1995: 158). Although this space is intercultural in a specific sense, marking the articulation of Aboriginal law and 'mainstream' Australian law, the forms of practice through which it is constituted are overwhelmingly based on the norms and interests of non-Indigenous parties. Further, given the fraught histories of relationships between Aborigines and white pastoralists in areas like central Cape York Peninsula, there is a considerable danger of reproducing the culturally biased character of the formal recognition space in the other forms of recognition through which native title is realised as a total social fact.

If Patton's hope for the possibility of more open outcomes from native title claims is to be realised within the complex zone of interactions between Aborigines and settlers, then more open forms of coexistence will need to be realised in day-to-day interactions between settlers and Aborigines than are provided for in native title determinations. Further, these forms of coexistence will necessarily have to be more inclusive of specifically Aboriginal forms of knowledge and practice in order to avoid the cultural hegemony that marks native title's formal recognition.

In the central Peninsula, consent determinations of native title between Aboriginal claimants and station owners typically depend on the negotiation of Indigenous Land Use Agreements (ILUAs). These negotiations are often been bogged down by discussions over formal sets of rules regarding Aboriginal land use. Nonetheless, despite an often stated dislike of 'lawyers and paperwork', settler pastoralists, as well as their legal representatives, are typically convinced of the ability of such formal arrangements to deliver them the 'certainty' that they require in order to consent to a native title determination. The need for such rules is typically argued for as providing 'certainty' for the continued running of a cattle business. For instance, pastoralists have argued that they require temporary exclusion zones on their properties during the mustering of cattle, or that they require explicit agreement that gates will be shut after they have been used. But pastoralists also seek 'certainty' regarding their lifestyles, for instance in seeking formal agreement about privacy zones covering a large area surrounding a homestead.[13]

---

[13] In ILUA negotiations, pastoralists in the central Peninsula have also sought certainty about who and what they are dealing with in the context of native title, requesting lists of those Aboriginal people who claim traditional connection with their properties, so they know exactly whose enjoyment of native title rights they have consented to, as well as maps of 'sacred sites' to be avoided during station work.

Arguments of this kind have often threatened the considerable goodwill of Aboriginal claimants, who see no need for formal delineation of such matters. Rules intended to ensure the proper running of cattle stations have proved particularly irksome. As one man put it, allowing himself an unusual display of public irritation, 'we've been working on stations all our life … we know what to do and what not to do'. Such irritation is not simply due to a denial of Aboriginal knowledge about how a station operates; it is also a reaction to an implicit denial of shared working and life histories between white station owners and Aborigines.[14]

Although seemingly irritated by the need for formal agreements regarding their use of their country within pastoral leases, Aboriginal claimants tend to be more sympathetic to pastoralists' concerns about privacy. In the negotiations I have observed or taken part in, such concerns are typically met with assurances that the right of the pastoralists to enjoy their privacy is accepted by the claimants, as is their need to be able to run their stations properly. This sympathetic reaction demonstrates a widespread acceptance by Aboriginal people across Northern Australia's pastoral regions of settlers' own rights in relation to stations they have established often over several generations (Redmond 2005: 242; Smith 2003: 37). Similar rights also seem to be extended to those pastoralists who have bought and taken up their station properties more recently.[15]

The kinds of formal arrangement discussed during the negotiation of ILUAs appear to be far from satisfactory, despite Aboriginal sympathy for some of the outcomes sought by pastoralists. In the central Peninsula, such arrangements are likely to lead to one of two results. Firstly, the literacy requirements for the use of formal agreements will, in most cases, lead to their being ignored or their contents guessed at or remembered by native title holders. Secondly, the legal formality of such agreements, combined with the adversarial character of the negotiations leading to a consent determination, may well dissuade native title holders from seeking to enjoy their 'rights and interests', even where these are found to be legally coexistent with those of station owners.

Enjoyment of native title rights on cattle properties is instead more likely to occur where such formal arrangements have been put to one side, and where Aborigines have been encouraged by station owners to 'ring up and drop in for a cup of tea and a yarn' on their way to fishing on a creek or river within the

---

[14] In one ILUA negotiation, pastoralists attempted to mitigate the offence caused by their assertions for formal rules for native title holders' conduct on stations by displacing the reason such rules were needed onto 'younger [Aboriginal] people … who might come onto the place and leave beer cans everywhere, leave gates open or not put out [camp] fires'. But this attempted displacement only caused further offence.

[15] Such sympathy also seems to draw on a common norm in Aboriginal Australia that even on someone else's country, the space of a person's camp is their own, and should not be trespassed upon by even senior men and women upon whose country the camp is located.

station boundaries. This outcome is more likely when friendly relations have been established, regenerated or reiterated between pastoralists and claimants in the course of native title negotiations.

For Aboriginal claimants in the central Peninsula, the power of this kind of invitation to shape future outcomes from a native title claim extends beyond general social niceties. Within local Aboriginal life-worlds, an insistence on not 'just going past' someone, but stopping to 'yarn' and share food and drink, is a clear statement of social connectedness. Not to do so is to mark one's relationship (or lack thereof) as one between 'strangers' or 'stranger people'.[16]

Likewise, negotiations that open out towards a more general, informal sociality resonate with local Aboriginal social norms, whilst negotiations that lead only towards the recognition of formalised rights and interests held in opposition to those of station owners do not. In the central Peninsula's 'Aboriginal domain', the normative expectation is of the maintenance of informal, friendly sociality among consociates. Despite the fact that the Aboriginal domain contains a series of potential forms of recognition constitutive of social differentiation or personal autonomy, the general tendency is one of social inclusion and an emphasis on relatedness rather than social distinction.[17] Unlike those accustomed to the cultural norms that inhere in nation-states, Aboriginal people remain predisposed not to understand—let alone enact— 'rights and interests' outside the context of lived social relationships.[18] As such, the idea that one might simply enjoy 'rights and interests' on the basis of 'paperwork' is at best puzzling, and at worst practically impossible.

In order to lead to the realization of *meaningful* property rights, native title in places like the central Peninsula must involve ongoing informal mutual recognition between local Aborigines and pastoralists on an 'open' basis. This kind of recognition, where it takes place, has restored meaningful forms of local community in which it is not only formalised rights and interests, but the ways in which such rights and interests become locally meaningful that come to constitute coexistence.

'Open' coexistence of this kind also tends to be restorative of meaningful forms of community (something that both Aborigines and settler pastoralists have claimed that they would like to see happen following ILUA negotiations). Rather than a homogenous community defined by a shared identity or lack of

---

[16] Importantly, the sharing of food—or the provision of separate food for Aborigines and whites—during past station employment is seen as marking the character of employment by white 'bosses' for many of the region's Aboriginal people.
[17] On the interplay of autonomy and relatedness in the Aboriginal domain, see Martin (1993) and Myers (1986).
[18] A key means by which social relatedness is affirmed is in the sharing of resources, including acquiescence to requests for access to land and waters. Importantly for the purposes of the present argument, such requests are only made where a warm and positive response is anticipated.

differentiated interests, or an array of formally differentiated social and legal persons, this community is instead constituted through the fundamental coexistence of its members' sharing of locale and event as the subjects of ongoing local histories (Wagner 1988: 59). As such, it is a community that is fundamentally *un*certain, this uncertainty being a reflex of the 'openness' through which it continues to be enacted.

The possibility for this kind of 'openness' now seems to be excluded within the increasingly 'juridified' domain of the Native Title Act,[19] which increasingly delivers judgements of ownership that are 'uncontestable, certain, concrete [and] decontextual—in short, monumentalising abstractions' and which are 'far from the multivalent determinations of custodianship that once marked indigenous ritual-political life' (Austin-Broos 2004: 213, citing Povinelli 2002: 227). As I have argued above, even given the forms of abstraction that now predominate within the formal 'recognition space', this kind of uncertain community can nonetheless still exist between Aborigines and settlers in their day-to-day recognition of each other's involvement with country. But despite Northern Australian pastoralists' general dislike of formality, state bureaucracy and legal processes (cf. Kapferer and Morris 2003), subscription to the Australian notion of a 'fair go', and commonly stated desire to return to what are seen as previous 'good relations' with local Aborigines, it has taken the force of Australian law and a more general societal shift towards the recognition of Aboriginal 'rights' to impel local whites towards this more equitable form of local recognition.

Conclusion

In contradistinction to the certainties aspired to in codifying a 'community of native title holders' and their 'rights and interests', it remains possible for whitefellas and Aborigines in central Cape York Peninsula to coexist as members of an *uncertain* community. This community is constituted through a more 'open' and processual style of recognition than that provided for in formal determinations of the coexistence of native title and pastoral leases. Given that this style of recognition—where it occurs—is reminiscent of the forms of sociality that characterise the 'Aboriginal domain', it seems to represent a move towards a culturally heterogenous space of interaction, rather than one dominated either by the legal and social norms of 'mainstream' Australian society, or earlier local forms of white hegemony.

Aborigines in the central Peninsula have long understood such coexistence to exist, despite the long history of their domination by white 'bosses' on the region's cattle stations. But a meaningful engagement with this kind of coexistence by pastoralists has depended on the force of Australian law and a

---

[19] Here I follow Martin and Mantziaris (2000) in referring to the increasing juridification of native title.

growing realisation that, in the longer term, any future certainty depends on their accommodation of the aspirations of their Aboriginal neighbours.

With this in mind, comments made by pastoralists and their solicitors during a court hearing for a consent determination of a native title claim in the central Peninsula are particularly interesting. In their comments, the pastoralists emphasised the importance of interpersonal relationships between pastoralists and the Aboriginal claimants both in reaching the consent determination, and in translating this determination of native title back into meaningful day-to-day relationships:

> MR K_ [solicitor and co-owner of S_ station]: Thank you, your Honour. The pastoralists that I represent consent to the determinations of Native Title. Your Worship, the Court cannot make any order, nor can any government legislate, in respect of how the parties, the pastoralists and the Native Title holders can co-exist and work together to build relationships for the future. This has been achieved by agreement, and it is a tribute to the foresight and open mindedness displayed by the parties and is an example to others as to how outcomes might be achieved by negotiation. Thank you, your Honour.
>
> HIS HONOUR: Thank you. Mr F_?
>
> MR F_ [co-owner of S_ station]: May it please the Court, the lessees of S_ [station] consent to determination. I also would like to pay tribute to the traditional owners of this place and, in particular, the W_ People. I would also like to mention, especially, the traditional owners for [S_ station]. It might interest the Court to know that approximately five years ago we decided we weren't progressing fast enough, I guess is the terminology, and insisted, for the first time, that we meet the traditional owners face-to-face. And I think from that point on we made a lot of progress, and I think it is fair to say today that, with the lessees of S_ and myself, that those relationships in some cases have developed into friendships. So it looks very good for the future.
>
> And I do have to say that, ... that when you sort of look around and have a look at all the time we've been working on this and realise that this is what we wind up at the end of it, the people sitting in the gallery could really be forgiven for wondering what the blazes we've been doing.

So what *had* the various parties been doing all this time? A number of things, but not least bringing about a situation in which the pastoralists and their legal representatives, as well as other parties, were prepared to recognise the 'traditional owners' as such.

The fraught process by which consent determination was reached in this claim indicates the interminable interrelation between law and justice. In central Cape

York Peninsula, where there has been a long history of injustice, the forms of recognition offered by the Native Title process, flawed though they may be, have nonetheless provided a means to return station owners to a more open and just dealing with local Aborigines.

While the native title process can produce its own injustices through the particular style of formal recognition on which it depends, it can also act to re-open a space for more just forms of coexistence. This uncertain space of interaction between Aboriginal people and settler pastoralists is marked by a 'face-to-face' style of recognition and interaction which continues to build relationships into the future, It seems that in allowing for a more open, processual style of interaction, even as it excludes openness from its formal operation, the native title process may potentially lead to the social justice hoped for by Patton, despite the limited results often offered by determination itself.

References

Austin-Broos, D. 2004. 'Anthropology and Indigenous alterity: book review essay (E. Povinelli, 2002. *The Cunning of Recognition: Indigenous Alterity and the Making of Australian Multiculturalism*)', *The Australian Journal of Anthropology*, 15 (2): 213–16.

Deleuze, G. and Guattari, F. 1987. *A Thousand Plateaus: Capitalism and Schizophrenia*, University Of Minnesota Press, Minneapolis.

Derrida, J. 2002. 'Force of law: the "mystical foundation of authority"', in J. Derrida, *Acts of Religion* (ed. G. Anidjar), Routledge, London.

Gaonkar, D. P. 2002. 'Towards new imaginaries: an introduction', *Public Culture*, 14 (1): 1–19.

Gluckman, M. 1949. *An Analysis of the Sociological Theories of Bronislaw Malinowski*, Rhodes Livingston Institute Papers 16, Oxford University Press, Cape Town.

Hinkson, M. and Smith, B. R. (eds), 2005. *Figuring the Intercultural in Aboriginal Australia*, Special Issue, *Oceania*, 75 (3).

Kapferer, B. and Morris, B. 2003. 'The Australian society of the state: egalitarian ideologies and new directions in exclusionary practice', *Social Analysis*, 47 (3): 80–107.

Keen, I. 2004. *Aboriginal Economy and Society: Australia at the Threshold of Colonisation*, Oxford University Press, Melbourne.

Mantziaris, C. and Martin, D. F. 2000. *Native Title Corporations: A Legal and Anthropological Analysis*, Federation Press, Sydney.

Martin, D. F. 1993. Autonomy and Relatedness: An Ethnography of the Wik People of Western Cape York Peninsula, PhD Thesis, The Australian National University, Canberra.

Martin, D. F. 2003. 'Rethinking the design of indigenous organisations: the need for strategic engagement', *CAEPR Discussion Paper No. 248*, Centre for Aboriginal Economic Policy Research, The Australian National University, Canberra.

Martin, D. F. 2004. 'Designing institutions in the 'recognition space' of native title', in S. Toussaint (ed.), *Crossing Boundaries: Cultural, Legal, Historical and Practice Issues in Native Title*, Melbourne University Press, Melbourne.

Merlan, F. 1998. *Caging the Rainbow: Places, Politics, and Aborigines in a North Australian Town*, University of Hawai'i Press, Honolulu.

Merlan, F. 2005. 'Explorations towards intercultural accounts of socio-cultural reproduction and change', in M. Hinkson and B. R. Smith (eds), *Figuring the Intercultural in Aboriginal Australia*, Special Issue, *Oceania,* 75 (3): 167–82.

Myers, F. 1986. *Pintupi Country, Pintupi Self: Sentiment, Place, and Politics Among Western Desert Aborigines,* University of California Press, Berkeley.

Nancy, J.-L. 1997. *The Sense of the World* (translated by J. Librett), University of Minnesota Press, Minneapolis.

Nancy, J.-L. 2000. *Being Singular Plural* (translated by R. Richardson and A. O'Byrne), Stanford University Press, Stanford.

Nancy, J.-L. and Ten Kate, L. 2004. '"Cum"…revisited: preliminaries to thinking the interval', in E. Ziarek and H. Oosterling (eds), *Intermedialities*, Continuum, New York.

Patton, P. 1995. 'Post-structuralism and the Mabo debate: difference, society and justice', in M. Wilson and A. Yeatman (eds), *Justice and Identity: Antipodean Practices,* Allen & Unwin, Sydney.

Patton, P. 2000. *Deleuze and the Political*, Routledge, London.

Pearson, N. 1997. 'The concept of native title at common law', in G. Yunupingu (ed.), *Our Land is Our Life*, University of Queensland Press, St Lucia.

Peters-Little, F. 2001. 'The community game: Aboriginal self definition at the local level', in F. Morphy and W. Sanders (eds), *The Indigenous Welfare Economy and the CDEP Scheme*, CAEPR Research Monograph No. 20, Centre for Aboriginal Economic Policy Research, The Australian National University, Canberra.

Povinelli, E. 2002. *The Cunning of Recognition: Indigenous Alterity and the Making of Australian Multiculturalism*, Duke University Press, Durham.

Redmond, A. 2005. 'Strange relatives: mutualities and dependencies between Aborigines and pastoralists in the Northern Kimberley', in M. Hinkson and B. R. Smith (eds), *Figuring the Intercultural in Aboriginal Australia*, Special Issue, *Oceania,* 75 (3): 234–46.

Rigsby, B. 1995. 'Tribes, diaspora people and the vitality of law and custom: some comments', in J. Fingleton and J. Finlayson (eds), *Anthropology in the Native Title Era: Proceedings of a Workshop*, Australian Institute of Aboriginal and Torres Strait Islander Studies, Canberra.

Scott, J. C. 1998. *Seeing Like a State: How Certain Schemes to Improve the Human Condition Have Failed*, Yale University Press, New Haven.

Smith, B. R. 2000a. Between Places: Aboriginal Decentralisation, Mobility and Territoriality in the Region of Coen, Cape York Peninsula (Australia), PhD Thesis, Department of Anthropology, London School of Economics and Political Science, London.

Smith, B. R. 2000b. 'Local and diaspora connections to country and kin in Central Cape York Peninsula', *Native Title Research Unit Issues Paper Vol.2, No.6*, Native Title Research Unit, Australian Institute of Aboriginal and Torres Strait Islander Studies, Canberra.

Smith, B. R. 2002. 'Pastoralism, land and Aboriginal existence in central Cape York Peninsula', *Anthropology in Action,* 9 (1): 21–30.

Smith, B. R. 2003. 'Whither "certainty"? Coexistence, change and some repercussions of native title in Northern Queensland', *Anthropological Forum,* 13 (1): 27–48.

Sullivan, P. 1996. *All Free Man Now: Culture, Community and Politics in the Kimberley Region, North-Western Australia*, Aboriginal Studies Press, Canberra.

Sullivan, P. 2001. Paper presented at the session 'Articulating culture: understanding engagements between Indigenous and non-Indigenous lifeworlds', Australian Anthropological Society Annual Conference, The Australian National University, 3 October.

Sullivan, P. 2005. 'Searching for the intercultural, searching for the culture', in M. Hinkson and B. R. Smith (eds), *Figuring the Intercultural in Aboriginal Australia*, Special Issue, *Oceania,* 75 (3): 183–94.

von Sturmer, J. R. 1984. 'The different domains', in *Aborigines and Uranium*, Australian Institute of Aboriginal Studies, Canberra.

Wagner, R. 1967. *The Curse of Souw: Principles of Daribi Clan Formation and Alliance*, University of Chicago Press, Chicago.

Wagner, R. 1988. 'Visible sociality: the Daribi community', in J. F. Weiner (ed.), *Mountain Papuans: Historical and Comparative Perspectives from New Guinea Fringe Highlands Societies*, University of Michigan Press, Ann Arbor.

Weiner, J. F. 2003 '*The Law of the Land*: a review article', *The Australian Journal of Anthropology*, 14 (1): 97–110.

Weiner, J. F. n.d. 'Anthropology, law and the recognition space', unpublished MS.

7. Native title and the Torres Strait: encompassment and recognition in the Central Islands

Julie Lahn

It seems that contemporary perspectives on native title have shifted rather dramatically from the early optimism that saw the Mabo decision described as a 'moral and historical statement of truth [that provides] the strongest justification yet for the claims of those dispossessed', potentially even challenging (or at least problematising) settler sovereignty itself (Pearson 1993: 82). Former director of the Northern Land Council, Mick Dodson, has described native title as providing relatively few benefits for Aboriginal people, and as forming part of a process of 'further dispossession'.[1] In a recent address he described the *Native Title Act 1993* (Cwlth) (NTA) and its amendments as embodying a racist doctrine of native title extinguishment (Dodson 2007).

One of the most forceful critiques along these lines has been that provided by Wolfe (1999), who argues that the principal function of native title is 'paradoxically as much to provide grounds for delimiting indigenous relations to land as for their recognition' (1999: 203). Put differently, to accept the terms of recognition within which the notion of 'native title' is framed is to endorse the terms for its extinguishment as well as the radical assumption of sovereignty upon which both are based. This view is a compelling one; the Mabo decision, the NTA (and associated legislation) and the growing corpus of native title case law, together certainly embody the power that defines sovereignty—the arrogation of authority to set the ultimate terms of exclusion and recognition, to delineate the space of rights and non-rights (see also Agamben 1998). And in this sense it is certainly possible to contend that native title is as much implicated in the continuing dynamics of colonisation as it can ameliorate aspects of it.

This theme is elaborated by Morris (2003), where he argues that the various determinations under the NTA have done more to limit and extinguish Indigenous claims to land than to facilitate them. He describes the original High Court Mabo determination as 'essentially perverse' in that it 'did not concede, the right to indigenous communities to exercise traditional law and customs over their lands—and nor could it without undermining its own authority' (2003: 140). At the same time, the decision enshrined a 'continuation of traditionalism' as the basis of native title claims, where 'indigenous identity and

---

[1] Mick Dodson in conversation, *Awaye!* ABC Radio National, 10 February 2006.

culture must put itself through a trial, and demonstrate its members' authenticity' (2003: 140).

Aspects of the limits of native title are now well-rehearsed among anthropologists, though their critical observations have usually been both less trenchant and less political. Among the most prescient early commentators were Kondos and Cowlishaw (1995), who drew attention to the potential for native title to reify notions of tradition, while Merlan (also in 1995), pointed to the risk for a 'regimentation' of customary practices. A closely related concern seeks to problematise any stress on systematicity in native title at the expense of contingency and reflexivity (Weiner 2000). These views in some respects parallel Wolfe's notion of 'repressive authenticity', where native title is depicted as displacing the 'burden of history' from 'the fact of expropriation to the character of the expropriated' (1999: 202).

But anthropologists have often also maintained an interest in exploring the transformative cultural and social potential in the arena of native title. Weiner (2003), for example, writes against the grain of a 'space of recognition' perspective of native title (see Smith, Chapter 6) in arguing for a more complex anthropological engagement with native title processes themselves as a 'total social fact', with productive potential in terms of the cultural and social practices of an indigenous population that has a long history of 'conjunctural engagement' with Euro-Australian institutional practices. At the same time, Weiner acknowledges the danger of an overall diminution in what the public and the legal establishment acknowledge as the 'total condition of recognisable Aboriginality in Australia' (Weiner 2003: 103).

In what is an excerpt from a larger study (Lahn 2003), I want to reflect on a similar question, that of the relation of native title to the total condition of recognisable *indigeneity* in Australia (rather than Aboriginality), with a specific focus on the Central Islands of the Torres Strait. As Keen (1999: 2) points out, indigeneity is an *a priori* interpretive concept within native title. I argue here that multiple forms of indigeneity are acknowledged among Torres Strait Islanders. I focus on the two contrasting modes with which I am most familiar, and which form a key distinction Islanders themselves draw in the Central Islands: that of being a 'native' or a 'foreigner'. It is important to note that both these terms refer to people recognised in local terms as Torres Strait Islanders. But they are differentiated in the Central Islands as distinct states of being indigenous. It is equally important to stress that neither term is pejorative; in fact, the descriptive 'foreigner' has generally been associated with a degree of status in the Central Islands. Both labels are used for self-description (as well as ascription) though they are not expressions that appear in everyday interactions.

This situation is a difficult one to render in English, which lacks adequate means to characterise such a contrast in a way that still affirms an embracing state of indigeneity. It could be helpful perhaps to return to one of the specific etymological significances of the term 'autochthony', which involves the notion of 'arising in situ' (i.e. rather than arriving from elsewhere). In this sense, the labels of native and foreigner in the Central Islands could be understood as drawing a distinction between 'indigenous autochthons' and 'indigenous non-autochthons'.[2] But such an approach is limited by the degree to which the term indigenous has come to be regarded among English-speakers as synonymous with the term autochthonous—to all intents and purposes, an indigene is regarded as an autochthon. With this difficulty in mind, I will utilise the Torres Strait Creole terms *neitiv* (native) and *porena* (foreigner) for the remainder of the discussion. While still somewhat recognisable to English speakers, their clear difference from their English cognates serves as a reminder that the terms do not bear the same conceptual baggage.

My intention here is to briefly explore the meeting between this *neitiv/porena* identification in the Central Islands and the representational requirements of native title. I argue that native title's regime of value marginalised, and potentially stigmatised this kind of local identificatory distinction. My focus is Warraber Island, the southernmost of the Central Island group. I have been working there since 1996, conducting doctoral fieldwork and native title research. Warraber people first represented themselves as a claimant group within a claim based on the *Torres Strait Islander Land Act 1991* (Qld) (TSILA); shifts in representation occurred in engaging with the different demands of native title.[3] These shifts illustrate aspects both of the unequal social relations inherent in the representational demands of native title as a state-sponsored regime of recognition, and of the capacity of local people to respond creatively to such demands.

Neitiv ('native') and *porena* ('foreigner')

Warraber residents use the *neitiv/porena* terminological division both when discussing their ancestors, and in expressing contemporary forms of local identity. It forms a profoundly significant expression both in their understanding of the past, and in their perception of their contemporary community. The primary significance of the *neitiv/porena* distinction involves a view that *neitiv* figures were present in the islands before the sudden influx of various foreigners or outsiders (*ausaid man*) into the Torres Strait from the mid-nineteenth century.

---

[2] This kind of a distinction is widespread throughout insular Southeast Asia, where indigenous groups—sharing a single distinct language and name—frequently distinguish within themselves descent from autochthonous and non-autochthonous ancestors. Where this occurs, specific realms of authority have often been historically divided according to this status, for example ritual leadership (often linked to local fertility) associated with autochthons, and secular community leadership with the 'outsiders' or non-autochthons. I thank Phillip Winn for drawing this parallel to my attention.

[3] I observed the TSILA proceedings while conducting doctoral fieldwork at Warraber and later became a participant in their native title claim as the anthropologist compiling the 'connection report'.

This occurred as part of the arrival of European marine industries to the region, which brought with them a labour force composed predominantly of Pacific Islanders, though with a number of Europeans in supervisory roles (see Beckett 1977, 1987; Mullins 1990, 1995; Shnukal 1992a, 1992b, 1995).[4] Pacific Islands of origin included Vanuatu, Samoa, Fiji and New Caledonia.

Some of the Pacific Islanders remained in the Torres Strait, marrying local Torres Strait women and producing children. The influence of these Pacific Islander residents and their descendants is especially marked in the Central Islands, which formed a key centre of marine industry activity. Aspects of Pacific Island music and dance forms, for example, have become a thorough part of contemporary Torres Strait Islander performance (see Lahn 2004; Lawrence 2004). Crucially, and as a result largely of colonial systems of racial classification, Pacific Islanders not only held superior positions in the marine workforce but generally served as intermediaries between Europeans and Torres Strait Islanders in various capacities, including Christian missionising activity. A legacy of this role was that the Pacific Islanders and their descendants, now referred to as *porena*, were regarded by local people as possessing special abilities—in particular the skills necessary to interact effectively with Europeans and European institutions (and, as a consequence, to buffer locals from the demands of these spheres).[5] *Porena* people in the Central Islands still dominate such quasi-governing bodies as Island Councils, and are regarded by *neitiv* residents as well-suited *by their ancestry* for playing such a role.

In fact, all Warraberans can potentially trace some form of genealogical connection to both *neitiv* and *porena* ancestors. The basis of contemporary identification as *neitiv* or *porena* relates to the status of male apical ancestors. Among Warraberans, as with other Central Island populations, there is a pronounced patrilineal emphasis in local thinking about descent. Female ancestors tend to be marginalised by comparison to their male counterparts; when Warraber people describe their personal lineage, as few females as necessary will be included in tracing connections to a male apical ancestor. Wherever possible, a patrilineage will be traced (or as near to a patrilineage as practicable). This parallels a general predisposition to depict men as the most active and influential social agents. All narratives concerned with historical events stress male

---

[4] The notion of 'foreigners' is not exclusive to Warraber. In the Eastern Islands, for example, the term *nog le* ('outside men') is used to designate 'foreigners' or 'outsiders' (Shnukal 1992a: 13) in much the same way that *porena* is used on Warraber. Interestingly, the Meriam used the term *salmis* to refer to Pacific Islanders and the term *nog le* was used to refer to other Torres Strait Islanders who were excluded from the Malo-Bomai cult (Jeremy Beckett pers. comm. 2004).

[5] Another factor in the rise to prominence of *porena* in the Central Islands, and likely a critical one, involved significant declines in local populations there (as elsewhere in the Torres Strait) linked to a combination of factors but particularly successive waves of epidemic disease. These were most serious in the latter half of the nineteenth century, but continued into the early decades of the twentieth century (Mullins 1995).

ancestors, in particular the part played by exceptional and powerful men.[6] The role of women is generally overlooked or disregarded.

Those able to trace descent in this way from male apical ancestors who were *porena* are those who consider themselves today as also being *porena*. The most important and earliest of these ancestors for Warraber people is an individual from Vanuatu named Bubarei. Similarly, those who trace descent from a male apical ancestor who was *neitiv* (i.e. someone deemed present in the islands before the outsider influx) consider themselves to be *neitiv*. A large majority of Warraber residents do not possess any male *neitiv* ancestors. They describe their descent wholly in terms of male *porena* figures, rather than including female *neitiv* ancestors with whom they could assert a connection. Therefore, the majority segment of Warraber's contemporary population represent themselves as *porena*.

The key factor in categorising significant personal ancestors in terms of a *neitiv/porena* contrast involves their presence on Warraber before or after the arrival of the marine industries. It is engendered by temporal association rather than ideas about ultimate origin. For Warraber people, this in turn generates further multifaceted associations that give rise to particular discourses of value. The first might be called the *neitiv's* 'power of precedence'. By pre-dating the arrival of others, *neitiv* figures are recognised both as being the original local landholders and also as possessing an intimate relation to locality, manifest in their close relation to particular significant sites in the landscape (some of which are associated with the fertility and productivity of island resources, such as the *wongai* fruit—a pre-colonial staple that retains symbolic importance). *Porena* ancestors are instead valorised as being 'agents of change', linked to what is regarded as a generally positive historical transformation of pre-existing life on Warraber Island. In this respect, for the wholly Christian Warraber population, the arrival of the marine industry is inextricably entwined with the arrival of Christianity. As noted, Pacific Islanders were prominently involved in both, as missionaries and as boat crew and owners (Lahn 2003).[7]

Importantly, while both valorising discourses coexist in Warraber society, they cannot be said to convey equal contemporary status or prestige on the two sections of the population. There are very few contexts where the 'power of precedence' asserted by the minority *neitiv*-identifying population is relevant, and to date, it has not provided a basis for eminence or influence in the Warraber community. By contrast, *porena* descendants, the majority population, have monopolised positions of formal and informal authority for some period on the island. During the involvement of Warraber and Poruma populations in NTA

---

[6] This tendency of prevailing gender norms to shape historical accounts has been highlighted elsewhere in the Torres Strait (for example Davis 1998).
[7] Jeremy Beckett (pers. comm. 2004) suggests that the position of Pacific Islanders in marine industries played a more critical role in their local prominence than involvement in the activities of the London Missionary Society. See Lahn (2004) for a discussion on the arrival of Christianity to the Torres Strait.

claim processes, issues of the contemporary significance of *neitiv* and *porena* ancestry re-emerged in potentially novel ways. But it is necessary first to trace the mode of collective representation that Warraberans developed in response to a first wave of land claims under the TSILA.

The Torres Strait Islander Land Act and the Gau Clan

Before engaging with native title, Warraber Islanders pursued a successful claim using the TSILA. This Act establishes procedures by which Torres Strait Islanders can make application to the Queensland state government to claim lands designated as 'transferable'.[8] Between 1996 and 1998 Warraber residents pursued a claim under this legislation over five uninhabited nearby islands: *Yarpar* (Roberts), *Ullu* (Saddle), *Bara* (Bet), *Guiya* (Poll) and *Aurid* (recorded by Haddon (1935) as *Yaywad*). These islands were regularly visited by Warraber and Poruma people, though none had permanent residents. In the past some of these islands had also been used in intermittent gardening and camping, largely linked to movements in marine industry activities.

The TSILA claim was lodged on grounds of 'customary affiliation'.[9] The legislative terms delineating this basis for establishing a land claim state that the Land Tribunal assessing the claim must be:

> satisfied that the Torres Strait Islander has a connection, or that members of the group have a common connection, with the land based on spiritual or other associations with, rights in relation to, and responsibilities for, the area of land under Island Custom.[10]

Clearly, this approach to customary affiliation is quite broad in scope. Particular core terms (for example 'connection', 'associations', 'responsibilities') are not specifically defined. Instead, there is repeated recourse to 'Island custom', which is presumed *a priori* to elucidate such concepts. The TSILA offers the following definition of Island custom:

> Island custom, known in the Torres Strait as Ailan Kastom, is the body of customs, traditions, observances and beliefs of Torres Strait Islanders generally or of a particular group of Torres Strait Islanders, and includes any such customs, traditions, observances and beliefs relating to particular persons, areas, objects or relationships.[11]

As a result, the terms of TSILA have a rather encompassing and inclusive tenor, notwithstanding its design as an alternative to native title (and notable limitations

---

[8] These include Deed of Grant in Trust (DOGIT) lands, reserve lands, and crown lands deemed available for transfer (see Brennan 1991 and Malbon 1996 for a discussion of DOGIT lands in relation to TSILA).
[9] 'Customary affiliation' is one of three bases through which a claim under TSILA may be lodged. The others are 'historical association' and 'economic or cultural viability' (TSILA s. 50-57).
[10] TSILA s. 50 (1)
[11] TSILA s. 8.

in the forms of tenure it makes available to successful claimants). Indeed, this appears to have formed an aspect of the policy intentions of the government of the day. For example, the phrase 'spiritual or other associations' in the first passage cited above originally read 'spiritual *and* other associations' (as it does in the equivalent Queensland *Aboriginal Land Act 1991*). The alteration was explained in parliament by the then Queensland Minister for Family Services and Aboriginal and Islander Affairs:

> The Torres Strait Islander Land Act will also be amended to ensure that the basis upon which land is claimed in the Torres Strait appropriately reflects islander relationships with land. I am advised that the principles of traditional affiliation with land in accordance with Torres Strait Islander custom may not necessarily include a notion of spiritual association with land. Consequently, the definition of traditional affiliation will permit but not require a claimant to demonstrate a spiritual relationship with the land (Warner 1991, cited in Neate 1997: 14).

The claim itself takes the form of an application of transfer, essentially an administrative rather than judicial process.[12]

In the case of the Warraber claim, an entity known as the Gau Clan formed the claimant group. The Gau Clan derives its local coherence from visions of the Vanuatuan ancestor figure of Bubarei. Bubarei is the earliest known outsider to father children on Warraber Island with an Islander woman named Wawa (who resided on Warraber, but whose own origins were in fact from a different island in the Torres Strait). Their 10 children formed the first generation of *porena* Warraberans, who were provided with land by *neitiv* landholders at that time, and hence incorporated by custom into Warraber's population. As the earliest known *porena* male ancestor, and as a prolific progenitor, Bubarei is a figure to whom all residents of Warraber in fact possess traceable genealogical links. The Gau Clan is not, then, a 'clan' in the classic anthropological sense; membership is not limited to descent but can be asserted on the basis of any combination of consanguineal or affinal connection to any of Bubarei's descendants. In this way the Gau Clan was able to encompass the entire population of Warraber (who are all in fact related in some sense) while simultaneously stressing the majority status of the *porena* population and the special regard given to *porena* historical figures.

---

[12] Essentially, there is an investigation by the Department of Natural Resources, aided by a consultant employed by the applicant/s. Its focus concerns the identity of the persons making the application and the grounds on which the application is being made. Consultation takes place with those people designated as 'particularly concerned with the land' subject to the transfer claim. Under the Act, this includes people who are connected to the land by 'Island Custom'; who live on or use the land; or live on or use neighbouring land (State of Queensland 2000: 2). Once these consultations are complete, a Land Tribunal established under the TSILA arrives at a decision and makes a recommendation to the relevant Queensland Minister. The Minister must grant approval for a transfer to occur.

Clans, and their associated totems, were not part of everyday discourse at Warraber during my period on the island, nor did they play any role in shaping social relations. Once reputedly critical in defining marriageability, kinship has long displaced clanship in this role (an observation Haddon makes in reference to the Western Islands as early as 1904 (1904: 160–1). Sugimoto (1983: 92), who conducted brief fieldwork on Warraber in the 1970s, noted that 'the totem clans seem to have played an important role in village life before the advent of Christianity, but they are hardly functioning now.' Intent on linking local patronyms to specific totemic clans, Sugimoto remains ambiguous as to what these residual functions may have been. He described eight totems as extant among Warraberans; some 25 years later I could identify only two—*gau* (associated with *poren* people, as described) and *womer* (linked to *neitiv* identity).[13]

However varied the presence, meaning and contemporary relevance of totems and clans throughout the region, Warraber people have been aware for decades of the role of totemic clans as identificatory categories associated with territorial interests in island communities in the Torres Strait. As a vehicle for representing the Warraber population as a whole in the context of the TSILA claim, the emergence of the Gau Clan can certainly be seen in terms of the dynamics of objectification discussed by Glaskin (Chapter 3), where self-conscious definitions of culture are fostered that may have an important role in internal group definition and reproduction. Totemic symbols and clan names are now undergoing something of a contemporary renaissance in the Torres Strait, appearing on gravestones and in the speeches associated with tombstone unveilings—an iconic event within 'Torres Strait Islander culture'.

In the context of Meriam people and the revitalisation of the Malu-Bomai cult, Beckett (1995: 30) has discussed the capacity for cultural reflexivity and objectification in the Torres Strait, the development of what he terms a 'relativistic view' of their own culture by the Meriam, influenced in part by their reading of Haddon. He also suggests that renewed interest in the cult would have been unlikely had it not resonated with the contemporary life of Meriam people, and points to the 'sensuous everyday experience' (1995: 30) of presence on Mer Island as pivotal in this regard.

Importantly, local discourse surrounding the Gau Clan on Warraber stressed its ability to reflect locally salient notions of social relatedness that are rooted in the idioms of Christianity and kinship. This is most aptly expressed in the local phrase '*ol wan pamli*' ('all one family'), which communicates an ethical sensibility

---

[13] Other totems are certainly present on Warraber in association with residents originating on other islands; for example, Mabuiag. According to Sugimoto (1983), Warraber totems in addition to *gau* and *wamer* [sic] were: *dangal* (dugong), *ger* (marine snake), *kadal* (crocodile), *kuzi* (eagle), *baidam* (shark), *umai* (dog), and *samu/emu* (cassowary or emu).

linked to idealised notions of island community and sociality. The Gau Clan, as a representational vehicle, was able to reflect these overt values in embodying an inclusive and seamless group of landholders, undifferentiated by local *neitiv/poren* distinctions. In this sense the Gau Clan effectively represented Warraber as a community of co-residents, with equal rights in land, given additional coherence and moral content through residents' collective identification as Christians. In other words, existing 'representational flows' (Merlan 1998: 180), which in this case included those of Torres Strait and Australian ideas concerning indigeneity as well as local understandings of Christianity, were engaged by local people themselves to produce images partaking of the past but also expressing and satisfying contemporary sensibilities.

Native title

In 1999, the year following the success of the TSILA claim, Warraber residents initiated a native title claim over Warraber and surrounding islands. The NTA demanded a demonstration of emplaced social identity that was subject to much more sharply delimited terms of authenticity and legitimacy than was the case in the TSILA. In particular, the native title process embodies a regime of value that valorises specific forms of continuity with the pre-colonial past.

Warraber people were well aware of the Mabo decision and approved of the idea that this involved the Australian nation recognising Islander possession of Torres Strait islands. However, they also generally considered the 'hand-over' ceremony under TSILA in 1998 as being akin to the Mabo outcome. The central issue that created interest among Warraber people in pursuing a native title claim was the gradual realisation that the TSILA land transfer did not actually include Warraber Island itself, but focused solely on surrounding, uninhabited islands. While some residents already knew this, many clearly did not until this was raised in information provided by the Torres Strait Regional Authority (TSRA), the native title representative body for much of Torres Strait.

In 1999 I was engaged by the TSRA to compile a Connection Report (CR) as part of a Warraber native title application covering the terrestrial areas of Warraber, Bara, Guiya, Buboi, Ullu, Ugain, Miggi Maituin, and Dugong islands. Senior staff in the TSRA's Native Title Office acknowledged that the CR criteria and associated research activities were limited in scope and/or complexity, certainly falling short of anthropological-style explanation. Nevertheless, they sought to address the requirements as fully as possible for the purposes of pursuing a negotiated settlement on behalf of the claimants in the most straightforward manner. To this end, the TSRA research brief followed the preferred structure and guidelines provided by the Queensland government. Some elaboration and interpretations of native title case law at that time were also offered as additional thematic foci in the research task. These included now familiar elements: detailing principles of group membership, genealogical information linking the claimant group to people who possessed the area before annexation, and with respect particularly to the criteria of rights and interests, descriptions of 'coherent social structure' and 'cultural logic' deriving from sources independent of relations with the colonial regime. There was an awareness that the CR could be called into evidence were this or other related claims to be contested in court at a future time.

In many respects, evidence in support of the native title claim appeared relatively straightforward. Identifiable Warraber ancestors were present on the island at annexation in 1872; land ownership is vested in Warraberan families and individuals who together formed the claimant group and who regularly engaged in local negotiations over the use of their own and others' land. Many of the documented social and cultural practices in which their ancestors were engaged (e.g. gathering marine resources, performing certain rites) remained in evidence in the contemporary period.

But a fundamental problem emerged concerning residents' orientation to group identification and ancestry as expressed through the Gau Clan. As discussed, the apical ancestor of the Gau Clan—Bubarei—was not a Torres Strait Islander. And while his children were gifted land according to local custom, Bubarei was not. He remained an outsider; in local terms, he is not considered to have been 'made a brother' by local people (i.e. incorporated by island custom). Indeed, he was reputedly not welcome at Warraber Island, and never resided there.

The Gau Clan, as a collectivity that exists essentially in reference to Bubarei, potentially infringe core requirements for native title, at least as it has come to be defined through the CR process, in turn drawing on *a priori* conceptualisations of indigeneity. As both a non-Islander and a non-Warraberan, Bubarei did not provide a suitable foundation for 'identification of a [relevant, indigenous] claimant group' (Department of Premier and Cabinet 1999). As someone who was never provided with land on the island, and did not reside there, Bubarei possessed no 'rights and interests in the territory claimed, which must derive from traditional law and custom' nor could he represent a source of 'continuous connection, that is, between claimant group and claimed area from a time before annexation' (Department of Premier and Cabinet 1999). Bubarei's Warraber-based children were certainly able to be regarded as indigenous to the Torres Strait under the terms of the NTA (as they were under TSILA) on the basis of their mother's status, that is of Bubarei's Torres Strait Islander spouse Wawa. However, native title required that Warraber claimants demonstrated descent from land-holding pre-colonial ancestors, that is, from *neitiv* figures, not from an outsider like Bubarei, a fact that rendered the Gau Clan irrelevant under the NTA.

Warraberalgal

In effect, the demands of indigeneity under native title offered recognition to only one set of Warraber ancestors, those who were *neitiv*. The native title process elevated the prominence of these figures over *porena* ancestors—a reverse of the existing local situation. In addition, the genealogical links that it was necessary to document among Warraberans involved tracing links to a range of *neitiv* ancestors who were largely female. I asked residents how they would refer to a group thus defined (in Torres Strait Creole). The consistent response was 'Warraber people'—the discourse of totemic clans was subverted in this new framing. I asked how this concept would be expressed in *prapa tok* or *langus* (i.e. in the Kulkalgaw Ya language). The answer was *Warraberalgal*, meaning 'people belonging to Warraber'. This became the name of the native title claimant group.

Elicited from Warraber people themselves, the term *Warraberalgal* was certainly an apt illustration of the importance of place within local representations of collective identification, but clearly marked a shift from the Gau Clan, with its emphasis on *poren* ancestors esteemed by the bulk of Warraber's residents. Both male and female informants on Warraber struggled to reconcile their sentiment of male ancestral value with the state's valorising of a definition of continuity and connection that marginalised many of these same figures. They fully comprehended the requirements placed before them, but those with *porena* male ancestors in particular were dissatisfied by a requirement to shift the existing local emphasis in matters of descent in order to secure native title to an island they already occupied and considered theirs. It especially rankled that the State of Queensland had already transferred other islands to them in the previous year as the Gau Clan, a collective form of representation that was successful without recourse to female or *neitiv* ancestors.

Far more than the Gau Clan, *Warraberalgal* marked an instance not simply of cultural objectification, but of native title as a realm of intercultural production—a form of representation occupying a discursive ground where a regime of value imposed by the nation-state intersects with the existing reality of an indigenous population. In this sense it belongs wholly to neither, but is inseparable from both.[14] For the state, a conception of 'native title' that relies very much on precursive cultural assumptions concerning an authentic indigeneity couched in terms of autochthony requires descent-based continuity of physical occupation. For most Warraberans, a valorised identification with apical male ancestors takes preference over visions of absolute ancestral emplacement. It is imperative to note that the outcome of such a meeting is an

---

[14] See the edited volume by Hinkson and Smith (2005) for explorations of the 'intercultural' in Aboriginal contexts.

expression of unequal social relations—as is native title itself (Merlan 1998: 176,181).

But while it is fair to state that, as a point of personal or collective identification, the new basis of group boundedness for the NTA claim was far less intuitively meaningful, it is notable that the new claimant group emerged as being just as embracing and inclusive as the Gau Clan had been. In this sense the level of 'violence' involved in the form of recognition offered to Warraber people by native title (see Smith, Chapter 6) could be described as somewhat muted.

Reflections

That the term 'native' featured in the expression 'native title' was not lost on some Warraberans. Initially, those persons who regarded themselves as *neitiv* asked me privately if the claim related specifically to them; that is, if they were the 'natives' being referred to in 'native title'. However, as the importance of female *neitiv* ancestors among *poren* residents within the claim became widely apparent, those regarding themselves as having apical male *neitiv* ancestors did not advance their suspicions that native title may have referred only to them. It became locally understood as involving every resident possessing either male or female *neitiv* ancestors.

The first successful Warraber native title determination occurred on 6 July 2000 with a special local session of the Federal Court of Australia, presided over by Justice Drummond.[15] At this event there were signs that many residents were tending to ignore the specific framing of the native title claim as a *Warraberalgal* event, while embracing the general recognition of shared emplacement it offered to the community. Residents—both *neitiv* and *poren*—have tended to refer to the event and to native title itself as affirming the earlier Gau Clan claim, rather than acting in any way to distinguish residents along lines of ancestral emphasis.

In any case, as I have described, those identifying as *neitiv* envisaged the descendants of foreign male ancestors (*porena*) to be legitimately *of* Warraber. They had acquired land from *neitiv* figures and thus belonged to Warraber. In addition, they regarded each other as kin, sharing their lives, religious practices and work interests for over a century. In this sense, Warraber thinking about the 'total condition of recognisable *indigeneity*' can be said to diverge from the preconceptions informing native title. But at the same time, the emergence of 'Warraberalgal' as a form of collective representation distinct from, but as encompassing as the Gau Clan, marks an instance of native title as a field of representational engagement where the ability of the Warraber community to

---

[15] Unlike other indigenous claimants, including the Meriam, and the Yolngu (see Morphy, Chapter 2), Warraber residents were not subject to court examination and cross-examination. Their determination was reached by consent. Their first experience of court processes in this matter was at the determination hearing in 2000.

maintain a commitment to their core terms of local relatedness was relatively succesful (the notion of a Warraber population that was 'ol wan pamli').

The *naitiv/porena* or autocthonous/non-autocthonous distinction may not be directly relevant to views concerning indigeneity among Aboriginal communities. But the wider relevance of the Warraber situation, outside the realm of native title, may simply be in reminding us of the historical part played by the European presence in shaping multiple modes of being indigenous, some of which are likely to have been as much a productive expression of indigenous/outsider interaction as they draw on extant aspects of pre-colonial lifeworlds. And that these modes may vary between specific locations, specific groups and specific sets of historical interactions (indeed, this is so even within Torres Strait itself). While certain modes are unlikely to be intuitively recognised by state-sponsored processes like native title, such processes may nevertheless play a part in continuing forms of expressing a 'total condition of indigeneity' that exceeds the expectations of the processes themselves.

References

Agamben, G. 1998. *Homo Sacer: Sovereign Power and Bare Life*, Stanford University Press, Stanford.

Beckett, J. 1977. 'The Torres Strait Islanders and the pearling industry: a case of internal colonialism', *Aboriginal History*, 1 (1): 77–104.

Beckett, J. 1987. *Torres Strait Islanders: Custom and Colonialism*, Cambridge University Press, Cambridge.

Beckett, J. 1995. 'The Murray Island land case', *The Australian Journal of Anthropology*, 6: 15–31.

Brennan, F. 1991. 'The Queensland Aboriginal Land Act 1991', *Aboriginal Law Bulletin*, 2: 10–12.

Davis, R. 1998. Epochal Bodies and Gendered Time, PhD Thesis, The Australian National University, Canberra.

Department of Premier and Cabinet 1999. *Guide to Compiling a Connection Report*, Native Title Services, Department of Premier and Cabinet, Brisbane.

Dodson, M. 2007. Annual Mabo Lecture extract, 7 June 2007, available at <http://www.abc.net.au/news/stories/2007/06/08/1945698.htm>. Accessed 25 August 2007.

Haddon, A. 1904 [1971]. *Reports of the Cambridge Anthropological Expedition to Torres Straits*, Vol. 5, *Sociology, Magic and Religion of the Western Islanders*, Cambridge University Press, Cambridge.

Haddon, A. 1935 [1971]. *Reports of the Cambridge Anthropological Expedition to Torres Straits*, Vol. 1, *General Ethnography*, Cambridge University Press, Cambridge.

Hinkson, M. and Smith, B. (eds) 2005. *Figuring the Intercultural in Aboriginal Australia*, Special Issue, Oceania, 75 (3): 157–66.

Keen, I. 1999. 'Cultural continuity and native title claims', *Land, Rights, Laws: Issues of Native Title*, 1 (28): 1–8.

Kondos, V. and Cowlishaw, G. 1995. 'Introduction: conditions of possibility', *The Australian Journal of Anthropology*, 6 (1 & 2): 1–14.

Lahn, J. 2003. Past Visions, Present Lives: Sociality and Locality in a Torres Strait Community, PhD Thesis, James Cook University of North Queensland, Townsville.

Lahn, J. 2004. '"Living in the light" and island dance: morality and temporality in Warraber Christianities', in R. Davis (ed.), *Woven Histories, Dancing Lives: Torres Strait Islander Identity, Culture and History*, Aboriginal Studies Press, Canberra.

Lawrence, H. 2004. '"The great traffic in tunes": agents and musical and religious change in eastern Torres Strait', in R. Davis (ed.), *Woven Histories, Dancing Lives: Torres Strait Islander Identity, Culture and History*, Aboriginal Studies Press, Canberra.

Malbon, J. 1996. 'Torres Strait conference on land and sea claims', *Aboriginal Law Bulletin*, 3 (78): 16–18.

Merlan, F. 1995. 'The regimentation of customary practice: from Northern Territory land claims to Mabo', *The Australian Journal of Anthropology*, 6 (1 & 2): 64–82.

Merlan, F. 1998. *Caging the Rainbow: Places, Politics, and Aborigines in a North Australian Town*, University of Hawai'i Press, Honolulu.

Morris, B. 2003. 'Anthropology and the state: the ties that bind', *Social Analysis*, 47 (1): 137–44.

Mullins, S. 1990. '"Heathen Polynee" and "Nigger Teachers": Torres Strait and the Pacific Islander ascendancy', *Aboriginal History*, 14 (2): 152–67.

Mullins, S. 1995. *Torres Strait: A History of Colonial Occupation and Culture Contact 1864–1897*, Central Queensland University Press, Rockhampton.

Neate, G. 1997. 'Torres Strait Islander Land Act 1991', *Indigenous Law Bulletin*, 4 (7): 13–16.

Pearson, N. 1993. '204 years of invisible title', in M. Stephenson and S. Rathapa (eds), *Mabo: A Judicial Revolution*, University of Queensland Press, St. Lucia.

Shnukal, A. 1992a. 'Pacific Islander immigrants in Torres Strait', *Voices*, 2 (2): 5–14.

Shnukal, A. 1992b. Pacific Islanders and Torres Strait 1860–1940', *Australian Aboriginal Studies*, (1): 14–27.

Shnukal, A. 1995. *'Practically White Men': Maori in Torres Strait*, Aboriginal and Torres Strait Islander Unit, University of Queensland, Brisbane.

State of Queensland 2000. The Torres Strait Islander Land Act 1991: *An Act Providing for the Transfer, Claim and Granting of Land as Torres Strait Islander Land*, Department of Natural Resources Land Facts, Department of Natural Resources, Brisbane.

Sugimoto, H. 1983. 'Sue Island (Warraber)', in G. Oshima (ed.), *Torres Kaikyo Wo Hitobito: People of the Torres Strait*, Koko Shoin, Tokyo.

Weiner, J. 2000. 'The anthropology of and for native title', *The Asia Pacific Journal of Anthropology*, 1 (2): 124–32.

Weiner, J. 2003. '*The Law of the Land*: a review article', *The Australian Journal of Anthropology*, 14 (1): 97–110.

Wolfe, P. 1999. *Settler Colonialism and the Transformation of Anthropology: The Politics and Poetics of an Ethnographic Event*, Cassell, London.

8. 'No vacancies at the Starlight Motel': Larrakia identity and the native title claims process

Benedict Scambary

> I feel the government has let us down. This Government has let the Larrakia people down. We don't want smiles and we don't want you know slaps and so forth on the back. What we want is to sit down and negotiate outcomes for all concerned.
>
> Bill Risk, Larrakia leader[1]

Darwin, the capital of the Northern Territory is built on Larrakia country. When it comes to elections in the Northern Territory, winning the hearts and minds of residents in the northern suburbs is critical. Election campaigns based on the issue of land rights, and hence race, played a significant role in keeping the Country Liberal Party (CLP) in government for 23 years. Notably, the 1983 election was fought almost exclusively on the issue of the return of Uluru to the Mutitjulu Land Trust (Gibbins 1988: 41). More recent elections have focused on Indigenous law and order and the detrimental impact of native title claims on the Northern Territory economy (Newman 1997). In its first term of government the Martin Labor (ALP) government had usefully engaged with Indigenous groups, the Larrakia Nation in particular, to address the issue of Indigenous itinerants in town through the 'Community Harmony' project. However, like the CLP government before it, which had strenuously opposed the Larrakia land claim to the Cox Peninsula, the Martin government was at the same time vigorously opposing the Larrakia Native Title claim over the city of Darwin, generating portrayals of Larrakia as a people who had 'lost their culture'. Fearful of not being re-elected for a second term, the ALP went into the 2005 election with an aggressive platform to address anti-social behaviour, a policy clearly aimed at the Northern Territory's homeless Indigenous residents. In urban centers of the Northern Territory such people are often referred to as 'long grass people' or simply 'long grassers'. The similarities between the ALP campaign and previous CLP campaigns were not lost on many. In April 2006 Justice Mansfield of the Federal Court dismissed the long running Darwin native title claim. In attempting to find a continuing tradition of law and custom that would allow recognition of native title, Mansfield J stated:

---

[1] Australian Broadcasting Commission (ABC), 'Larrakia native title claim', *Stateline Northern Territory* 21 April 2006. ABC, Darwin.

A combination of circumstances has, in various ways, interrupted or disturbed the presence of the Larrakia people in the Darwin area during several decades of the 20th Century in a way that has affected their continued observance of, and enjoyment of, the traditional laws and customs of the Larrakia people that existed at sovereignty. (Mansfield J 2006: [812])

In his summary to the decision, Mansfield J notes that Larrakia claims to the Darwin area 'were vigorously contested by the main respondents, the Northern Territory and the Darwin City Council' (Mansfield J 2006: [7]). This chapter focuses on the struggle of Larrakia to assert their rights to their traditional estate, and how successive governments have on one hand generated negative portrayals of Larrakia in their opposition to such claims, while on the other hand they have utilised idealised constructions of Larrakia in the pursuit of political gain.

Native title and the colonial process

Mansfield in his determination specified that under s. 223 (1) of the *Native Title Act 1993* (Cwlth) (NTA) Larrakia had to satisfy three criteria to be successful in their claim. These were: that Larrakia were united in and by their acknowledgement and observance of a body of accepted laws and customs at 1825 when sovereignty over Larrakia country was assumed by the colony of New South Wales; that such laws and customs now are 'in essence' the same as those practiced by Larrakia ancestors; and finally that there has been a continuation and substantial non-interruption of the acknowledgement and observance of such laws from 1825 to the present (Mansfield J 2006 [6–8]). The histories of Larrakia people are diverse, and subject to the many vagaries of the colonial process in Australia. Mansfield found that Larrakia had satisfied the first criterion of the NTA with evidence being drawn from the archaeological, linguistic, and historic record. He noted, 'the Larrakia community of today is a vibrant, dynamic society which embraces its history and traditions' (Mansfield J 2006: [11]). Despite this the judge found that the settlement of Darwin, an influx of Indigenous people into the claim area, and the impacts of assimilationist government policy had adversely impacted on the ability of Larrakia people to maintain a continuation of traditional laws and customs (Mansfield, 2006).

The decision demonstrates the narrow focus of the NTA in accounting for of the impacts of the colonial process on Indigenous rights and interests, and its limited ability to recognise the dynamics of change that are encompassed by the term tradition. As Glaskin notes, 'Aboriginal tradition in the native title context tends to be reified towards a pre-colonial moment so that contemporary traditions must be demonstrably continuous from this period' (Glaskin 2005: 297–8). This is despite an increasing body of research highlighting that reinterpretation, reinvention and in some cases revival of cultural practice are integral elements to the maintenance and assertion of tradition (Glaskin 2005; Hobsbawm and Ranger 1983; Keesing and Tonkinson 1982; Otto and Pedersen 2005; Weiner and Glaskin 2006) David Martin, in an interview on *Stateline Northern Territory* noted that the necessity to prove a continuity of tradition between the present and the society in existence at the time of sovereignty clearly confronts Indigenous people with a test that is not applied to the rest of the Australian population. He cited revitalisation of the celebration of ANZAC day as an example that would not meet the test of 'continuing tradition' as applied by the NTA.[2]

From its earliest establishment Darwin was a segregated city. In 1911 the Commonwealth assumed responsibility for the Northern Territory from South Australia and adopted the *Aborigines Act 1910*. Under the provisions of this Act, Larrakia became institutionalised within Darwin, their place of residence confined to reserves, and their movement at the discretion of the Chief Protector of Aborigines. Larrakia camps at Lameroo Beach in the city centre, which predated European settlement of the area, were relocated to the Kahlin Compound around 1911. Children of mixed descent were further segregated within the camp. Mansfield J in his decision notes an early report of Beckett, a Protector of Aborigines, that the intent of establishing Kahlin compound was aimed at 'keeping the unemployed natives out of Darwin' (Mansfield J 2006: [247]). Early assertions by Larrakia in the media of their 'special' status vis-à-vis other Indigenous people resident in Darwin, particularly in relation to rations and housing provisions at Kahlin Compound were dismissed by Mansfield J as not being demonstration of a traditional right (Mansfield J 2006: [179-183], [255-256]).

With increasing expansion of Darwin, the Kahlin compound was closed and Larrakia were moved further away from the European population to the Bagot Reserve. Those who had been granted an exemption from the restrictive provisions of the *Aborigines Act 1910, and* the *Aboriginals Ordinance 1918 (NT)*, and also the later provisions of the *Northern Territory Welfare Ordinance 1953*, by law had to cease contact with 'full blood' relatives. Exemption allowed the right to undertake paid employment, which was denied those subject of the various laws. Unable to reside in the town centre, or designated reserves, many of these people lived primarily in the enclaves of the Parap Camp and Police Paddock. Darwin also had a significant Chinese and Malay population who were engaged in activities such as gold mining, pearling, and market gardening. Intermarriage between these groups and Larrakia people was common. Stigmatised by their Aboriginality in the white town of Darwin, many Larrakia came to expediently identify as being of Asian descent, and to deny publicly their indigeneity. World War II saw further disruption to Larrakia identity and social institutions with the evacuation of many Larrakia to southern States.

---

[2] ABC, 'The future of native title', Stateline Northern Territory 21 April 2006, ABC, Darwin.

Intermarriage also occurred with members of other proximate Indigenous groups, particularly from the Daly River and West Arnhem regions, who were also residing in Darwin, and upon Larrakia land. In addition members of the Kiuk, Beringgen, Emienthal, Wadjigyn and Mariatjben have occupied Larrakia country on the Cox Peninsula west of Darwin in a caretaker role since migrating north from the Daly River region around the turn of the twentieth century. These groups are now commonly referred to as 'the Belyuen' (Povinelli 1993).

The conditions of control in early Darwin have dictated the identity of contemporary generations of Larrakia and significantly and unevenly affected both the extent and transmission of traditional knowledge of the Larrakia estate. Familiarity within the Larrakia polity was also heavily impacted in these years of administration, and has lead to much disputation in relation to Larrakia identity and group membership. Despite this, many Larrakia have maintained and developed their identity as Larrakia through a complex of family and social relations, centred on continued residence in the Darwin area and in reserves, the Parap Camp and Police Paddock. Institutions such as the Sunshine Club, and the Buffaloes sporting club, which have typically been the domain of 'Darwin Aboriginal families', and loosely the Larrakia, have also been an important focus of Larrakia identity.

Modern Larrakiya identity and native title

Larrakia assertions of their ownership of Darwin have been present at all points in Darwin's history. In 1971, spurred by the Gove Land Rights case, and the ever-decreasing reserve land in Darwin, Bobby Secretary led Larrakia people and other long-term Indigenous residents of Darwin in a series of protests under the banner of 'Gwalwa Dariniki', 'our land'. These protests, which included sit down blockades of Darwin streets and the hoisting of the Larrakia flag,[3] brought the plight of Larrakia, and particular the struggle to gain title of the Kulaluk town camp, to national attention (Day 1994). Justice Woodward enquired into the issues at Kulaluk in his enquiry into Aboriginal Land Rights (Woodward J 1973). However, his recommendation that land rights be recognised in town areas was not incorporated into the *Aboriginal Land Rights (NT) Act 1976* (Cwlth) (ALRA).

The Kenbi land claim was one of the first land claims to be lodged under the ALRA, and having run for 23 years was the longest. It is a claim to Larrakia country on the Cox Peninsula outside the Darwin town boundary. The area is predominantly occupied by the 'Belyuen' who have a custodial relationship with the Larrakia in relation to their residence on Larrakia country. The initial

---

[3] The Larrakia flag is coloured red at one end to represent the 'blood of the old people who were shot', and red at the other end for the blood of the protesters. In the middle is a shady tree on a jungle fowl's nest which represents the location of the early protest meetings at Kulaluk (Day 1994).

unsuccessful claim concluded in 1991. Justice Olney, the Aboriginal Land Commissioner at the time, indicated that he had only been able to identify one Larrakia person who had 'a "spiritual affiliation" to one site within the meaning of the Act; however, one person cannot be a group, and land rights can only accrue to groups under the Act' (Olney J 1991; and see Parsons 1998).

A successful appeal was lodged and the entire claim was heard again. The claims process required Larrakia to give representations about their prior ownership of the Darwin area, and indeed themselves. Given the colonial history of Darwin, some Larrakia claimants did not publicly acknowledge their Larrakia ancestry, or had kept it hidden, and in some cases they simply did not know about it. The Kenbi land claim brought about a resurgence of Larrakia identity, and with it contestation from within the group and from opposing parties about the substance and basis of Larrakia identity. Justice Mansfield found that such a resurgence of knowledge did not constitute a continuing Larrakia tradition in the native title claim over Darwin (Mansfield J 2006: [839]).

In the second run of the Kenbi land claim before Justice Gray (1995–2000), the Northern Land Council (NLC) made a strategic decision to divide the claimant group into those descended patrilineally from apical ancestor Tommy Lyons, and the wider Larrakia, who claim their descent cognatically from nine Larrakia apical ancestors. This division fuelled intense contestation about membership of the group. Many Larrakia found their authenticity as Larrakia was challenged by inclusion in the larger group, which, because of its descent model had less chance of fitting the criteria of the Act. In the course of the land claim many of the senior Larrakia passed away. With increased disputation, the long-standing cooperative arrangements with the 'Belyuen' became tenuous. The decision of the 'Belyuen' group to also contest the claim as traditional owners, despite their custodial relationship with Larrakia in regard to the claim area, created considerable tension, and further challenged the authenticity of Larrakia.

Justice Gray handed down a positive recommendation in 2000, finding in favour of the six descendants of Tommy Lyons (Gray J 2000). The decision, though successful, was devastating for the approximately 1600 Larrakia people who were not recognised as primary traditional owners. The Northern Territory government, which had opposed the Kenbi land claim throughout its 21 year history, asserted that the Commissioner's decision was 'bound to have far reaching detrimental effects on the entire population of the Northern Territory' (Commonwealth of Australia 2001: 22262). Prominent journalist Paul Toohey summed up the adverse public opinion in Darwin in relation to Larrakia in an article in *The Australian*:

> The people Darwin folk grew up with have suddenly become Aborigines ... Twenty years ago, these people were not thought of as Larrakia, perhaps because back then they did not loudly proclaim themselves as

such ... will the majority of the Larrakia, who live in houses, watch TV and speak only English, now cross the harbour to dress in lap-laps, and dance in ochre paint? In Darwin, there is a widely held view that these people never were real Aborigines. But if they have suddenly become Aborigines, then let's see the spears and corroborees.[4]

Whilst the Land Commissioner made his positive recommendation in 2000 the grant of title by the federal Minister for Aboriginal Affairs has not occurred and is still pending the settlement of detriment issues.

Prior to the conclusion of the Kenbi Land Claim, three non-claimant applications under the NTA were lodged by the Northern Territory government in respect of a proposed subdivision in Palmerston,[5] the new East Arm Darwin port,[6] and the site for the liquid natural gas plant at Wickham Point[7] in Darwin Harbour. Native title claims lodged in response were cast as Larrakia attempts to halt these major developments, and as an attempt by Larrakia to claim the 'backyards' of Darwin residents (Stone 1998).

In 1994, on the eve of a Northern Territory election, a prominent member of the Danggalabba clan, who assert their separateness and primacy over the 'post-classical' new Larrakia Tribe as described by Sutton (Sutton 1998), held a press conference in the public bar of Darwin's Don Hotel to announce a native title claim over all of Darwin. The claim was not lodged, but the impact on the election result was spectacular, with the CLP increasing its already considerable margin over the ALP. The election campaign itself was characterised by the incumbent CLP government's platform that the ALP intended to introduce a separate legal system for Indigenous people. This position was central in a campaign of 'push polling', a practice that was relatively new in Australian politics (Williams 1997). Speculation and debate that the announcement was made in return for $50 000 grant funding from the incumbent CLP occurred in the 1994 Sessional Committee on Constitutional Development (Northern Territory Government 1994). The announcement of this claim had a divisive impact on the already fragile Larrakia polity and prompted a considerable public backlash, which expressed itself in the election outcome. The leader of the ALP in attempting to downplay the claim announced that the Larrakia could not demonstrate continuing occupation of the Darwin area, while the incumbent CLP government used the announcement to vigorously state that the claim would halt development in Darwin.

Debate about the vexatious nature of Larrakia claims continued until 1996 when the first proactive Larrakia native title claim over all vacant crown land and

---

[4] Toohey, P. 'The traditional owner next door', *Weekend Australian*, 16 December 2000.
[5] National Native Title Tribunal (NNTT) file no. DC94/1.
[6] NNTT file no. DC94/4 &94/5.
[7] NNTT file no. DC95/1.

reserve land in Darwin was lodged. It was the first such claim over an Australian capital city. Larrakia claimants sought to assure the residents of Darwin that their aspirations for public beaches and reserves concerned Larrakia involvement in the management of these culturally important areas, not the exclusion of non-Larrakia (Carey and Collinge 1997). However, a public backlash occurred, fuelled by political comment from the Darwin Lord Mayor, Chief Minister Stone, and Prime Minister Howard—the latter describing the claim as 'an extravagant ambit claim' (Carey and Collinge 1997: 21). The NLC received a significant amount of mostly anonymous hate mail, including a newspaper photograph of Larrakia claimants at a press conference that had been modified by the drawing of targets with bullet holes on their foreheads (Wells 2003).

Due to the unknown nature of native title in these early years, and significant development proposals within the city limits, increased pressure came to bear on Larrakia people to respond to the demands of developers, the government, the general public and agencies such as the NLC and the Aboriginal and Torres Strait Islander Commission (ATSIC). In addition a heightened awareness and recognition of prior Indigenous occupation nationally meant that there was an increased demand for Larrakia people to open events such as conferences, art exhibitions, and festivals. At a number of these occasions Larrakia individuals publicly contested each other's affiliations and therefore rights to perform as Larrakia in such forums. At an organisational level, a number of competing Larrakia organisations, whose membership was based around family and historical association, competed for the authenticity of their memberships in the arena of native title consultative processes, and within the newly formed Larrakia Nation Aboriginal Corporation (LNAC). This organisation is a coalition, initially facilitated by the NLC, of Larrakia families, individuals and factions, with the primary purpose of providing a corporate identity for Larrakia against increased pressure from external agencies to 'know' whom the Larrakia were. Mansfield J, in his assessment of Larrakia tradition, pointed to a 'breakdown in decision making structures', noting 'it is clear that the decision making process among the Larrakia people has been largely transferred to the Larrakia Nation. Its composition is not traditional' (Mansfield J 2006: [832]).

Larrakiya and the 'long grassers'

In the mid 1990s the perennial issue of illegal camping in Darwin, with its portrayals of drunken 'long grassers' begging, fighting, and defecating in public, by an act of media convenience, public ignorance, and government collusion, became in part attached to the native title debate and hence conveyed negative portrayals of Larrakia as being a people without culture.

The Darwin fringe dwelling population is a diverse group which is predominantly Indigenous, and consists of short-term visitors, and medium to long-term migrants deriving from a variety of Top End communities. It is thought that the itinerant population, which fluctuates seasonally, is in the vicinity of 150 to 200 people, although some estimate that the figure is as high as 1000 (Memmott and Fantin 2001). A number of the temporary camps, or 'Starlight Motels' as they are sometimes called, are well established and have been populated by Indigenous migrants for many decades. As Bill Day notes, in relation to the residents of Fish Camp, a long term camping area on the Kulaluk special purpose lease, these migrants not only maintain links with their original country, but over time have forged new links with Larrakia people and their land that legitimate by agreement their presence on, and use of Larrakia country (Day 2001: 11). The political support of the fringe dwelling community for Larrakia assertions of traditional ownership has been an ongoing feature of the relationship with Larrakia.

The native title process however, has impacted this informal relationship. Larrakia through their involvement in the native title process were increasingly gaining legitimacy through the advocacy of the NLC, but more critically through the corporatisation of the Larrakia polity in the form of the Larrakia Nation. The fringe dwellers, however, were excluded from the consideration of native title, and as they came under increasing pressure from the Northern Territory government and the media, they were not supported by the NLC, ATSIC, North Australian Aboriginal Legal Aid Service, or the Larrakia Nation Aboriginal Corporation.

The fringe dwellers became increasingly politicised in response to forced evictions of Barada people from a long-term informal camp at Lee Point.[8] The Northern Territory government rejected their request for title of the area on the grounds that the Larrakia native title claim prevented the granting of third party interests. This is despite successful negotiation of the native title process by the Northern Territory government with Larrakia to allow for the construction of the East Arm Port and the granting of land title to Conoco-Phillips for the construction of the Wickham Point liquid natural gas plant. The negotiations in relation to these projects ultimately all resulted in positive and potentially lucrative economic outcomes for the Larrakia Nation.

The establishment of the 'Darwin Longgrass Association' by prominent Larrakia woman June Mills assisted the politicisation of the fringe dwellers (see Fig. 8.1), and also demonstrated that the informal relationship between some members of Larrakia and the fringe dwelling community still existed. However, the intense consultative load associated with development and native title, disputation within Larrakia and the disengagement of Indigenous representative organisations from fringe dwelling issues, greatly reduced the capacity of Larrakia to respond as a group and in a formal sense to the needs of the fringe dwelling community.

---

[8] Barada people are from near Maningrida on the central Arnhem Land coast.

Fig. 8.1 Itinerant protestors in Darwin

Photo: Courtesy of W. Day

Harassment of fringe dwellers increased under mandatory sentencing laws introduced by the CLP government in 1997. A Darwin City Council 'by-law' made it an offence to sleep in a public place and attracted a $50 fine for contravention. Under the mandatory sentencing regime unpaid fines of this nature became a property offence and attracted a mandatory jail term when brought before the courts (Howse 2000).[9] In response to such harassment fringe dwelling communities around Darwin became increasingly politicised. The Darwin Longgrass Association, and community advocates campaigning on their behalf, were able to project positive images of fringe dwellers as 'traditional people' living off the land, both in the mainstream media and the newsletters *Longgrass* and *Kujuk* (Figs 8.2 and 8.3).

In a perverse twist, such images were incorporated into the discourse of Larrakia having lost their culture, and therefore having no claim on Darwin. Newspaper articles highlighted the assumption that Indigenous people from elsewhere utilised the natural resources of Darwin to a greater extent than Larrakia. In addition non-Indigenous Darwin residents on occasion proclaimed that they too were more engaged in the activities of hunting and in particular fishing, than those asserting native title rights. The notion of 'anti social behaviour' which became a euphemism for being black and being in town, however, was conflated

---

[9] The Territory Infringement Notices Scheme which is contained in Division 2A of the *Justices Act (NT)*, was challenged by the Aboriginal Justice and Advocacy Committee (NT) which successfully sought to have the 'sleeping in public' by-law declared *ultra vires* (see Howse 2000).

by media and politicians with native title to create negative representations of Larrakia and fringe dwellers alike. Chief Minister Shane Stone, well known for his opposition to Larrakia claims in the Darwin area advocated 'harsh retribution' for itinerants, and stated that Aboriginal people with drinking problems deserved to be monstered and stomped on.[10]

Fig. 8.2 Cover of *Kujuk*

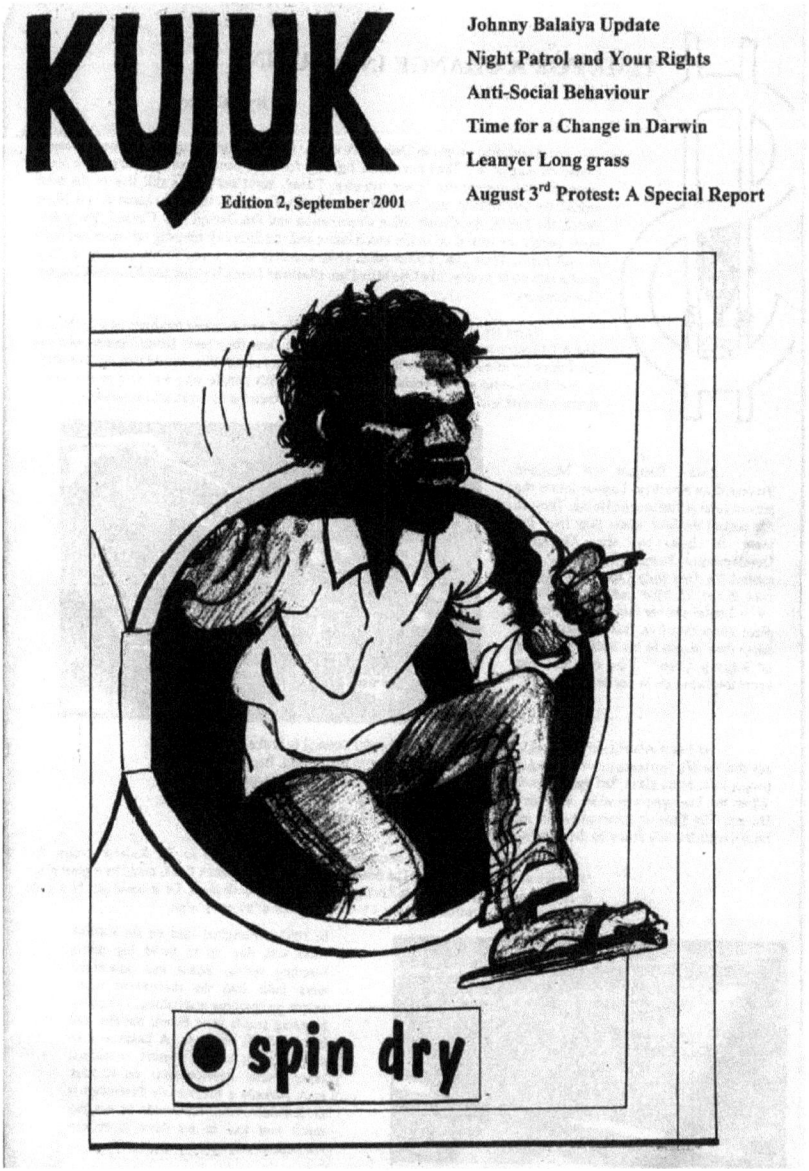

---

[10] ABC, 'Home calls NT itinerants', *The 7.30 Report* 6 January 2004, ABC, Canberra.

Fig. 8.3 Cover of *Longgrass*

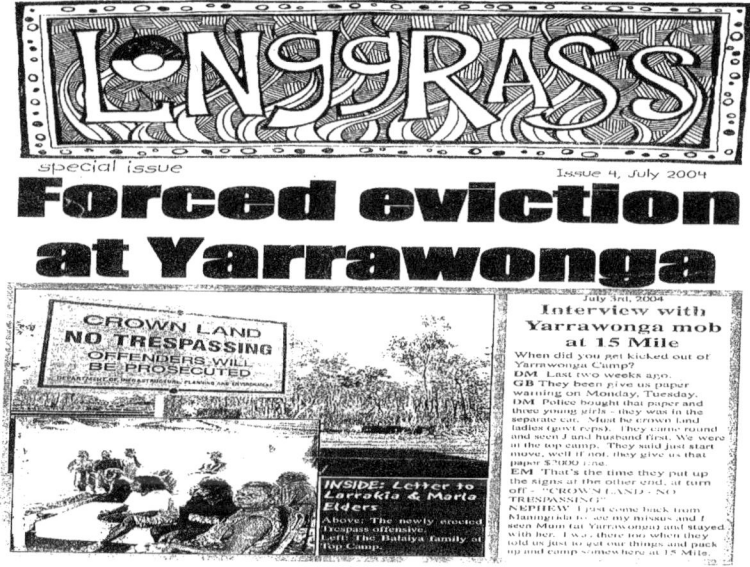

The Larrakia claim over Darwin

In 1997–98, due to a backlog in native title claims nationally, the Federal Court and the National Native Title Tribunal (NNTT) both received a dramatic increase in funding, which resulted in the Larrakia claim over Darwin being called forward for hearing. Given the levels of disputation within Larrakia, and the divisive history of the Kenbi Land Claim, a negotiated or mediated settlement was arguably the preferred course of action by the applicants. As noted a number of commercial deals had already been negotiated on the basis of claims lodged but not heard, including the lucrative Darla urban development agreement in Palmerston and an agreement in relation to the Wickham Point gas plant (NLC 2003: 46).

Hearing of traditional evidence in the major claim over 216 areas of land and waters in and around Darwin began in September 2002. The claim, and in particular the evidence of traditional owners was hotly contested by the Northern Territory government and the Darwin City Council. Justice Mansfield stated, notably:

> The respective positions of the parties could hardly have been more diametrically opposed, save for the realistic acknowledgments the applicants made in respect of the extinguishing effect of a number of those past legislative and executive actions (Mansfield J 2006: [30]).

And later:

> The issues on the hearing have been hard fought. Apart from facilitating the course of the evidence, the Territory and the other respondents have made no admissions (Mansfield J 2006: [59]).

Constructions of Larrakia as having lost their traditions and having no system of law that had plagued Larrakia in the Kenbi Land Claim and throughout the 1990s, were used to aggressively refute the evidence of Larrakia witnesses, and in some cases humiliate them. The historical record, with its many assertions of Larrakia 'dying out', and no longer practicing 'traditional culture' ultimately outweighed the oral evidence of contemporary Larrakia people.

As a mark of the government's opposition to the claim, and as an indication of the belief that the claim would be highly contestable, the Northern Territory government submitted a respondent anthropologist's report, which had never occurred in a Northern Territory native title claim before. Given that the hearings were public, reports of the evidence have seeped into the public domain. Ken Parish, an ex-ALP politician, local barrister and academic posted the following on his Northern Territory University sponsored blog site, *The Parish Pump*:

> I recently sat through significant parts of the 'traditional' evidence in the Larrakia native title claim. I don't know what the judge will make of it, but I must say I found most of it totally unconvincing. Even I knew more about Aboriginal culture, law and tradition than most of the Larrakia 'traditional' witnesses! (Parish 2002).

Larrakiya identity co-opted

The Martin ALP government, which came to power in 2001, was at pains in its first term to distance itself from the negative approach to Indigenous affairs of the previous CLP government. In seeking to address the issue of 'antisocial behaviour', rather than jail itinerants, it sought to engage the Northern Territory Indigenous community leadership, and in particular the Larrakia as 'traditional owners' of Darwin, in the 'Community Harmony Project'. This program focused on alcohol rehabilitation, increased community or night patrols, and repatriation of itinerants to their home communities. The Larrakia Nation received a grant of $500 000 to facilitate its involvement. The Larrakia Nation, in consultation with its membership, established a behaviour protocol for visiting Indigenous people that is widely advertised around Darwin in the form of posters in shop windows and signs in known 'anti-social behaviour' hot spots, that proclaim Larrakia authority over Darwin on the basis that they are the 'traditional owners'. Despite opposing prior Larrakia claims to the Darwin area the Northern Territory government utilised opportunistically the corporate identity of Larrakia as the 'traditional owners' of Darwin as a way of ridding the city of homeless Indigenous people.

Conclusion: an uncertain identity

While there have been positive economic outcomes for the Larrakia Nation from this process, the future is by no means clear. Chief Minister Martin has indicated that a dialogue between the government and Larrakia is ongoing, but that the government 'is unlikely to consider handing over land outside the court process'.[11] Using representations of Larrakia as 'traditional owners' and custodians of the Darwin area, the government through the Harmony project has made Larrakia complicit in the demonising of the fringe dwelling population of Darwin, while giving Larrakia no formal recognition of their rights within their country.

In the 2005 election campaign, in a move clearly aimed at the conservative voters of Darwin's northern suburbs, the Martin government retreated from the initiatives of the Harmony Project and campaigned on the basis of increased law and order. Election advertising material indicated that existing community night patrols would be replaced by police patrols to combat the issue of anti social behaviour and 'itinerants'. A key element of the campaign was the pronouncement that habitual drunks would face jail if they refused rehabilitation. The ALP election campaign was widely reported as being focused on race (Eastley 2005; Murdoch 2005),[12] and even attracted the critique of the CLP opposition that the campaign was 'chasing the redneck vote'. The *Alcohol Court Act 2005* (NT) and the *Antisocial Behaviour (Miscellaneous Amendments) Act 2005* (NT) passed subsequent to the election establishes a mechanism for the placing of prohibition orders on habitual alcohol abusers. However, rather than making habitual alcohol use the offence, the legislation allows for such orders to be made when an offence is committed.

Justice Mansfield's decision recognises that a Larrakia polity exists and that the process of 're-establishing traditional laws and customs adapted to the modern context … is enriching the lives of Larrakia people, and of the Darwin community (Mansfield J 2006: [836]), a sentiment also conveyed by Norman Fry, CEO of the NLC:

> Everybody in the Northern Territory … all know who the Larrakia are. They are not invisible people, they are here … To expect that people would remain stagnant, in some sort of time capsule, is quite silly. The Larrakia people are the heart and soul of this place.[13]

---

[11] ABC, 'Larrakia dialogue ongoing despite native title ruling, says Martin', *ABC News Online* 17 April 2006, ABC, Canberra.
[12] For example Eastley, T. 'Proposed anti-social laws in NT to make it tougher for long grassers—featuring David Gulpilil', *AM* 28 August 2005, ABC, Canberra; and Murdoch, L. 'The race is on', *Sydney Morning Herald* 17 June 2005.
[13] Cited in Michelmore, K. 'Larrakia fail in bid for Darwin native title', *National Indigenous Times*, Issue 103, 20 April 2006.

Justice Mansfield's decision was unsuccessfully appealed before the Full Bench of the Federal Court in 2006. The negative decision of the Full Bench is an emphatic blow to the assertions of Larrakia rights to their traditional estate within the city of Darwin. Negative depictions of Larrakia generated by successive governments in their opposition to the claims process and the pursuit of political gain have served to position Larrakia somewhere between the dominant white society of Darwin, and idealised notions of 'traditional Aborigines', a place that for many Larrakia is all too familiar.

References

Carey, C. and Collinge, A. 1997. 'Larrakia native title: the long march', *Indigenous Law Bulletin*, 4 (2): 21.

Commonwealth of Australia 2001. *Senate Official Hansard*, No. 2, 2001, 39th Parliament, First Session, Eighth Period, Parliament of Australia, Canberra.

Day, W. 1994. *Bunji: A Story of the Gwalwa Dariniki Movement*, Aboriginal Studies Press, Canberra.

Day, W. 2001. Aboriginal Fringe Dwellers in Darwin, Australia: Cultural Persistence or a Culture of Resistance? PhD Thesis, University of Western Australia, Perth.

Gibbins, R. 1988. *Federalism in the Northern Territory: Statehood and Aboriginal Political Development*, North Australia Research Unit, The Australian National University, Darwin.

Glaskin, K. 2005. 'Innovation and ancestral revelation: the case of dreams,' *Journal of the Royal Anthropological Institute*, 11 (2): 297–314.

Gray, J. 2000. *The Kenbi Land Claim, Report of the Aboriginal Land Commissioner*, Australian Government Publishing Service, Canberra.

Hobsbawm, E. and Ranger, T. (eds) 1983. *The Invention of Tradition*, Cambridge University Press, Cambridge.

Howse, C. 2000. 'Towards a dealing just and kind', *Alternative Law Journal*, 25 (3): 108–30.

Keesing, R. M., and Tonkinson, R. (eds) 1982. 'Reinventing traditional culture: the politics of Kastom in Melanesia', *Mankind* (Special Issue) 13 (4): 297–399.

Mansfield, J 2006. *Risk v Northern Territory of Australia*, FCA 404, 13 April 2006.

Memmott, P. and Fantin, S. 2001. *'The Long Grassers': A Strategic Report on Indigenous 'Itinerants' in the Darwin and Palmerston Area*, Version 2, Vol.

1, Aboriginal Environments Research Centre, University of Queensland, Brisbane.

Newman, G. 1997. 'Northern Territory election 1997', *Research Note 7 1997-98*, Parliamentary Library, Parliament of Australia, Canberra.

Northern Land Council (NLC) 2003. *Northern Land Council Annual Report 2002–2003*, NLC, Darwin.

Northern Territory Government 1994. Debates: Sessional Committee on Constitutional Development, Seventh Assembly First Session 27 June 1994, *Parliamentary Record No: 1*, Northern Territory Government, Darwin.

Olney, J 1991. *The Kenbi Land Claim: Report of the Aboriginal Land Commissioner*, Australian Government Publishing Service, Canberra.

Otto, T, and Pedersen, P. (eds) 2005. *Tradition and Agency: Tracing Cultural Continuity and Invention*, Aarhus University Press, Aarhus.

Parish, K. 2002. *The Parish Pump* [blog site, Darwin], available at <http://www.ntu.edu.au/faculties/lba/schools/Law/apl/blog/stories/gen-law/170.htm>. Accessed 16 October 2005.

Parsons, D. 1998. 'Kenbi Land Claim: 25 Years On', *Indigenous Law Bulletin*, 4 (8): 15–17.

Povinelli, E. A. 1993. *Labor's Lot: The Power, History, and Culture of Aboriginal Action*, University of Chicago Press, Chicago.

Stone, S. 1998. *Eighth Assembly First Session 17/02/98 Parliament Record No.3*, Northern Territory Government, Darwin.

Sutton, P. 1998. *Native Title and the Descent of Rights*, National Native Title Tribunal, Perth.

Wells, S. 2003. Negotiating Place in Colonial Darwin. Interactions between Aborigines and Whites 1869–1911, PhD Thesis, Sydney University of Technology, Sydney.

Williams, G. 1997. 'Push polling in Australia: options for regulation', *Research Note 36 1996-97*, Parliamentary Library, Parliament of Australia, Canberra.

Woodward, A. E. 1973. *Aboriginal Land Rights Commission: First Report*, Australian Government Publishing Service, Canberra.

Weiner, J. and Glaskin, K. (eds) 2006. *Custom: Indigenous Tradition and Law in the 21st Century, The Asia Pacific Journal of Anthropology*, Special Issue 17 (1).

9. What has native title done to the urban Koori in New South Wales who is also a traditional custodian?

Dennis Foley

> Native title is a concept in the law of Australia that recognises the continued ownership of land by local Indigenous Australians … it is also an example of two distinct systems of law operating within the same geographic, national and jurisdictional space … however, to the extent of any inconsistency between Australian law and customary Aboriginal law, non-indigenous rights will generally prevail (*Wikipedia* 2007).

The *Wikipedia* definition of native title seems straightforward; non-indigenous rights prevail and native title recognises Aboriginal ownership of land—or does it? What does native title mean to the urban Koori who is born, raised and educated on their customary lands now called Sydney? These same lands are now occupied by some 4.2 million people who are representative of settler society. The Sydney population also includes a large number of growing Indigenous groups who are not the descendants of traditional owners. Rather the majority of Indigenous Australians in the specific example of Sydney and its environs are themselves usurpers.

This is a paper on native title as it applies to Sydney: what native title is and what it isn't, how it has been adopted by the black usurper and white coloniser and used as a process to deny Traditional Owners a voice in their rightful lands. The denial process is entwined within the legislation that is the *Land Rights Act No. 42 1983* (NSW) (LRA).

Background to the New South Wales Land Rights Act

In June 1983 the Wran Labor Government enacted the LRA, which subsequently allowed Aboriginal land councils to claim empty Crown land not needed for essential public purposes. This Act had its initiative in the early South Australian lands trust; in 1974 the New South Wales Coalition government had sponsored the establishment of a Lands Trust. The Trust's main activity was the purchasing of residential properties. In time it became the landlord to around 20 per cent of the State's Indigenous population. Much of this property later ended up as valuable assets for land councils and Aboriginal housing groups. The advent of the Wran Labor Government in 1976 was hailed as a necessary first step towards the granting of inalienable land rights to Indigenous people. After much delay and despite heated debate and opposition from some Indigenous groups, the parliament of New South Wales passed the LRA. It gave certain groups freehold title over current Aboriginal reserves but had no process for claiming former Aboriginal reserves. The only non-reserve land that could be claimed was Crown land that had no future use and was not being used. There was no recognition of traditional ownership (Bennett 1999: 104; Wilkie 1985).

Our traditional custodians were ill-prepared for what followed. Aboriginal Land Councils were established very quickly and began a land grab. This was often without any involvement or consent from local Aboriginal people who were direct descendants of the traditional people of the lands in question. Guringah people generally were still recovering from wearing the brunt of nearly 180 years of physical and psychological trauma (dating from the establishment of Sydney town adjacent to our lands in 1788 through to the 1967 referendum which removed discriminatory clauses from the Australian constitution). These traumas included firstly dispossession of our land, enforced segregation and discrimination, and then assimilation and the denial of our culture. Guringah people were not fully conversant with the new opportunities that the Act bestowed upon them, nor savvy enough about the workings of the new legal system. There was a lag in the granting of these opportunities and in local resolution as to how to respond to them. Another group of Indigenous people however stepped into the vacuum and took advantage of this significant historical event. We Guringah custodians could not believe other Aboriginal people could act against us to both deny our existence and then steal our traditional lands from under us. But they did and history will show that the medium to allow this was the LRA.

It is important to understand the overall ramifications of the 1983 Act for other Aboriginal people throughout New South Wales. The Wran government was not the benefactor to Aboriginal people by the enactment of the 1983 legislation with an offer of 6000 acres of land (a 'fund' together with the subsequent opportunity of claiming unwanted Crown lands) as some would suggest. Rather the Act was a smokescreen to cover what the government had realised in 1979, four years previously, when they and their legal advisors understood a legal ambiguity that had been created in 1913. For between 1913 and 1969 some 25 000 acres of 'old reserves' in New South Wales had been confiscated, at times forcibly with the use of police firearms (Goodall 1988: 37). Many of these old reserve properties were productive farm lands, developed and managed with pride by enterprising Aboriginal families. In 1979 the Wran Government's legal people concluded that the Aboriginal Crown lands seized were in fact vested in the Protection and Welfare Boards until 1969, not the Lands Department as previously thought. Therefore in 1983 the freehold title over the old reserves was invalid and the Aboriginal people as the beneficiaries of the now defunct Directorate of Aboriginal Affairs could have had a successful claim on 25 000 acres of land that was arguably theirs. Many firmly believed that the reserved land was decreed or granted to them by Queen Victoria in recognition of their traditional ownership (Goodall 1996: 376-8).

The Wran government would only pass the 1983 Act on the condition that Aboriginal people would not oppose a new parallel law; the *Retrospective Validation of Revocations Act* which enforces a conscious theft of title to some 25 000 acres of Aboriginal land.

In 1988 the chairperson of the New South Wales Aboriginal Land Council defended their own actions in support of the introduction of the 1983 Act: '[L]ets face it—this is the only opportunity that we have had to implement self-management, self-determination and to give us the opportunity to establish an economic base; to give us the opportunity to be less of a burden to the taxpayers of this state.'[1]

Honorable rhetoric, the outcomes of which in the Sydney example are anything but self-management, self-determination and the opportunity to establish an economic base, as is illustrated by observations made by two political journalists discussed later in this paper (Jopson and Ryle 2004).

It seems that native title issues under (British) Australian law in New South Wales results in a continuous passage of pain and discrimination for Aboriginal people. The key discussion point of this paper concerns the perceived or actual financial benefit that usurping Aboriginal groups have made under the 1983 Act which has in many ways protracted local Indigenous impoverishment and marginalisation. It also highlights the process of native title and how the beneficiaries of the Act (that is the NSW Aboriginal land councils) become cultural auditors for the federal native title legislation.

Historical background

The Sydney region has had a strange allure for Aboriginal people from further afield, from the time that smallpox first decimated our people in 1789. Some travelled to the burgeoning town for medical assistance, or for food, because many Indigenous people were starving. Some came because everything they knew or valued was disrupted during the early days of colonisation. Others came to trade or obtain the rum that seemed to soothe the confusion and pain of colonial cultural chaos. Others just watched from the periphery. The Guringah, Darug and southern clans tried as much as possible to stay away from the newly arrived visitors. But the British stayed and we struggled to maintain a sustainable existence.

By the 1880s small pockets of traditional owners and others continued to exist in various locations of Sydney. They included Manly, Neutral Bay, Double Bay, Blues' Point, the north shore of Botany Bay, La Perouse, Kurnell, Sans Souci and

---

[1] Tiga Bayles, in Chalk 1988a).

a noisy camp at Circular Quay (Nugent 2005: 47). Other settlements have been recorded at Pittwater, Narrabeen Lakes and in isolated pockets along the Hawkesbury and its tributaries (Brook 1999; Foley 2001). Darug families could still be found along the Hawkesbury, the Nepean and Colo Rivers, on the Sackville Reserve, near Rooty Hill, and in and around the various farms working on the western urban fringe (Goodall 1988: 35).

As early as the 1880s the housing developments around what would become the Enfield Rail yards provided small, low cost housing for people of 'colour'. Pockets of Koori families in rented housing were well established in the Glebe Point, Forest Lodge, Ultimo, Chippendale and Camperdown-Newtown areas as the inhabitants provided a reliable, cheap labour source for the stevedoring industry, and various merchants and factories which operated in the area. By the 1890s, Aboriginal families whose members worked on the railway began to concentrate around the 'block' area in Redfern. Numerous housing enclaves for railway workers were constructed in easy walking distance to the main rail workshop areas. Many of these workers were Aboriginal. By the early 1900s an increasingly diverse group of people (including southern Europeans, Indigenous Australians and Chinese) were well established in the tight narrow streets of the inner west.[2]

Published histories of Sydney, written between the late 19th century and the 1960s, have failed to account for the Aboriginal presence. After George Thornton was appointed Protector of Aborigines in 1881, he pursued a campaign to remove Aboriginal people from Sydney. He forcibly closed down the metropolitan Aboriginal camps and prohibited the provision of rations to city-dwelling Aboriginals (Nugent 2005: 50–7). Despite Thornton's attempts however, many Koori families were not dependent on welfare. They had access to employment; and rented, lived and continued to work on their traditional lands. These people managed ingeniously to stay outside the Protector's watch and reach. Their invisibility from the Protector is reflected in the public record, and their stories have been omitted from the historical landscape of Sydney (Nugent 2005: 54–7). This is not the time nor place for speculations as to whether this was an unconscious oversight or a strategic 'whitewashing' by historians however its occurrence is noteworthy.

The lure of jobs in Sydney during the Great Depression and the rural decline during the 1920s and 1930s saw an influx of Indigenous people from country areas. This precipitated a turning point in Indigenous affairs in Sydney as Indigenous peoples seeking to relocate from country New South Wales to the metropolitan area, increasingly outnumbered the small groups of surviving traditional custodians. In the 1950s and 1960s Eora peoples were provided with an opportunity to move to the outer Sydney fringe where inexpensive rental

---

[2] Gordon Foley, pers. comm., c. 1970.

accommodation was made available in new housing commission estates in the western suburbs.³ These included Chester Hill, Bass Hill, Regents Park, Yagoona, Cabramatta, Warwick Farm, Merrylands and a multitude of other postwar housing estates. Other impoverished inner city dwellers who could afford these rentals went with them seeking healthier living conditions. People of Koori, southern European and Anglo-Celtic backgrounds became mixed in the western sprawl. Those Eora peoples who preferred to remain in city camps or could not afford the rents, were rounded up by authorities and subsequently 'disappeared'. Their camps—including the well-known one at Narrabeen Lakes—were demolished. The whereabouts of many of these people remained forever unknown to other members of their families, many of whom were too afraid to ask questions. Shortly thereafter, the inner city area around Redfern became a magnet for Indigenous people from rural regions searching for employment or political activity similar to that led by Afro-American Martin Luther King in the United States (King's anti-segregation campaigns commenced in the mid 1950s). The combination of the two spatial flows of city and country Aboriginal groups (the westerly dispersal of traditional custodians from urban Sydney and the centralisation of rural arrivals towards Redfern), together with the emergence of a new generation of Aboriginal activists fired by the success of international events, had significant consequences for power relations between local and newly arrived Indigenous groups. This was a migration of Aboriginal people, the traditional owners of Sydney were dispersed, and the migrating Aboriginal people from Moree, Dubbo and Cowra (as examples) became the usurpers. This had serious implications for the traditional owners in subsequent generations.

During the early 1970s Indigenous people formerly from rural areas became increasingly vocal and active in community management. For example, the Federal Council for the Advancement of Aborigines and Torres Strait Islanders (FCAATSI) became an 'all black' institution. This trend towards Indigenous-only managed organisations continued to both strengthen and broaden in scope (Horner 2004). As previously mentioned by Bayles (1988) Aboriginal people saw land rights legislation as an opportunity. However, this opportunity was dominated by the usurping Indigenous groups.

Whilst the Eora voice had once been strong, it became increasingly silent in Indigenous affairs around Sydney. In the inner-city areas it was replaced by the streetwise, union-trained Indigenous voices that maintained strong links to areas such as Dubbo, Cowra and Moree. These same areas were strongholds of unionism

---

³ Eora peoples are loosely recognised as the traditional clans of the lands located between the Hawkesbury, Georges and Nepean Rivers. The southern Guringah (the Gai-mariagal) are included within the Eora distribution as they cover the Lane Cove River catchments, the northern side of Sydney Harbour and northern coastal suburbs. The word Eora, 'I-yora' or the many other forms of phonetic spelling, simply means people (Smith 2004). For the purposes of this paper Eora refers to the Indigenous custodians pre-contact within the Sydney geographic basin. The northern suburbs comprise the northern rim of that basin.

within the shearing industry, which was the training ground for many iconic leaders of the Aboriginal resistance movement. This included Mr. Jack Patten, Mr. Bill Ferguson and Mr. William Cooper. The shearing industry and later the waterside industries were the schools for 19th and 20th century Aboriginal activists. The Eora peoples had little to no contact with unionism.

In time it appears respect for traditional custodianship was lost in the struggle for Aboriginal rights. This prolonged battle became too much for many of our Elders who we lost between the mid 1960s and the early 1970s. A power vacuum was created at a critical period. The new usurping black power brokers failed to recognise many of us with our fair skin and blue eyes. Whilst once we had shared our tables, our friendship and our land as Aboriginal peoples, many of us were now not black enough for the politically active. It was not until the late 1980s and early 1990s—during a period of increased understanding about the effects of government policies to biologically 'absorb' Aboriginal people into settler society—that we began to receive formal recognition once more as traditional custodians. Unfortunately this timing was inconvenient for some. It was then not in the best interests of some local Aboriginal land councils to recognise us. Indeed some took steps to exclude us from participating within 'their' organisations, that were first established to assist us.

The traditional owners of Sydney were 'black-washed' from the historical landscape. This was made clear to the writer and 80 other attendees and bystanders at a book launch at Gleebooks, Glebe on Tuesday 30 August 2005 when a heckler and a self-identified spokesperson for a Sydney Aboriginal land council boasted to the assembled group that 'they' (i.e. the Aboriginal land council) had proven that Colin Gale was not Aboriginal and that all other people who claimed to be of Darug descent were 'all liars'. When the writer questioned this elderly person as to his identity he stated that he was originally from Queensland. Further he added that as a member of the Sydney land council 'it' had the right to speak on Aboriginal issues as they were the 'real' Aboriginal people.

This illustrates the way in which land councils now assume the power and legal right to determine who is Aboriginal and who is not. This goes against the judgments of The *Commonwealth v Tasmania* [1983][4] and *Gibbs v Capewell* [1983].[5] Neither individuals nor the New South Wales Aboriginal land council have the legal capacity to determine the Aboriginality of individuals or groups.

It needs to be noted that Mr Colin Gale (on behalf of the Darug people) was unsuccessful in the Federal Court of Australia before Madgwick J on 31 March

---

[4] *The Commonwealth v Tasmania* 1983. 158 CLR 1, 274.
[5] *Gibbs v Capewell* 1995. 128 ALR 577.

2004 in a native title claim.[6] Court records show this decision was based on Mr. Gale's contemporary way of life rather than his Darug descent. For example, 'Mr. Gale is living a suburban way of life indistinguishable from that of many non-Aboriginal Australians', and 'there is no evidence that there is now anything like a body of traditional laws and customs, having a normative content in relation to rights or interests in land, which any member of the claimant group now acknowledges or observes'.[7] .

The transcripts of this case have been carefully analysed. Mr Gales' Aboriginality was not in question. The claim made by the land council representative in Glebe on 30 August 2005 was misinformed and reflects the general attitude underlying attempts to usurp the rights and deny the existence of traditional owners. The LRA facilitates this process in its creation of New South Wales Aboriginal land councils.

The New South Wales land councils were established well before the landmark Mabo and Wik cases and operate in a fashion that has little in common with the objectives and practices envisaged by the Federal Court in the National Native Title Tribunal. However the New South Wales land councils have become cultural auditors through their recognition under State law. They deliver little if anything for the traditional people of the northern suburbs of Sydney as they are not recognised and are not admitted as members of an exclusive club composed of people from other Aboriginal nations. Many do not want to subject themselves to the same public humiliation administered to Mr Gale and do not register themselves on the Register of Native Title Claims. Further, many do not have the financial or political resources (or the family unity) to do so.

It is a matter of public record that the Minister responsible for native title utilises tactics that run dangerously close to an abuse of process against Aboriginal claimants. In the Winbar appeal Stein J remarked:

> it is difficult not to feel some sense of intense surprise at the apparent conduct of the Minister and those who represent or assist him ... I do not make these remarks lightly since it is no pleasure to be critical of a Minister of the Crown. However, I find such conduct to be contrary to the spirit and intent of the Land Rights Act and particularly the recitals to the Act [8] (Chalk 1988b: 35).

The local Indigenous peoples of Sydney are aware that the Federal court is hostile. They have witnessed the loss of the Darug and they are all too aware of the opposition of the local Aboriginal land council, which is supported by State

---

[6] *Gale v Minister for Land and Water Conservation for the State of New South Wales* 2004, FCA 374 (31 March 2004).
[7] *Gale v Minister for Land and Water Conservation for the State of New South Wales*, ALR 2004: 8–9, lines 116, 121. Available at http://bar.austlii.edu.au/au/journals/AILR/2004/11.html, accessed 5 May 2007.

legislation through the 1983 Act. The way in which the land rights system operates is difficult to both contest and accept on moral or legal grounds if you are a local, urban traditional owner.

The Hon Brad Hazzard has highlighted in 'parliamentary debate' that of the 130 000 Aboriginal people in New South Wales less than 10 per cent are voting members of land councils (Legislative Assembly of New South Wales 2005: 17881) and 'many Aboriginal people ... are fed up to the back teeth with the failings in the Aboriginal land rights system. They are fed up with the fact that very few people in some land councils get the opportunity to benefit' (*Hansard* 2005: 17881). This Member of Parliament has raised two important issues; firstly, the poor representation of Aboriginal peoples in New South Wales land councils, and secondly, that only a few share the benefits.

To be a native title claimant in New South Wales you must successfully lodge a registration with the National Native Title Tribunal. In the registration process for native title, traditional owner groups require the support of their New South Wales land councils if they are to be successful native title claimants, otherwise the federal Minister could use the land council as an opposing body or land council members as opposing claimants. The urban traditional owner is in a perilous legal situation within an environment that is characterised by poor representation, poor delivery of benefits, poor administration, and a hostile federal Minister in the Native Title Court. It is important now to review some recent literature on Sydney and what constitutes an Aboriginal land council to ensure that the reader can begin to understand what New South Wales Aboriginal land councils are mandated to do and what is happening in Sydney.

What constitutes an Aboriginal land council?

It must be realised and accepted that the 1983 Act has not relieved the general poverty of New South Wales Aboriginal people. It has however been effective in delivering about 79 000 hectares of land into the clutches of land councils since their inception. There are 122 local Aboriginal land councils in the State. In August 2004, 11 were under the control of a government-appointed administrator and the peak body, which had been operating under a cloud of accusations of financial and administrative mismanagement for several years, was also under the control of an administrator (Jopson and Ryle 2004: 30). From a series of reviews and inquiries, it is clear that New South Wales land councils have, since their inception, suffered 'problems with misappropriation and mismanagement' (Bayles in Chalk 1988a: 4)

When the 1983 Act was created, it did two things. First, it created a fund to finance the 122 local Aboriginal land councils by setting aside 7.5 per cent of all land tax collected for 15 years. Some of these funds were used to finance the land councils. The balance was set aside to provide funding for the future. When the scheme ceased in 1998, this fund amounted to approximately $500 million. It was planned to pay a stipend to each council of around $110 000 per annum.

Secondly, the new Act enabled the Indigenous people of New South Wales to claim any Crown land that was not needed for an essential public purpose. Local government councils resisted this move until 1991, when the peak body, the New South Wales Aboriginal Land Council, pointed out to them they could collect rate payments on any lands granted to local Aboriginal land councils. More than 2100 land claims have since been awarded to local Aboriginal land councils. This has made some of them very large property owners. This is particularly so for some operating along the coast and within the Sydney region. The Office of the Registrar of the Land Rights Act conservatively values these lands at $770 million. The administrator of the New South Wales Aboriginal Land Council believes the figure could be closer to $3 billion. These local Aboriginal land councils could collectively be a larger landowner than Lend Lease or Mirvac. Recent enquiries have revealed that a serious lack of necessary infrastructure has left the door open to corruption. One report makes the claim that land councils have been drawn into questionable dealings by lucrative offers from real-estate developers (Jopson and Ryle 2004: 30).

Many land councils are controlled by families and factional groups. Under the 1983 Act, a quorum of just 10 is needed for a legally constituted meeting. Of that number just eight can vote to legally approve a multimillion-dollar land sale (Jopson and Ryle 2004: 30).

There is little monitoring of the lands successfully claimed by local Aboriginal land councils and it is impossible to determine what lands they have inappropriately sold. Given their dealings are poorly monitored and are regularly conducted with little, or no, input or consultation with the traditional people of the lands in question, some of the coastal Aboriginal land councils' land sale dealings are of serious concern.

Individual members of land councils have publicly voiced their concerns about some of the mis-dealings that occur within their institutions (see e.g. Bayles in Chalk (1988a) quoted above). Other concerns include decision-making processes, powerful factions, and strivings for personal gain rather than the betterment of local Aboriginal people. For example, members have made the following claims which are not exhaustive. First, that notices of meetings are often 'tucked away' in obscure publications that most members never read. Secondly, powerful factions organise to meet alone and take various steps to prevent the attendance of others, so as to ensure voting delivers the outcomes desired by that particular group of members. Thirdly, most members of local Aboriginal community groups and councils are kept out of the 'deals' as they are not members of local Aboriginal land councils. While some make voluntary decisions not to associate with land councils, others are precluded on the basis that they do not meet the necessary criteria. The reasons for this exclusion are rarely disclosed. And finally, only a select few seem to receive any benefits from their membership of local Aboriginal land councils, be they financial or otherwise (Jopson and Ryle 2004: 30, 2004b: 31).

The 2001 census revealed that 135 319 people living in New South Wales identified as Aboriginal (ABS 2002). Almost half of this group was living in financial stress. Most of them were existing on incomes classified as being below the poverty line. Almost one in five was unemployed and one-third lived in sub-standard housing. Of the 135 319 Aboriginal people in the State, only 20 459 or 15 per cent are members of Aboriginal land councils (Jopson and Ryle 2004a: 30). As previously mentioned, the logical deduction is that the great majority of Aboriginal people in the State are not receiving any flow-on benefits from the 1983 Act. Despite their chronic poverty, they have not received any benefit from the 79 000 hectares of land granted to Aboriginal people or the sale of prime coastal property by Aboriginal land councils.

Land lies at the heart of Indigenous cultural heritage. If the land is being managed (and sold) by a small minority of Aboriginal people who have no historical connections with that land—be they spiritual, cultural, intellectual, ceremonial or economic—then surely the claim can be made that the New South Wales Aboriginal land councils are little more than real estate speculators. They are by their own actions usurpers.

The Sydney experience

In March 2003 an investigator revealed the Sydney based local Aboriginal land council was bordering on mismanagement and it faced the risk of losing its land bank which had been built up through years of government grants. He concluded that this Aboriginal land council's 'adherence to standard corporate governance procedures was almost non-existent' (Robert Jackson, cited in Jopson 2003a). It would appear that responsible fiduciary management was not evident.

Just prior to this investigation, this Aboriginal land council had sold five parcels of land, which collectively were valued conservatively at over $13 million. They were located at Belrose, Terry Hills, Frenchs Forest and Asquith. All of this land lies within Guringah language borders. So too do the following properties that they allegedly hold (if they have not already sold them):

- 17 Belrose parcels valued at $22 million
- 9 Cromer parcels worth $18.5 million and
- 6 Terry Hills parcels estimated at $4.5 million (Jopson 2003b).

When *Sydney Morning Herald* reporter Debra Jopson interviewed the former chairperson of this Aboriginal land council, she was advised the land sales were necessary to ensure the economic self-sufficiency of the council, as it was land-rich but cash-poor (2003b). In other words, land had to be sold to keep the body financial. For all accounts and purposes, this appears to be an unfinancial organisation with almost non-existent corporate governance procedures (Jopson 2003a). The sale of Aboriginal land goes against the very ethos of Aboriginal peoples' struggle since colonisation, which is the fight to preserve and maintain Aboriginal land.

The investigator also noted the cash blowouts in this council's current expenditure. For example, their forward commitments at the time were budgeted at approximately $2.5–$2.8 million. There was however, only $2.4 million in the term deposit account, which was supposed to earn sufficient interest to fund running costs. The council would therefore have to withdraw its term deposit to fund these running costs. This would then deprive it of future interest and result in still further land sales to enable the ongoing life of the organisation (Jopson 2003a).

It seems the council will have to continue to sell land to fund the administration of this organisation. This raises important questions. Firstly, where is the money going? Secondly, what are the details of the successful projects this organisation espouses? Thirdly, how long will this be allowed to continue?

The land bank is limited. The cultural heritage landscapes that the Aboriginal land councils are selling are irreplaceable. Yet land councils continue to sell land to meet operational expenses.

These land sales are being carried out with total disregard for the spiritual/cultural importance of this land to local Aboriginal people and traditional 'owners'/custodians. There is no consultation; the land is being treated like a common chattel. It is being sold with contempt for the traditional Indigenous belief that we do not own the land, the land owns us. We ask, how can they be permitted to continue to sell off our Mother earth?

If Guringah people went to Cowra, Dubbo or Moree and began to sell land there in much the same way as the executive of the Sydney-based land council is doing, there would be a major outcry. Yet in Sydney the usurpers have successfully stifled the voice of the traditional 'owners'/custodians. It is important to understand how they have managed to achieve this.

The Aboriginal land council executive have declared that the local traditional 'owners' are extinct and have disseminated this mistruth through their extensive networks within the New South Wales National Parks and Wildlife Service, Local Government Councils situated on Guringah lands, and various other government departments and agencies. This is, however, in sharp contradiction to their public relations material. For example, one public notice makes the claim that 'contrary to white propaganda the original inhabitants, the Eora people, were not wiped out after the European invasion' (Madden 2000). Yet a letter from their former Chairperson dated 18 March 2003 addressed to the General Manager and Mayor of the North Sydney Council, and copied to eight other local government councils (Lane Cove, Hornsby, Kuring-gai, Willoughby, Mosman, Manly, Warringah and Pittwater Councils) declared it was 'unaware of any traditional owners of the North Shore Peninsula'. This is incorrect, for a simple membership check of the Registrar of Aboriginal Corporations ICN 4270 reveals Guringai Tribal Link Aboriginal Corporation incorporated on 11 August 2003. Their list of members are Guringai people (other spelling Guringah) or they identify as descendents of Guringah people. The claim of the Aboriginal land council in question, as to the existence or non-existence or traditional owners is unfounded and misleading to the public.

This same Sydney Aboriginal land council had previously communicated with the writer on the basis that I was then recognised as a traditional custodian. Ironically, the State's Governor General, Attorney General and Minister for National Parks and Wildlife, and the Royal Society for the Arts all formally acknowledge the writer as a member of the Guringah people. So likewise do countless numbers of professional people, organisations, Indigenous groups and other individuals. The local Aboriginal land council, however, continues to state it is unaware of any traditional owners when it is convenient for them to do so.

Its actions in managing the recent burial of human remains on North Head on March 4, 2005 typifies the land council's contempt towards Aboriginal people outside of its own circle of direct influence. The media and a select group of Aboriginal people were advised when and where the burial was to occur, and invited to attend. The Indigenous heritage staff of the overseeing government department omitted to invite the local Aboriginal community or relatives of the deceased. No Guringah persons were invited despite numerous telephone calls to the New South Wales National Parks and Wildlife office and the Australian Museum staff by the writer. It is difficult to explain the pain of being deliberately excluded from the interment of your own ancestors; yet a further example of usurping.

These mixed public messages, questioning of Aboriginality and in some cases the denying of it without investigation or proof, in addition to limited membership and somewhat questionable management practices is a moral concern. In May 2004, the former NSW Minister for Aboriginal Affairs, Dr Andrew Refshauge, released a media statement that both admitted the NSW Aboriginal land council system was 'clearly not working well enough' and announced the establishment of a special taskforce to overhaul the system and fix fundamental problems (Refshauge 2004). Two issues papers have since been prepared by this taskforce. They go some way towards suggesting land councils have been given too loose a rein in the desecration of Indigenous cultural heritage through the sale of coastal ancestral lands to developers (NSW Aboriginal Land Rights Act Review Task Force 2005a, 2005b).

The control and power systems that the Aboriginal land councils enforce also have a direct influence on the cultural heritage industry, which needs to be reviewed, and a system of professional accreditation implemented. Presently qualifications and regulation is blurred as political correctness has reduced any form of questioning if a person of Indigenous heritage has the right to adopt/create or steal knowledge of an area and disseminate it. This problem was summed up by the well-known Indigenous businessman, Mr John Moriarty who at the time of writing is also a member of the National Indigenous Council. Mr Moriarty told me directly he was concerned with the 're-invention of Aboriginal knowledge' by Indigenous people who were not from Sydney who were developing their own agendas.[8] It is important that only people of a professional, accredited standard be appointed as Cultural Heritage Officers. The ability to communicate the holistic knowledge and the cultural intricacies of particular lands calls for much more than just Aboriginal descent.

The legal implication regarding cultural heritage management entrusted to Aboriginal Land Councils who are usurping the resources of the traditional custodians is a concern if it affects Native Title decisions. If we review the Native Title Cases of *Gale*[9] (2004 FCA 374) and *Yorta Yorta*[10] (2002 194 ALR 534) the concept of what is tradition; (and it could be argued cultural heritage from the traditional custodian's perspective) reflects the fundamental nature of native title rights and interests. In many cases claimants will invite the Court to infer from evidence in the trial as to the content of traditional law and custom (s. 233 *Yorta Yorta* 2002). If usurping Aboriginal land councils have the legal position within NSW to dominate cultural heritage management practices then we are already experiencing a manifestation in the 'creation of culture' to earn income from property developers, the tourism industry and so on. This purported creation of culture by unsuitably qualified cultural heritage management staff will ensure conflicting information for the legal and anthropological professions to interpret and appraise. The 're-invention of Aboriginal knowledge' (Moriarty 2005) by Indigenous people who were not from Sydney who were developing their own agendas has the potential to distort or confuse at the very least, knowledge for the Native Title Courts.

Conclusion

The *Land Rights Act 1983* (NSW) (as amended) and the subsequently established NSW Aboriginal Land Councils which are actively usurping the resources of

---

[8] John Moriarty, pers. comm.. c. 2005.
[9] *Gale v Minister for Land and Water Conservation for the State of New South Wales* 2004. FCA374, 31 March 2004.
[10] *Yorta Yorta Aboriginal Community v Victoria 2002.* 194 ALR 534.

traditional owners/custodians in the sale of their land and control of cultural heritage matters are an impediment on the federal native title process.

Critics of the NSW Department of Aboriginal Affairs could also claim collusion and nepotism are rife within the land rights and cultural heritage systems and there is little monitoring to prevent it. At the present time many local Aboriginal land councils are closed shops, selling off lands and heritage for short-term profits. There is an urgent need for a bipartisan agreement in the NSW Parliament to amend the Act to remedy this situation; at the time of writing this paper the recent review does not facilitate this. Traditional 'owners'/custodians need to be included on the executive committee of local Aboriginal land councils. This should not be a token appointment, and if these have to be legislated then so be it. Perhaps this is where self-determination is not working when such actions need to be legally enforced. Indigenous people should be working together without division or hatred. There should be respect for country and its inhabitants. What has evolved in Sydney is shameful.

As Moreton-Robinson comments, 'questioning the integrity and legitimacy of Indigenous ways of knowing and being has more to do with who has the power and whether their knowledge is commensurate with the west's rational belief system' (2002: 3). The NSW Aboriginal land councils have power; this is undeniable under the 1983 legislation, and they have legitimacy within the west's belief system. It is time that this power was dissipated into socially accepted interaction; we could do so much more working together in lieu of faction fighting.

There is need for a sale register to be lodged with the NSW Department of Aboriginal Affairs and maintained on an ongoing basis to protect the interests of the greater majority of NSW Indigenous people who are not members of Aboriginal land councils. All sales should be vetted by the Minister. This is not to take opportunities for self-determination away from Aboriginal people. Rather it is a necessary measure to protect the majority of Aboriginal people from the questionable actions of an enterprising few. This would ensure the cultural heritage of local Aboriginal people and traditional 'owners'/custodians are not sold from underneath them.

Under Australian trust law, the following three institutions have a fiduciary responsibility to Aboriginal 'owners'/custodians: the NSW Government, the executive of local Aboriginal land councils, and local government authorities within which Aboriginal land councils operate. Each has an important responsibility to remedy this situation before all of the land has been sold and the proceeds squandered.

The 1983 Act was purportedly established to improve the living conditions and life-chances of Aboriginal people in New South Wales and redress some of the hardships they have suffered as a direct result of their dispossession from their ancestral lands. The Act has now become less effective in achieving these aims. It needs urgent revision to correct the current injustices being experienced by some Aboriginal people in New South Wales. The recent amendments and review do not appear to have resolved the concerns expressed above.

In conclusion, Aboriginal people have suffered much over the generations; let us no longer continue to suffer, rather let us work together for the betterment of our people. This is my wish. Native title is a dream to the urban Koori; the Act effectively stole 25 000 acres of trust land away from Koori people and has given us 24 years of turmoil and hate. It is time to correct these issues and for Koori people once again learn to respect one another and live together as one in Eora pemul.

Acknowledgments

A version of this paper was presented at the 'Effects of Native Title Workshop', Old Canberra House, The Australian National University, Canberra, November 1-2, 2005. Special thanks go to the organising committee of CAEPR and the financial support of AIATSIS and CAEPR to run the two day seminar. Special thanks also go to Professor Mick Dodson of the National Centre for Indigenous Studies for his support in allowing me to attend the workshop, to Dr Benjamin Smith for inviting me, to Professor Peter Read (a true warrior in the struggle for equity and peace for Aboriginal people), to the staff of CAEPR (particularly Professor Jon Altman for his inspiration and support), to various Federal and State Members of Parliament, local Mayors and Local Government staff, together with a long list of historians, anthropologists and archaeologists; in addition to staff within museums and the NSW National Parks and Wildlife Service for their moral support in a battle that seems to have no ending (their privacy is maintained due to their fears of recrimination), and the Indigenous inhabitants of the Northern Suburbs of our land, especially Ms Susan Moylan-Coombs for her untiring support. Di-goori goor to my Guringah family for their voice and prayers, and to the various church leaders and their congregations of the Northern suburbs for their spiritual support in this struggle.

I would like to thank participants at the workshop for their helpful feedback as it surprised me to learn that our people were not the only ones who were being denied their heritage by other Indigenous usurpers who were in control of the very organisations that were set up to protect our culture.

My special thanks also go to Jill Barnes for her editorial eye and untiring enthusiasm while reading and commenting on my work.

References

Australian Bureau of Statistics (ABS) 2002. *Australian Social Trends 2002*, available at <http://www.abs.gov.au/>, accessed 11 May 2007.

Bayles, T. 1988. 'The NSW Land Rights Act', Interview, Radio 2BL, 12 April 1988.

Bennett, S. 1999. *White Politics and Black Australians*, Allen and Unwin, St. Leonards.

Brook, J. 1999. *Shut Out from the World: The Hawkesbury Aborigines Reserve and Mission 1889–1946*, Deerubbin Press, Berowra Heights, NSW.

Chalk, A. 1988a. 'The NSW Land Rights Act: Interview with Tiga Bayles,' Aboriginal Law Bulletin, 21 (2): 1–2. Available at <http://kirra.austlii.edu.au/au/journals/AboriginalLB/1988/21.html>, accessed 11 May 2007.

Chalk, A. 1988b. 'NSW Land Rights: All Just an Act?' Aboriginal Law Bulletin. 30 (2): 32–8.

Foley, D. 2001. *Repossession of Our Spirit*, Aboriginal History, Canberra.

Goodall, H. 1988. 'Aboriginal calls for justice: learning from history', *Aboriginal Law Bulletin*, 37 (2): 33–8.

Goodall, H. 1996. *Invasion to Embassy: Land in Aboriginal Politics in New South Wales, 1770–1972*, Allen and Unwin, St. Leonards.

Horner, J. 2004. *Seeking Racial Justice: An Insider's Memoir of the Movement for Aboriginal Advancement, 1938–1978*, Aboriginal Studies Press, Canberra.

Jopson, D. 2003a. 'Report warns land council property bank is running out', *The Sydney Morning Herald*, July 7. Available at <http://www.smh.com.au/cgi-bin/common/popupPrintArticle.pl?path+articles/2-003/>. Accessed 19 January 2004.

Jopson, D. 2003b. 'Metro land council claims million-dollar stake in the northern suburbs', *The Sydney Morning Herald*, March 7. Available at <http://www.smh.com.au/cgi-bin/common/popupPrintArticle.pl?path+articles/2-003/>. Accessed 19 January 2004.

Jopson, D. and Ryle, G. 2004a. 'A gift with strings attached', *The Sydney Morning Herald*, 31 July: 30.

Jopson, D. and Ryle, G. 2004b. 'Black land white shoes', *The Sydney Morning Herald*, 31 July: 23.

Legislative Assembly of New South Wales 2005. New South Wales Aboriginal Land Council Management', *Hansard*, 15 September 2005: 17881.

Madden, A. 2000. 'The art community and the Sydney Metropolitan Land Council', *ARTnews*, April 2000. Available at <http:/www.artnews.com.au/madden.htm>. Accessed 14 January, 2004.

Moreton Robinson, A. 2002. 'I still call Australia home', in S. Ahmed and M. Sheller (eds), *Uprootings/Regroundings*, Berg, London.

New South Wales Aboriginal Land Rights Act Review Task Force. 2005a. *Review of the Land Dealings Provisions of the Aboriginal Land Rights Act 1983*, Issues Paper 1, August 2005, NSW Department of Aboriginal Affairs, Sydney.

New South Wales Aboriginal Land Rights Act Review Task Force, 2005b. *Structure, Representation, Governance and Benefits*, Issues Paper 2, November 2005, NSW Department of Aboriginal Affairs, Sydney.

Nugent, M. 2005. *Botany Bay Where Histories Meet*, Allen and Unwin, Crows Nest, NSW.

Refshauge, A. 2004. 'Overhaul to NSW Aboriginal Land Council system', Media Release by Deputy Premier, Minister for Education and Training, Minister for Aboriginal Affairs:, 26 May.

Smith, K. 2004. Language of Port Jackson and Coastal Sydney in Eora Clans, MA Thesis, Macquarie University, Sydney.

Wikipedia Encyclopedia 2007. 'Native title'. Available at <http://en.wikipedia.org/wiki/Native_title>. Accessed 17 May 2007.

Wilkie, M. 1985. *Aboriginal Land Rights in NSW*, Alternative Publishing Co-operative, Sydney.

10. Beyond native title: the Murray Lower Darling Rivers Indigenous Nations

Jessica Weir and Steven Ross

> I never gave up my Country to you people. You can destroy the River all you like but in the end we'll still be here.
>
> Mary Pappin, Mutti Mutti Elder, Up the River Forum, Message Sticks 2004.

Introduction

The recognition and development of native title law has focused attention on Indigenous peoples' traditional identities. Indigenous peoples who collectively hold traditional laws and customs are now explicitly recognised as holding rights to their traditional country and implicitly recognised as forming political systems of self governance (Strelein 2001). Native title has been described as a 'recognition space' where traditional laws and customs intersect with the Australian legal system (Mantziaris and Martin 2000: 2). Native title is thus produced by a combination of traditional laws and the common law. However, this interaction of laws has been incredibly problematic, and is at times experienced by Indigenous people as being at odds with the continuance of their laws and customs (Smith 2005: 230).

Moreover, the notion that Indigenous peoples' traditional laws and customs are operating in a realm distinct to and outside of the Australian legal system and colonial administration is unsustainable (Weiner 2003: 99). Indigenous and non-Indigenous histories and lives are so intertwined that a 'profound syncretism' has occurred (Smith 2003: 28). Today, Indigenous peoples' cultural life and traditions are a part of contemporary intercultural Australia (Merlan 2005), and engagements over native title are no exception. Despite this, the influence of native title has been to continue an emphasis on the separateness of Indigenous traditions that are unchanged by 'civilisation' (Smith 2005: 223).

In the more densely settled south east part of Australia, narrow understandings of 'tradition' at the common law, and the extinguishing effect of certain categories of land tenure, has limited the potential of native title to recognise the laws and customs of traditional owners. Instead, traditional owners are asserting their traditional authority irrespective of native title outcomes. This paper engages with this context in relation to the Murray Lower Darling Rivers Indigenous Nations (MLDRIN), an organisation that has formed as an alliance of 10 traditional owner groups from along the River Murray and its tributaries (see Fig. 10.1). It is argued that the rhetoric of this alliance consolidates the native title trend of emphasising a traditional authority that exists in a distinctly separate Indigenous domain. However, the work of the alliance is deeply intertwined with government structures and processes within intercultural Australian society. Indeed, native title law has had a particular effect on the mobilisation of this alliance.

Fig. 10.1 The Indigenous nations of the Murray–Darling system

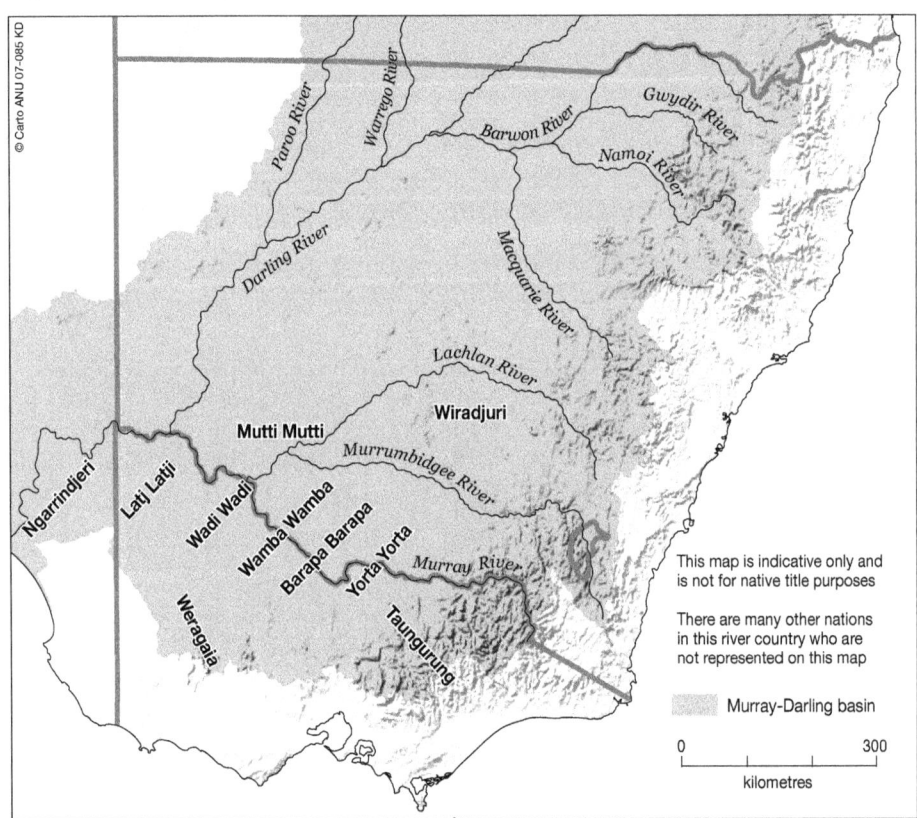

MLDRIN: a brief introduction

In August 1999, the Yorta Yorta people organised a two-day meeting in the Barmah Forest for traditional owner groups whose country is along the Murray River. The meeting resolved to develop a stronger voice for traditional owners in policy and management responses to the severely degraded Murray River, including strengthening the relationships between traditional owner groups through the development of 'Nation to Nation' protocols (see also Morgan et al. 2006: 142–3). At a second meeting two months later, the traditional owners decided to create an umbrella body that could represent traditional owners and be a platform to engage with government. Specifically, a board of delegates was proposed which would have representation from each traditional owner group. A broader consultation process with traditional owners followed, undertaken by Yorta Yorta woman Monica Morgan (working for the Yorta Yorta Nation Aboriginal Corporation) and Mutti Mutti elder Jeanette Crew (working for the New South Wales Department of Land and Water Conservation), and in 2001 MLDRIN held its inaugural meeting. Since then, MLDRIN has consolidated its organisational structure and election processes, and has incorporated under the *Corporations Act 2001* (Cwlth). MLDRIN usually meets four times a year with two delegates attending for each traditional owner group. Crucial to its ongoing operation, MLDRIN has also been able to secure its funding base. In 2003, MLDRIN secured a three-year funding agreement with the Murray–Darling Basin Commission which included funding for meetings and a full-time coordinator. This three-year funding agreement was renewed in 2006.

Today MLDRIN remains an alliance of 10 traditional owner groups, also known as Nations: the Wiradjuri, Yorta Yorta, Taungurung, Wamba Wamba, Barapa Barapa, Mutti Mutti, Wergaia, Wadi Wadi, Latji Latji, and Ngarrindjeri. These traditional owners have country in the southern part of the Murray–Darling Basin (see Fig. 10.1). A lot of the work of the alliance is focused on increasing the involvement of traditional owners in natural resource management and planning, particularly ecological restoration projects, and it is lobbying for an Indigenous water allocation. The MLDRIN alliance is also supportive of the work and aspirations of each traditional owner group. However, MLDRIN has a principle that the alliance cannot interfere with Nation business, because it argues that traditional authority is vested in the Nation group and not the alliance.

In 2007, the delegates established a web presence for MLDRIN at www.mldrin.org.au, which details that the role of MLDRIN is to perform the following functions for the traditional owners of the Murray–Darling River Valleys:

- to facilitate and advocate the participation of 10 Indigenous Nations within the different levels of government decisions on natural resource management
- to develop responses on the cultural, social and economic impacts of development on Indigenous traditional country, and
- to be a collective united voice for the rights and interests of their traditional country and its people.

MLDRIN is thus a creation of the traditional owners that seeks to consolidate the traditional owner identity by forming a regional alliance within which traditional owner groups acknowledge and support each other. The alliance also emphasises the distinct responsibilities that traditional owners hold in their traditional country, and argues that that they require greater representation and rights in order to fulfil their responsibilities to country. It chiefly engages with State governments and departments, the Murray–Darling Basin Commission, and the Commonwealth government, and it also works closely with environmental groups who are concerned about river health. The support it has already received from government—funding, employment positions, inclusion on boards and in briefings—shows that the confederation is valued by government as a consultative body for policymakers. The political assertions of the delegates, that they are the ones who speak for country, have been acknowledged by government in Memoranda of Understanding signed between MLDRIN and the former New South Wales Department of Land and Water Conservation (in 2001), and the Commission (in 2006).

Traditional ownership, native title and establishing MLDRIN

Native title interacts in multiple ways with the arguments that the MLDRIN confederation makes about their traditional authority, and their identity as a confederation of Nations.

The 1992 High Court Mabo native title judgement has motivated traditional owners across Australia to assert a distinct traditional identity because native title recognises their collectively held traditional laws and customs. One of the ways traditional owners have asserted this identity and authority is to make native title claims over their country. A positive native title determination is a recognition of their traditional authority by the common law as it is developed in the Federal and High Courts. Another assertion of traditional authority that is responsive to the Mabo decision is the mobilisation and incorporation of traditional owner groups, and the formation of MLDRIN is an example of this.

However, the MLDRIN delegates emphasise a distinction between native title and their organisational basis as founded in traditional authority. Yorta Yorta woman Monica Morgan, who was a key figure in the establishment of MLDRIN, has spoken about how the MLDRIN alliance is founded in traditional authority and native title:

> the development of MLDRIN isn't something new, it is just with the advent of native title Indigenous peoples could then focus on their traditional selves, who they are, their makeup and regain their identity in making decisions that are around that ... So there is a natural progression from old days to now, and so this is a modern concept and Yorta Yorta were the first ones to invite people from along the Murray River to regain our self-determining process within our traditional frameworks.[1]

---

[1] Interview with Jessica Weir, 1 July 2004.

While Monica explicitly states the influence of native title in the formation of MLDRIN, at the same time she asserts the continuance and revival of traditional authority. They are both important, but MLDRIN is described as an extension of the traditional decision making frameworks of the traditional owners, and not as an alliance of native title groups. Indeed, on its website and in its documents, traditional authority is asserted to the exclusion of native title, or at least traditional authority is not contingent on a positive native title outcome. While there is an issue of scale here, in that native title claims are made by traditional owner groups, and not by large multi-state regional alliances, there remains a marginalisation of native title issues in the delegates' rhetoric and strategic planning. The changes being wrought to Australia's land management landscape by native title are not a noticeable part of the agenda for MLDRIN. Indeed, MLDRIN is a model of representation and governance which specifically circumvents the native title system, relying instead on self-identification which is endorsed through the informal networks, kinships and histories held and known between the traditional owner groups.

Many of the delegates who are on MLDRIN talk about how being self-determining makes MLDRIN a different organisation to the Indigenous organisations which are created by government law and policy, such as the land councils in New South Wales or the cultural heritage cooperatives in Victoria. This self-determination is grasped as a continuation of traditional authority from pre-colonial times. As MLDRIN delegate and Mutti Mutti elder Mary Pappin has said: 'We are still coming together, we are still enjoying a meal, we're still talking about country and rivers. What we're doing is tradition and that is the most important thing.'[2]

This repeated emphasis on traditional authority relates to the specific history of MLDRIN and the Yorta Yorta people, and the narrow 'recognition space' for claiming native title in the more densely settled south east of Australia. The Yorta Yorta people's native title claim was seen by many as a test case for whether native title rights and interests would be recognised in the rural south east. Unfortunately, the Yorta Yorta were the first people in Australia to receive a Federal Court decision that their native title rights and interests had not been continuously maintained through the experience of colonisation, or, as described by Justice Olney's gross euphemism, that their traditional laws and customs had been 'washed away by the tide of history'.[3] Thus, the Yorta Yorta were the first traditional owners who had to explicitly assert their traditional authority as

---

[2] Interview with Jessica Weir, 22 July 2004.
[3] *Members of the Yorta Yorta Aboriginal Community v The State of Victoria* [1998] 1606 (18 December 1998), para 19. This decision was unsuccessfully appealed to the Full Federal Court, and then to the High Court of Australia: *Members of the Yorta Yorta Aboriginal Community v State of Victoria* [2001] FCA 45 (8 February 2001); and *Members of the Yorta Yorta Aboriginal Community v Victoria* [2002] HCA 58 (12 December 2002).

distinctly separate to native title, that is, external to any native title rights that may be recognised by government. For the Yorta Yorta, gathering traditional owners from along the rivers together to work co-operatively on water issues was part of the reassertion of their own identity, their 'self-determining processes', against that determined by native title at the common law.

Under the *Native Title Act* there are provisions for the extinguishment of native title rights and interests, and a judge can make a determination that native title is no longer held by a traditional owner group, but these decisions are not part of the traditional laws and customs of traditional owners (Strelein 1999). It is not possible under Indigenous law to sever the intimate relationship held between a group of traditional owners and their country in this way. However, after a judge makes a negative native title determination, the traditional owners will not have the rights and interests of native title holders, nor the procedural rights they held while registered as native title claimants. This is a considerable loss as native title rights and interests provide traditional owners with opportunities to exercise their traditional authority, including being consulted on development applications on native title lands. Thus, native title law has the power to undermine the capacity of traditional owners to exercise their traditional authority. Indeed, this is just one aspect of how traditional authority is increasingly enmeshed with native title law.

The native title loss for the Yorta Yorta people was felt strongly by their neighbouring traditional owners, not least because of the precedent it set for south east Australia: that native title would not be recognised, or at least would struggle to be recognised, given the narrow legal parameters of the common law. Within the MLDRIN confederation, half of the traditional owner groups—the Ngarrindjeri, Latji Latji, Wamba Wamba, Barapa Barapa and Wadi Wadi—have native title claims, and some parts of Wiradjuri country are also subject to native title claims. The Wergaia are the only delegates who have had native title rights recognised, as part of the Wotjobaluk determination in December 2005 in western Victoria.[4] For those traditional owner groups whose country overlaps State boundaries, they have limited their native title claim to within State borders. This procedure has reduced the complexity of the claims process and the number of opposing parties, however it reminds us that native title is in many ways a compromise for traditional owner aspirations and identity. Native title is not a comprehensive response to traditional owner aspirations across Australia. For many traditional owner groups, making a native title claim is not something they are planning to do.

The combination of the philosophical change wrought by the Mabo decision, and the failure of native title to then recognise the traditional authority of the

---

[4] *Clarke on behalf of the Wotjobaluk, Jaadwa, Jadawadjali, Wergaia and Jupagulk Peoples v State of Victoria* [2005] FCA 1795 (13 December 2005).

Yorta Yorta people, did lead to the development of political will in government to respond positively to the aspirations of traditional owners. In fact, support for MLDRIN has come from the same government bureaucracies who had contested the native title claim, including the Murray–Darling Basin Commission and the Victorian, New South Wales, and South Australian governments. Government recognition of the Yorta Yorta as the traditional owners of country was formalised by the Victorian government in 2004 when the two parties signed off on the Yorta Yorta Cooperative Land Management Agreement for the Barmah-Millewah forest.[5] Thus, the behaviour of the Yorta Yorta as the traditional owners of country was understood by the Victorian government as a credible assertion of traditional identity. It is deeply ironic that the negative and traumatic experience of an unsuccessful native title claim was part of that validation process.

With a more mature government policy, the negative native title context in the south east is now changing. The trend is towards consent determinations, whereby native title claimants and government come to an agreed native title determination without resorting to litigation. However, the MLDRIN delegates continue to assert their confederation as a model that represents the traditional authority of traditional owners outside of the native title system. This MLDRIN model forms the basis of the following discussion.

A confederation of Nations

Native title and the traditional authority of traditional owners have been informing each other since the Mabo decision, and traditional authority and colonisation have had a much longer period of interaction, an interaction which has also informed the conceptualising of native title. The MLDRIN confederation is a particular example of how these interactions have been interpreted by traditional owners in south east Australia, and how the traditional owners have decided to organise and incorporate a regional governance structure.

While the delegates assert their distinct traditional identities, the formation of MLDRIN has occurred within a very complicated intercultural context. The term 'intercultural' has come into increasing use in Indigenous studies as part of a rejection of the notion of cultures as exclusively bounded, self-defining, and self-reproducing domains (Martin 2003: 4). James Tully describes what he calls 'interculturalism' as being where cultures overlap geographically, are interdependent in their formation and identity, existing in complex historical processes of interaction (2004 [1995]: 10–11). For example, the term 'nation' has a long history of interaction. The use of the term to describe the social and

---

[5] Yorta Yorta Nation Aboriginal Corporation and The State of Victoria, 2004. *Co-operative Management Agreement between Yorta Yorta Nation Aboriginal Corporation and The State of Victoria*, signed 10 June 2004.

cultural organisation of Indigenous peoples comes from the late 19th and early 20th century anthropologists who used 'nation' to describe Aboriginal groups that were cultural blocs based on genealogical descent. At that time, the term 'nation' did not carry implications about sovereignty, which have developed since the early 20th century (Blackburn 2002: 150, 153). By describing themselves as Nations, emphasised with a capital letter, the MLDRIN delegates assert the reference to sovereign authority that is now linked to the term. They are also connecting their experiences to the Indigenous rights struggles of First Nations people in North America. However, not all of the traditional owner groups within the alliance have adopted the term 'Nation' to describe themselves.

Interculturalism informed Indigenous peoples' way of life prior to colonisation. However, since colonisation Indigenous peoples' cultures have experienced radical upheavals in a very short space of time. As part of surviving and adapting to the colonial context, the identities of traditional owner groups have been transformed. The more finely defined relationships with country, such as clan and estate groups, have not always continued through colonisation, and the trend in south east Australia has been for traditional owners to broadly define themselves with language groups as their most important political identity (Sutton 1995: 47). In addition, the early anthropologists were keen to identify Indigenous people as part of broader groups—as tribes or nations—and to produce maps that fixed these groups to physical land boundaries (Blackburn 2002: 135). These simplistic maps have misrepresented the complex, indeterminate, and multi-layered relationships held between traditional owners and with country (Sutton 1995: 40, 49–50). However, this mapping of boundaries and peoples is a practice that influences how land claims are recognised today. The *Native Title Act 1993* (Cwlth) requires traditional owners to provide a clear explanation of how the group is defined, what laws and customs unite them, and the extent of their territory. The influence of native title in south east Australia has been to consolidate an already existing trend of describing relationships between traditional owners and their country in a more bounded way. The creation of the MLDRIN alliance has also contributed to this trend of articulating traditional owner identities and matching them to their particular country. Indeed, it is a consolidation of that trend into a regional alliance.

In such a confederation of diverse Nation groups based on the traditional owner identity there are complex issues concerning how identity relates to the political formation embedded in its governance structure. That is, the governance processes of the MLDRIN alliance are intertwined with how the identity of both a traditional owner and a traditional owner group is determined. For example, the Wamba Wamba and the Barapa Barapa have separate delegation on MLDRIN. However, kinship and language ties between the two groups are very close and some of their country is shared. The language of the Wamba Wamba is almost identical to their eastern neighbours the Barapa Barapa (Hercus 1992: 3). The identity networks move further outwards geographically, following this language heritage. Both Wamba Wamba and Barapa Barapa are part of what has been called the Kulin language group in western Victoria, which also includes the Mutti Mutti, Wergaia and the Wadi Wadi (Hercus 1992: 1). The positioning of identity is also being negotiated in the alliances which are being made over native title. The Wergaia are part of the Wotjobaluk native title determination, which includes the Jaadwa, Jadawadjali and Jupagulk peoples as well. There are relationships of scale and definition here: where does a family group, clan, tribe, nation and language group begin and end? A fraught example is that of the Yorta Yorta and the Bangerang. The Yorta Yorta Nation Aboriginal Corporation is a union of the Wolithiga, the Moira, the Ulupna, the Bangerang, the Nguaria-iiliam-wurrung, the Kwat Kwat, the Kailtheban and the Yalaba Yalaba clans (Atkinson 2004: 23). Since the unsuccessful Yorta Yorta native title determination, some members of the Bangerang have asserted a separate identity as a traditional owner group rather than as a clan within the Yorta Yorta Nation.

Identity issues and representation are important to the governance of MLDRIN, to ensure that an individual delegate is representative of their traditional owner group. For individuals, their personal genealogical history can link up with numerous traditional owner groups, connected by the marriages and alliances made through the generations. Individuals are born or adopted into their traditional owner group, and the complicated genealogical histories they inherit are accommodated by some flexibility in self-identification. Identity is influenced by family heritage—drawing on two parents, four grandparents, eight grandparents and so on—as well as the individual's own personal history and experiences (Davies 1995: 77).

When complex identity issues about an individual are presented to the alliance, the delegates defer to the authority of the Nation groups. The delegates argue that it is an internal matter for the traditional owner group to determine who is a member of that group. Yet, when it comes to issues of the identity of a Nation, arguably the traditional owner groups regulate the group identity of other traditional owners groups among themselves. This can be seen in the formation of the MLDRIN alliance. For example, the Manatunga Council of Elders, who are based in Robinvale on the Murray in Victoria, used to sometimes send a representative to the MLDRIN meetings. However, in the process of becoming incorporated, MLDRIN sent the Manatunga Elders Corporation a letter which clarified that, as they are not a traditional owner group in their own right, they are not eligible for MLDRIN delegation. These are politically sensitive decisions, and depend crucially upon the networks of knowledge and relationships held informally between the traditional owners.

By formalising their governance structures on a large scale, as a confederation of Nations, the delegates are exposed to, on very rare occasions, making decisions about group identity. While negative native title determinations can be discredited as an exercise in colonialism by the Australian legal system, and the decision making process of the traditional owners can be argued to be otherwise, MLDRIN's decision making processes are not being made in a realm external to the colonial experience. It is also a decision making process which is informed by native title. It is hard to predict whether the success or failure of the currently lodged native title claims will cause readjustments and realignments in the MLDRIN alliance, however, clearly assertions about distinct traditional owner authority are complicated by this interconnected intercultural life.

Election processes and the diversity of political identities

The complexity of this political context, and how MLDRIN operates today, can be examined in relation to the election processes for the MLDRIN candidates. Because the alliance is about respecting the self-determining decision-making processes of the Nations, there is no uniform election method for the delegates. Election depends on the governance structures of the respective Nation group. The election process of each Nation is influenced by a number of factors; put briefly these include:

- the traditional laws and customs of the Nation
- the geographic size of its country and where large concentrations of traditional owners live within their country
- the relationship with and reaction to colonial processes
- the history and changes within the population, such as forced removal or relocation of peoples
- the existing leadership and other capacity within the Nation, and
- organisations formed within the Nation and Nation membership to other organisations.

These influences can impact on the capacity of a Nation to choose its delegates and on how information is distributed throughout Nation networks. The Nations without the current capacity to meet regularly have been encouraged by MLDRIN to establish incorporated bodies to represent their Nation. With incorporation, that body could receive funding and administration support from the alliance for Nation meetings. Moreover, incorporation increases accountability for external Nation business, as the incorporation process includes a naming of the representatives of that Nation. This also creates a clear governance structure for government to communicate with. Knowing who to contact among the informal networks of traditional owners is often unclear for government (Forward NRM and Arrilla-Aboriginal Training & Development 2003: 77), and the current informality of these communication networks is open to manipulation both by individuals within the Nation and by the government. The MLDRIN coordinator is working with those Nations that have asked for assistance in the incorporation process.

The business of electing MLDRIN delegates in each Nation reveals both the diversity of governance structures in operation, and the way in which informal traditional authority makes use of Indigenous organisations that have been created and funded by government. Traditional owners are generally not funded to be traditional owners, or to mobilise themselves into an organisation of traditional owners. The logistical and funding constraints experienced by the Nations means that an opportunity to meet for a matter which is funded by government also becomes an opportunity to deal with other decisions that require a Nation meeting. The following information has been collated largely from the information supplied by each Nation at the time of election to the MLDRIN co-ordinator Steven Ross, one of the authors of this paper. At some of these meetings, Steven has attended and given a presentation about the work of MLDRIN prior to the election of the delegates.

The Wiradjuri face a problem common across most of the Nations, that of being a political identity with responsibilities to country but operating as such without organisational support. The Wiradjuri have an Elders Council which meets regularly, but there is no Wiradjuri organisation that is truly representative of all the families and/or communities. Some clan groups within the Wiradjuri Nation have formalised their governance to the extent of becoming incorporated bodies. MLDRIN is supporting a Wiradjuri governance project to assist this Nation and its delegates. This will involve establishing a traditional owner steering committee that will draft a governance framework, which will then be put to the Wiradjuri people at a series of Nation meetings for amending, endorsement and implementation. When it came to electing a MLDRIN delegate in 2004, the Wiradjuri were able to take time out from a meeting in Wagga Wagga that had been organised by the Murray–Darling Basin Commission as part of their consultation processes with Indigenous communities.

Another important forum for the election of MLDRIN delegates has been the meetings of the former North-West Clans Group in Victoria. The North-West Clans was a coalition of traditional owner groups—the Dhudoroa, DjaDjaRung, Wergaia, Wadi Wadi, Latji Latji, Wamba Wamba and Barapa Barapa—as organised within a Victorian government cultural heritage administration region. The Barapa Barapa and the Wadi Wadi selected their delegates through the North-West Clans heritage group meetings. In 2006, the passage of Victorian cultural heritage legislation disbanded this administration region, and cultural heritage is now administered differently. The Barapa Barapa have since become incorporated and will now select their delegate out of this legal entity. The Wadi Wadi will probably select their delegate through their native title meeting.

The two MLDRIN delegates for the Wamba Wamba represent the two geographic population centres of Wamba Wamba descendents—Deniliquin (in New South Wales) and Swan Hill (in Victoria). The Swan Hill Wamba Wamba delegation was originally selected at the meetings of the North-West Clans Group, and is now selected at their native title meetings in Victoria. The delegate from Deniliquin is selected through a process held between the Yarkuwa Indigenous Knowledge Centre and the Deniliquin Local Aboriginal Land Council. Yarkuwa is a traditional owner-based group that records genealogies and offers cultural services. The land council is a government legislative body whose membership is based on residence. However, because of the profile of the resident Indigenous population, approximately 95 per cent of this membership are Wamba Wamba. Together these organisations select a MLDRIN delegate, who is then endorsed at a land council meeting by the traditional owners. Deniliquin land council has an internal protocol that only traditional owners within their boundaries can make decisions on Nation matters.

The Yorta Yorta have formalised their governance structures through the process of incorporating under federal legislation as the Yorta Yorta Nation Aboriginal Corporation. This corporation is charged with advancing Yorta Yorta self-determination, which includes holding and managing Yorta Yorta rights and interests in trust. Yorta Yorta governance is established on genealogical connection to country, and is centred on 16 Yorta Yorta families. The 16 families elect a Council of Elders and a governing committee. The MLDRIN delegates are selected by this Council of Elders.

The Mutti Mutti have recently become incorporated as the Mutti Mutti Aboriginal Corporation, under a genealogical model similar to Yarkuwa, and will select their delegate through that corporation. Previously, their MLDRIN delegates were selected during Nation meetings, which were supported by the New South Wales Department of Natural Resources and MLDRIN. The Taungurung, the newest Nation member of MLDRIN, are already incorporated as the Taungurung Clans Aboriginal Corporation. Their MLDRIN delegates are selected at the annual general meetings of this Corporation.

Native title meetings also provide an opportunity to elect MLDRIN delegates. Both the Wergaia and the Latji Latji elect their delegates at their native title meetings. However, native title claims are not always organised along the lines of a match between traditional owners and their country, and are thus not as representative of the traditional owner group as they might be. As discussed earlier, some of the traditional owners have lodged 'single-state claims'. The Wamba Wamba have two election processes for their delegates to ensure broader representation. Native title has also influenced the Ngarrindjeri delegation from South Australia. In 2003 the Ngarrindjeri split their native title claim and the northern half of the claim became a separate body, which includes the Riverland peoples made up of Ngarrindjeri, Latji Latji and Mauraura claimants. In early MLDRIN meetings the Ngarrindjeri had four delegates to cover the north and south of their traditional country. The MLDRIN delegation currently comes from the southern part of Ngarrindjeri country, selected through their Ngarrindjeri Heritage Committee and Native Title Committee meetings.

The election processes of the delegates engage with issues of scale and identity, geography, logistics, interactions with existing Indigenous organisations, and the transformation of traditional owner identities since colonisation. One of the tools that MLDRIN has embraced to manage these complexities is the process of becoming incorporated. However, incorporation creates another layer of complexity, and is changing the way decision making is occurring within the Nations.

Incorporation, governance, and certainty

We have already shown how the MLDRIN alliance is influenced by the common law creation that is native title, and how it operates within the broader intercultural context of south east Australia. Within this context, MLDRIN is influenced by government requirements for Indigenous people to have organisational and legal structures that will create more security in transactions (Mantziaris and Martin 2000: 100–1).

Becoming an incorporated body under government legislation is now a common example of how Indigenous organisations adopt western administration structures to improve their engagement with government. This governance mechanism, which draws on the values and practices of the general Australian society, helps the Indigenous organisation to strategically engage with broader Australian institutions (Martin 2003: 9). The formation of western-style organisations to represent Indigenous peoples' interests has also become meaningful to Indigenous peoples as part of their experiences of living within intercultural Australia.

More than just engagement, the formalisation of organisational structures and the creation of a legal body through incorporation has become critical to how Indigenous peoples' rights are being recognised by governments. As Tim Rowse observes, group rights for Indigenous people are evolving in a piecemeal fashion as 'a series of loosely integrated organisational projects' (2002: 179). Rowse writes that, 'in practical terms, the collective subject of these rights is neither "the Indigenous people" nor "the Indigenous population", but the organised instances of their mobilisation' (2002: 179). The governance structure of MLDRIN needs to have the confidence of government if the Nations are to have their rights recognised and to exercise those rights, and going through the process of incorporation is part of achieving that confidence. Since becoming incorporated, the MLDRIN delegates have been able to have more substantive negotiations with State governments about the recognition of an Indigenous water allocation.

Native title is part of this trend. One of the reasons why the delegates have incorporated MLDRIN is to facilitate the type of agreement making between governments and traditional owner groups made possible by the influential policy changes wrought by native title. Since Mabo, governments across Australia have become familiar with making agreements with traditional owners who are asserting a collective identity and collective rights. Incorporated bodies have been designed by government as a part of this agreement making context. Under the NTA, native title groups are compulsorily required to become incorporated to hold their collective rights and to facilitate legal transactions with government and development proponents.

However, the mobilisation of traditional owner groups through organisational structures and incorporation raises concerns about the 'juridification' of what were previously informal decision making structures. Juridification is a trend in western legal systems to transform previously non-legal social relations into legal obligations (Mantziaris and Martin 2000: 127). While juridification does not necessarily have negative social consequences, for traditional owners the process of becoming incorporated does run the risk of supplanting their informally held decision making structures. Bureaucratic corporate practices such as annual general meetings, quorums, voting by proxy, the need to keep a register of members, and such like, are assumed to be a culturally neutral administrative regime, but they impose strong western cultural values which have consequences for how decisions are made (Sullivan 1996: 19–20).

One of the main concerns about incorporation is that it will narrow the group of people making decisions within the Nation. For MLDRIN, the incorporated body is the most efficient way to engage with the Nation, but there can be something important lost in this efficiency: the involvement of the Elders and the broader Nation group. The people who like going to meetings and are happy, or comfortable, with corporate structures, will likely be the people who have the most involvement in this mobilisation of traditional owner groups through legal entities. If the Nation is represented by very narrow interests only, the informed consent of the Nation group will be undermined, which then also undermines the legitimacy of MLDRIN.

MLDRIN is actively encouraging the incorporation of the unincorporated traditional owner groups within the alliance as a calculated risk. While incorporation may supplant their informal decision making processes, informal decision making structures are already supplanted when government consultation with traditional owners takes place through incorporated bodies which are not formed by traditional owners (such as some land councils and cultural heritage cooperatives). Several traditional owner groups within the MLDRIN alliance have already incorporated to address this problem with representation, as well as to pursue their own aspirations which require a contractual relationship with government. What is critical to ensuring informed consent is that robust relationships are established between the incorporated body and the informal political structures of the Nation (Martin 2005: 197).

Another risk of the incorporation process is the further consolidation of the traditional owner identity. The traditional owners have to create the organisational stability required by government, because the traditional owners are dependent on the government to accommodate their rights within the nation state (Tully 2004 [1995]: 165). However, there are complex issues of identity and scale for each traditional owner group. There is an instability that results from this difficult project of fixing dynamic and multi-layered relationships between people and their country. As this process of consolidation has been designed as fundamental to the governance structure of the MLDRIN alliance, the concomitant instability may hamper the realisation of the delegates' aspirations for MLDRIN. The MLDRIN alliance is going through processes of change and amendment as the delegates and the Nations determine how best to represent and organise themselves. Indeed, rather than expecting MLDRIN to achieve a design endpoint, these processes of change are a part of the exercising of their political authority.

The relationship between traditional owners and their country is a broad intellectual and spiritual framework that informs traditional owners where their responsibilities lie in relation to their neighbours. Country and identities move over time and shift as populations move and shift through marriage, other alliances, or through political manoeuvring. This includes the experience of colonisation, such as the location of towns, mission lands, and roads. Movements and shifts will always continue, because relationships between groups, and between groups and their country, are dynamic, living relationships. This dynamism complicates the organisation of structures that seek to fix and determine relationships between traditional owners and their country.

The shifts in identity that occur and continue to occur reflect the complexities and politics of identity formation. Such shifts can be manipulated to undermine the legitimacy of the MLDRIN alliance if the government expects a traditional owner identity that is more fixed and bounded than it is in reality. Because of the persistence of porous boundaries in both traditional and contemporary times, the people–language–country identity which is being consolidated in the south east will always struggle to keep within that definition.

Conclusion

Rather than populating organisations that are created for them by government, the MLDRIN traditional owners have come up with their own organisational approach. By organising themselves along the lines of traditional authority, they are seeking to consolidate their political identity, and build their governance capacity to take care of their Nation and country. The traditional owners are determining a form of engagement with government that is more meaningful to them, and thus potentially more resilient.

However, the rhetoric of a distinct and separate traditional authority is problematic and can expose the alliance to criticism. Native title has a problematic influence in this regard. Instead of fostering a more sophisticated understanding of Indigenous identity, the influence of native title has been to generate a lot of tension over the understanding of 'tradition', and has sought to fix Indigenous peoples' identity. The capacity of MLDRIN to negotiate this complexity and make agreements with government, reflects the capacity and power of the Nations to assert their rights in their own way, rather than through native title claims.

Acknowledgments

The authors acknowledge the support of the MLDRIN delegates in the preparation of this paper. Jessica Weir has a research agreement with MLDRIN, and has been attending MLDRIN meetings since mid 2003. Steven Ross is the MLDRIN co-ordinator. The authors thank Frances Morphy and Benjamin Smith for organising the workshop which has lead to the creation of this paper. The authors take full responsibility for the content of this paper, including any errors or omissions.

References

Atkinson, H. 2004. 'Yorta Yorta Co-operative Land Management Agreement: impact on the Yorta Yorta nation', *Indigenous Law Bulletin*, 6 (9): 23–5.

Blackburn, K. 2002. 'Mapping Aboriginal nations: the "nation" concept of late nineteenth century anthropologists in Australia', *Aboriginal History*, 26: 131–58.

Brennan, S., Behrendt, L., Strelein, L. and Williams, G. 2005. *Treaty*, The Federation Press, Sydney.

Davies, J. 1995. 'The uncertainty of the political', in P. Sutton (ed.), *Country: Aboriginal Boundaries and Land Ownership in Australia*, Aboriginal History Monograph 3, Aboriginal History, Canberra.

Forward NRM, and Arrilla-Aboriginal Training & Development 2003. *Scoping Study on Indigenous Involvement in Natural Resource Management Decision Making and the Integration of Indigenous Cultural Heritage Considerations into Relevant Murray-Darling Basin Commission Programs*, Murray–Darling Basin Commission, Canberra.

Hercus, L. 1992. *Wemba Wemba Dictionary,* Luise A. Hercus, Canberra.

Mantziaris, C. and Martin, D. 2000. *Native Title Corporations: A Legal and Anthropological Analysis,* The Federation Press, Sydney.

Martin, D. 2003. 'Rethinking the design of indigenous organisations: the need for strategic engagement', *CAEPR Discussion Paper No. 248*, Centre for Aboriginal Economic Policy Research, The Australian National University, Canberra.

Martin, D. 2005. 'Governance, cultural appropriateness and accountability', in D. Austin-Broos and G. Macdonald (eds), *Culture, Economy and Governance in Aboriginal Australia*, Sydney University Press, Sydney.

Merlan, F. 2005. 'Explorations towards intercultural accounts of socio-cultural reproduction and change', *Oceania*, 75 (3): 167–82.

Morgan, M., Strelein, L. and Weir, J. 2006. 'Authority, knowledge and values: Indigenous Nations engagement in the management of natural resources in the Murray–Darling Basin', in M. Langton, O. Mazel, L. Palmer, K. Shain and M. Tehan (eds), *Settling with Indigenous Peoples*, The Federation Press, Sydney.

Murray–Darling Basin Ministerial Council 2001. *Integrated Catchment Management in the Murray–Darling Basin 2001–2010: Delivering a Sustainable Future*, Murray-Darling Basin Ministerial Council, Canberra.

Rowse, T. 2002. *Indigenous Futures: Choice and Development for Aboriginal and Islander Australia*, University of New South Wales Press, Sydney.

Smith, B. R. 2003, 'Whither "certainty"? Coexistence, change and land rights in northern Queensland', *Anthropological Forum*, 13 (1): 27–48.

Smith, B. R. 2005. 'Culture, change and the ambiguous resonance of tradition in Central Cape York Peninsula', in L. Taylor, G. K. Ward, G. Henderson, R. Davis and L. A. Wallis (eds), *The Power of Knowledge, The Resonance of Tradition*, Aboriginal Studies Press, Canberra.

Strelein, L. 1999. 'Extinguishment and the nature of native title: *Fejo v Northern Territory*', *Land, Rights, Laws: Issues of Native Title*, 27 (February): 1–8.

Strelein, L. 2001. 'Conceptualising native title', *The Sydney Law Review*, 23 (1): 95–124.

Sullivan, P. 1996. *All Free Man Now: Culture, Community and Politics in the Kimberley Region, North-Western Australia*, Report Series, Australian Institute of Aboriginal and Torres Strait Islander Studies, Canberra.

Sutton, P. 1995. *Country: Aboriginal Boundaries and Land Ownership in Australia*, Aboriginal History, Canberra.

Tully, J. 2004 [1995]. *Strange Multiplicity: Constitutionalism in an Age of Diversity*, Cambridge University Press, Cambridge.

Weiner, J. F. 2003. '*The Law of the Land*: a review article', *The Australian Journal of Anthropology*, 14 (1): 97–110.

11. The limits of recognition

Manuhuia Barcham

The last 20 years have seen the indigenous peoples of Australia and New Zealand receive unprecedented levels of recognition. This process has involved the recognition of both their position as the indigenous peoples of these two countries and of the various historical injustices that had been visited upon them over the last 200 years. This recognition has in part been based on a desire to bring about justice for these indigenous peoples. This process has taken a number of different forms including the creation of the native title process in Australia and initiation of the Treaty settlement process in New Zealand. However, while these processes have led to a number of positive outcomes they have also opened up the opportunity for the emergence of new kinds of injustice. This chapter explores this phenomenon through the lens of the original Yorta Yorta ruling in 1998 and the fisheries settlement in New Zealand. Focusing on these two cases the chapter demonstrates the current limits of recognition of these two processes—limits based upon an inability to deal adequately with the issue of cultural change over time. In order to overcome these new problems of injustice we need to approach the issue of cultural change over time more seriously, and not necessarily equate change with a loss of identity or authenticity.

The recognition of recognition

In many respects the last 20 years has seen the issue of recognition become one of the pivotal concepts in social, political and legal theory in the Anglo-American world.[1] Indeed Nancy Fraser has gone so far as to claim that in the 1990s the politics of recognition replaced the politics of redistribution (Fraser 1995). Moreover, this shift in theoretical circles from a politics of redistribution to a politics of recognition was accompanied by a broader shift in public policy in a number of these Anglo-American countries. The 1990s were thus marked by a shift in New Zealand and Australia in their legislative and public policy frameworks towards the recognition of the special character of their indigenous peoples and towards the recognition that injustices had been committed against those peoples. In both countries these acts of recognition were explicitly linked to issues of justice.[2] More specifically these acts of recognition were concerned with overcoming issues of historical injustice and their ongoing negative consequences.

---

[1] There is a large and growing body of work on the issue of recognition in the social and political theory literature. For prominent examples of this literature see Taylor (1992) and more recently Fraser and Honneth (2003).
[2] So, for example, in the Australian case see *Mabo v Queensland (No. 2)* [1992] 175 CLR 1 at 29.

In New Zealand these processes were based on a growing recognition of the legitimacy of the Treaty of Waitangi while in Australia these processes flowed on from the recognition, in the Mabo case, that Australia was not *terra nullius* in 1788 at the imposition of British sovereignty. In New Zealand and Australia practical steps flowing on from this act of recognition led to, amongst other things, the creation of the Treaty settlement process and the native title process respectively. It is to an analysis of these two processes that we now turn.

Justice from recognition

Various Māori protest movements and successful court cases brought by Māori groups against the Crown in the late 20th century led to the emergence of increasing recognition by the state (through the introduction of a number of key pieces of legislation) that Māori filled a special place in New Zealand society as *tāngata whenua* (people of the land—that is, the indigenous people of New Zealand). In practice this recognition led to two main outcomes. The first was the emergence of the belief that wrongs committed against various Māori groups in the century and a half following the signing of the Treaty of Waitangi required restitution.[3] One of the key aspects of this recognition was the creation of the Waitangi Tribunal—a quasi-judicial body. The Tribunal's main function is to conduct inquiries and make recommendations on the basis of those inquiries for issues relating to breaches of the Treaty of Waitangi.[4] This then was the birth of the Treaty settlement process. The second outcome of this recognition, flowing on from the first, was that government policy and legislation increasingly came to contain specific reference to Māori and Māori groups. The last decades of the 20th century thus saw a dramatic sea-change in government's attitude to Māori that was predicated on the recognition of the continuing force of the Treaty of Waitangi and the subsequent recognition of the special status of Māori in New Zealand society. While these two processes were inter-related, I will focus in this chapter more on the issues which have flowed from the Treaty settlement process although some discussion of the broader social policy framework within which these events occurred will also be necessary.

Throughout the 1980s and 1990s the Waitangi Tribunal was kept busy with processing increasing numbers of claims. These claims spanned a wide number of issues stretching from the return of confiscated lands through to the challenging of government legislation concerning the sale and privatisation of

---

[3] The initial *Treaty of Waitangi Act 1975* allowed claims to be considered only for acts after the passage of this piece of legislation. However, the passage a decade later of the *Treaty of Waitangi Amendment Act 1985* meant that claims were able to be considered dating back to the signing of the Treaty of Waitangi in 1840.
[4] It should be noted that the findings of the Tribunal are only recommendations and have no binding force in law.

government assets.⁵ By the mid-1990s not only had a large number of claims been successfully processed, but sizeable quantities of money and resources had also begun to be transferred back to claimants as the New Zealand government began to act on the findings of the Waitangi Tribunal. The Ngāi Tahu and Tainui claims have been the largest and most prominent of these settlements to date. Both claims involved cash settlements approaching NZ$200 million as well as the direct transfer of other resources such as land and an apology by the government for past wrongs committed. The operation of the Treaty settlement process over the last 20 years has thus seen the New Zealand government actively addressing past injustices through a process of recognition.

Paralleling the rise of the Treaty settlement process in New Zealand, the *Mabo v Queensland* (No 2) 1992 High Court decision in Australia established that Australian common law recognised the existence of native title. This recognition was put into practical effect with the passage of the *Native Title Act 1993* (Cwlth). The recognition of native title was hailed as a great move forward in addressing the injustices of Australia's colonial past. Referring to the principle of *terra nullius* in the Mabo (No 2) decision Justice Brennan argued that 'judged by any civilised standard, such a law is unjust and its claim to be part of the common law to be applied in contemporary Australia must be questioned.'⁶ And, by the late 1990s, a number of positive native title determinations had been made, thereby helping to provide justice for those Aboriginal groups which had so long been denied title to their traditional lands. However, despite these initial successes in both New Zealand and Australia, trouble loomed on the horizon as the limits of the recognition offered in Australia and New Zealand to their respective indigenous peoples became clear.

The limits of recognition

In New Zealand, the first signs of trouble in the recognition process flowed from a 1992 government decision whereby Māori, in relinquishing their claims to fishing rights as recognised under earlier fisheries legislation, received NZ$150 million of commercial fisheries assets and 20 per cent of all future fisheries allocations.⁷ In determining how these assets were to be distributed the Waitangi Fisheries Commission looked to *iwi* as the 'natural' recipients of these resources as it was thought that since the settlement was in exchange for fishing rights that had previously belonged to *iwi* then the settlement could only go to *iwi* (Barcham 2000: 145).

---

⁵ It should be noted that these claims were not all necessarily being lodged by traditional (or neo-traditional) Māori organisations. Indeed, the claim against the privatisation of government assets without prior Māori consultation (where Māori interests would have been affected by the sale) was brought against the government of the day by the New Zealand Māori Council—a modern non-tribal organisation which was itself a product of earlier government legislation.
⁶ *Mabo v Queensland (No. 2)* [1992] 175 CLR at 29.
⁷ In this following section I draw upon Barcham (2000).

This determination was based around the generally held belief that traditionally Māori society had been organised along a framework of kin-based descent groups centred around three main units: *whānau* (immediate and extended family), *hapū* (clan), and *iwi* (confederation of *hapū*). When *rangatira* (chiefs) had signed the Treaty of Waitangi in 1840, they had signed in their capacity as leaders of *hapū* and *iwi*. The problem, in terms of the Fisheries settlement, flowed from the fact by the 1990s more than 80 per cent of Māori lived in urban areas and for many of these individuals *iwi* and *hapū* were no longer seen as being the sole focal point of their identity as Māori (Maaka, 1997: 7).[8] Nonetheless Māori in the urban environment still continued to identify as Māori. Thus while the Fisheries Commission looked to *iwi* as the most 'authentic' recipients of this settlement the extent to which this ideal matched the empirical reality was suspect. And so given the *iwi*-centric focus of both many Māori and New Zealand government departments in the 1990s, while no-one argued that Māori living in an urban environment were not entitled to receive these entitlements, both the Waitangi Fisheries Commission and *iwi* themselves argued that urban Māori should receive these entitlements through *iwi*. However, groups representing urban Māori, such as the Manukau Urban Māori Authority (MUMA) and Te Whānau o Waipareira Trust, argued that all Māori possessed rights to this particular settlement and they should be entitled to claim them through whatever organisational structure they wished—be it *iwi* or a more modern structure such as MUMA.

The last years of the 1990s and first years of the new millennium were thus marked by a number of acrimonious court battles between representatives of *iwi* groups and representatives of urban Māori groups as they argued over who was entitled to a share of the cash and assets from the fisheries settlement. The underlying argument was whether or not an *iwi* could be identified as 'a people' or only as a specific 'traditional' organisational structure. The problem was, however, that even the modern *iwi* structures of the late 20th and early 21st centuries were themselves relatively recent neo-traditional corporate constructs which had emerged in response to the changing government policy environment of the last two decades of the 20th century.[9] And so, although these *iwi* were seen by government as being the legitimate successors of the *iwi* of the nineteenth century they were not identical with those first *iwi*.

---

[8] In 1936, 81 per cent of the Māori population lived in their tribal areas, which more often than not were rural. Another problem with the decision to transfer these resources to *iwi* is that, as Angela Ballara has convincingly shown (1998), the idea that *iwi* were the main organisational form of Māori society appears to be a belief that emerged in the late 19th century. In a sense *hapū* dropped out of the equation—although recent battles over resources (once again concerning the Fisheries settlement) have seen the relationship between *hapū* and *iwi* come to the fore.

[9] For a more detailed discussion of these processes see Barcham (1998: 305–6).

In these court battles we see how the justice brought about by the recognition of Māori claims was in turn leading to new and different forms of injustice. Māori were being denied access to settlements *unless* they chose to access those settlements through *iwi* structures. No recognition was made of the fact that historical circumstance had meant that many Māori no longer either saw *iwi* as their major source of identity or necessarily wanted to utilise these structures in their modern lives. And for some Māori in the urban environment the shift to the city (sometimes as much as four or five generations ago) meant that even if they had wanted to identify with an *iwi* they were no longer able to do so as they did not even know to which *iwi* their family belonged, although this did not in any way lessen their identity as Māori. The injustice therefore emerged from the inability of then current legal and policy frameworks to take seriously the changes that occurred in Māori society since the signing of the Treaty of Waitangi.

Similar problems have occurred in the Australian case. One of the key aspects of any determination of native title is the demonstration of an ongoing and unbroken normative existence of an Indigenous Australian community through the continued existence and practice of their lore and custom. For many groups this involves demonstrating that they reach a threshold of 'cultural authenticity' in terms of their continued normative existence as a group. While native title determinations for groups such as Martutjarra or the Spinifex People are relatively unproblematic in terms of passing this threshold of cultural authenticity, the Yorta Yorta case has shown that this is not the case for all Aboriginal communities.

In order to establish native title a claimant group has to fulfil three requirements. These conditions of recognition are that the claimant group: establish that they are the descendants from the original inhabitants of the territory in question; show their continued occupation of the land; and demonstrate the continued maintenance of their law and custom. In his original ruling on the Yorta Yorta case, Olney J argued that the Yorta Yorta people did not possess native title as:

> the facts in this case lead inevitably to the conclusion that before the end of the 19th century the ancestors through whom the claimants claim title had ceased to occupy their traditional lands in accordance with their traditional laws and customs ... [As such,] the foundation of the claim to native title in relation to the land previously occupied by those ancestors having disappeared, the native title rights and interests previously enjoyed are not capable of revival.[10]

---

[10] *The members of the Yorta Yorta Aboriginal Community v The State of Victoria & Ors* [1998] 1606 FCA (18 December 1998) s. 129.

In reaching this decision Olney J based his argument on his belief that 'the tide of history has indeed washed away any real acknowledgment of their traditional laws and any real observance [by Yorta Yorta] of their traditional customs.'[11]

A number of points are to be noted in regards to this judgement. First, in coming to this conclusion, Olney J placed much more weight on the written evidence of the pastoralist E. M. Curr than he did on the oral evidence of Yorta Yorta individuals.[12] In doing this, apart from devaluing the importance of evidence from non-written sources, he explicitly argued that the cultural practices of the Yorta Yorta people of today (no matter how laudatory they were) did not match those of their ancestors as recorded in the Curr's writings.[13]

The key point to be noted here is that Olney was basing his decision on the belief that a group's present-day customs and laws needed to match those practiced by their ancestors at the imposition of British sovereignty (or at the least be strongly aligned—if not identical—with those recorded in the earliest written records) if native title was to be retained. That is, given the evidential weight that Olney J gave to the writings of E. M. Curr over the oral testimony of the current day descendants of the Yorta Yorta people, if native title by a group such as Yorta Yorta is to be achieved it now appears 'that contemporary observances [of their customs] must match the accounts we have of them in nineteenth century European documents' (Buchan 2002: s.12).

Effectively Olney J has argued that legal recognition of native title is dependent on the existence of an authentic form of Aboriginal culture; that is, an Aboriginal culture unchanged by contact with the west. In simple terms, he has argued that cultural change for Aboriginal groups extinguishes their native title. On one reading of the law—indeed this is how Olney read the precedents set by the case and statue law in the matter of native title—this may actually be the case, although this would involve a very strict and limited reading of the law. As I will argue later this narrow reading of the law is problematic in a number of ways.

However, even with a charitable reading of the decision, one would be hard pressed to understand Olney's claim in the Yorta Yorta case that 'no group or individual has been shown to occupy any part of the land in the sense that the original inhabitants can be said to have occupied it'[14] except in reference to a romanticised image of how Aboriginal Australians ought to live. In making this

---

[11] *The members of the Yorta Yorta Aboriginal Community v The State of Victoria & Ors* [1998] 1606 FCA (18 December 1998) s. 129.
[12] *The members of the Yorta Yorta Aboriginal Community v The State of Victoria & Ors* [1998] 1606 FCA (18 December 1998) S. 106.
[13] *The members of the Yorta Yorta Aboriginal Community v The State of Victoria & Ors* [1998] 1606 FCA (18 December 1998) s. 123.
[14] *The members of the Yorta Yorta Aboriginal Community v The State of Victoria & Ors* [1998] 1606 FCA (18 December 1998) s. 121.

claim Olney J has effectively argued that to change the content of a group's law and customs is to change that group's identity. While this *may* be true, this is not always necessarily the case. While Yorta Yorta no longer practice all the various customs practised by their ancestors it does not necessarily mean that they identify *any less* as Yorta Yorta. Indeed, the counter-factual argument would not necessarily hold given that even if colonisation had not occurred, an environmental disaster may have caused just as radical a change in Yorta Yorta customs and law.

In making his decision in the Yorta Yorta case Olney J has raised the evidential 'bar' such that the majority of Aboriginal groups of eastern and southern Australia may never be able to achieve native title.[15] In the Yorta Yorta case the quest for native title for some Australian Aboriginal groups is now dependent upon them matching an impossible standard of authentic traditional culture.

What we see emerging as a result of the Yorta Yorta case (and subsequent appeals) is a similar dynamic to that observed in New Zealand where an initial act of recognition has led to some instances of injustice. The key point from which this injustice flows is the inability of legal and policy frameworks to adequately deal with cultural change over time. That is, recognition within these frameworks appears to be dependent upon the maintenance of a fixed identity. In the Australian case this injustice means that some Aboriginal groups (such as Yorta Yorta) are, through the denial of the recognition of *their* native title rights, in a sense being denied their existence as authentic Aboriginal groups. Indeed, a Yorta Yorta woman Monica Morgan has recently gone so far as to say that the Yorta Yorta decision represents a form of bureaucratic genocide of her people (Morgan 2002: 4).

Recognising change

The key problem, as noted above, with the types of recognition of indigenous populations that have been achieved in Australia and New Zealand (and have formed the basis of the native title and Treaty settlement processes in these countries) is that these acts of recognition have been based on the maintenance of a prior identity by the group being recognised. This is problematic in a number of ways—most pressing being the inability for these strategies of recognition to adequately deal with the concept of change. As it stands the current frameworks mean that the content of the identity of the group being recognised must remain identical to that of the original group from which recognition flows if the current group's identity is to be recognised. As the Yorta Yorta case shows, deviation from an 'original' content is seen as reducing the authenticity of that identity and so too is seen as reducing the authenticity and legitimacy of their claim to recognition based on that identity.

---

[15] See Lavery (2003).

However, as has been briefly discussed above, this degree of the maintenance of a group's identity is something that has not been achieved even by groups generally seen by many as being extremely 'authentic'. Thus while modern *iwi* in New Zealand can, in many cases, be seen as the legitimate successors of the *iwi* of 19th century New Zealand, they are not identical with them. If anything, many of the modern corporate *iwi* structures in New Zealand more closely resemble a Western corporation than they do the descent groups of the past. Similarly the customs and lore followed by groups such as the Spinifex People who have achieved positive native title determinations are not identical to those of their ancestors. If this were the case then one would be hard pressed to understand the existence of particular lore and custom including cat dreaming (Cane 2002: 84). The problem thus appears not to lie in recognising change over time (for groups which have been recognised *have indeed* changed over time) but rather in terms of the extent of change undergone by the group in question.

Dealing with change over time

Different groups' cultures have adapted and changed (and continue to do so) dependent upon the environment within which they operate.[16] Groups in the south east of Australia have had to accommodate higher degrees of contextual change than those groups who, for instance, live in the Western Desert. Contact with Europe and the wider world has meant that all indigenous groups in Australia and New Zealand (and elsewhere too one would imagine) have had to change the way in which they relate not only to the world but also to one another. This change in content does not, however, necessarily lead to a change in identity.[17] And so, while the customs and laws of 21st century English men and women do not match the customs of their 19th century predecessors this change in no way lessens the 'authenticity' of 21st century English men and women's identity as English.

However, in the Australian case this issue seems to stem, in part at least, from a particular approach to the issue of native title by some sections of the legal establishment. As discussed briefly above Olney's approach to the recognition of native title was dependent upon the existence of an authentic form of aboriginal culture—an argument which can be seen to flow from the original Mabo ruling which argued that 'native title has its origins in and is given its content by the traditional laws acknowledged by and the traditional customs observed by the indigenous inhabitants of a territory.'[18] However, this original argument in no way negates the possibility that cultures, and so too a society's

---

[16] Indeed we could quite easily make the claim that change, in terms of adaptation to a changing external environment (be it physical or symbolic), is an inherent characteristic of culture.
[17] This is not to say that change in content does not lead to change in identity. It is rather to make the different claim that this is not necessarily the case.
[18] Mabo decision 1992, 42.

lore, norms and traditions, can change over time. Olney's reading of the law was thus *only one possible reading*, a reading that focused on the equivalence of the customs of the present day descendants of the original native title holders with the customs of these original native title holders. In the Yorta Yorta case Olney J thus based his decision on the belief that 'the traditions and customs observed by Curr were said to constitute the title that burdened the Crown and it seems that only through continued observance of these particular customs would the title survive' (Strelein nd: 2). However, as Lisa Strelein has argued 'the radical title of the Crown at the time of the acquisition of sovereignty was burdened not by the native title rights and interests then existing, but was burdened by the fact of the existence of native title' (Strelein 2005: 69). And so, in the Australian case at least, problems associated with the inability of the native title process to adequately deal with questions of change stem not from the law itself but rather from its interpretation.

The New Zealand Māori case is slightly more complicated in that the identity in question—that of Māori (as opposed to descent groups such as *hapū* and *iwi*) is itself an artefact of contact between Māori and early European explorers.[19] However, as I have noted elsewhere, many influential Māori leaders see no necessary contradiction between the fact that while the Treaty of Waitangi may have been signed with the representatives of *hapū* and *iwi* it is urban Māori authorities that should receive some of the benefits of Treaty settlements (Barcham 1998: 308). In some respects the signing of the Treaty of Waitangi froze Māori society (at least in terms of the territorial bounds of *hapū* and *iwi*) at 1840. If the Treaty had been signed 10 years earlier or later then the Treaty settlement process would look considerably different as those 20 years saw the fortunes of a number of *hapū* and *iwi* wax and wane quite considerably. However, despite this freezing process Māori society has continued to alter and change—the problem is that legislative frameworks have sometimes not taken this change into account.

Taking change seriously

What is required in New Zealand and Australia given the new forms of injustice that appear to be emerging from processes designed explicitly to bring about justice and right historical injustices, is that the process of change needs to be taken seriously. The problem is that the concept of change is a particularly difficult issue to accommodate in any legislative or policy framework as it necessarily entails a degree of uncertainty—and uncertainty is something of which bureaucratic and legal modes of organisation are not too fond. However,

---

[19] In pre-European contact New Zealand, groups identifies themselves in terms of the descent groups to which they belonged. Māori (a verb used to describe a state of normalcy) as a term of identity was used by New Zealand's indigenous inhabitants so as to differentiate themselves from the early European explorers (who by any standards would have seemed most abnormal to these original inhabitants).

just because particular frameworks do not easily adapt to change (the irony of this is clear) this does not mean that they cannot adapt. The Ward decision is a case in point of how change can be accommodated within a juridical framework.[20]

In their decision the Justices argued that in order to be traditional (as required under s. 223(1)(a) of the *Native Title Act*) the body of customs and law currently observed must originate and be given their content from the body of law and customs observed by the ancestors of the claimants. Now in making this claim the Justices acknowledged that some change or adaptation of law and custom over time would not necessarily be fatal to a native title claim. The problem, however, lay in assessing the degree and extent of change necessary for this change to be fatal to a native title claim. And so, as I noted above, the problem is not so much one of kind as it is one of degree.

To some extent then the issues I have discussed in this chapter are still to be overcome. However, precedents like the Ward case (in Australia at least) have opened up the space of possibility for a more serious engagement with issues of cultural change. The problem is not insurmountable, but overcoming it requires the realisation, by the legal fraternity at least, that issues of syncretism and authenticity are not inversely related. Early cases like the original Yorta Yorta case have unfortunately set a precedent in Australia where syncretism and adaptation are identified with assimilation—where, as has been shown above, this is not necessarily the case. Adaptation and assimilation are not necessarily linked. In New Zealand this link is not as strong as it is in Australia although it is still present. The process of recognition has thus still created an environment in New Zealand where non-traditional forms of Māori organisational form are devalued in the eyes of the courts at least.[21]

In many respects the problem is that people have been following the letter but not the spirit of the law in these processes of recognition.[22] Those involved in these processes of recognition in Australia and New Zealand need to remember why these processes were initially created. They were created to overcome injustice. Given this, one cannot fall back on positivistic arguments as to the separation of moral and legal arguments. The statues under which these processes were established were created for precisely moral reasons and so one must approach one's deliberation of these issues with at least a certain degree of openness in their ethical sensibility rather than allowing one's judgement to be

---

[20] The appropriateness of the 'bundle of rights' approach to native title being set to one side. For more on this see Glaskin (2003).
[21] As noted above though, the 'authenticity' of modern *iwi* is itself a question that needs to be asked if questions of funding are dependent upon the authentic status of groups.
[22] Although, as noted above, in the Australian case at least, there are a number of different ways in which the 'letter of the law' can be followed, some of which need not necessarily lead to new injustices being committed.

clouded by outmoded and outdated 'folk' conceptions of what constitutes cultural change.

Where these processes become most problematic is where people's identity is shaped not by their own desires and will but instead by legislative and juridical processes. Indeed, this is where the worst injustices are being committed. The content of peoples' identities changes over time although this does not necessarily change one's identity. What I mean here, using the Yorta Yorta case as an example, is that while the present day Yorta Yorta people identify as Yorta Yorta they (I would imagine) would readily admit that the various customs and lore which shape and structure their lives as Yorta Yorta are not identical to those which shaped the lives of their Yorta Yorta ancestors yet they nonetheless still see themselves as being Yorta Yorta. Instead it merely changes the way through which their identity is constituted and/or performed. Problems have occurred when this process has been ignored or devalued. This is particularly unfortunate as current legislative frameworks are, as the Ward case as shown, able to deal with processes of change. And, perhaps most sadly, not doing so is leading to injustice for the indigenous peoples of these two countries—the exact thing that these processes of recognition were created to overcome. What we need to do then is approach these cases with an openness to the idea of the legitimacy of change.

Conclusion

In a sense both the native title and Treaty settlement process have been a success. Both processes were created through acts of recognition in order to overcome historical injustice. In this respect both processes have been successful as a number of these cases of historical injustice have been settled—if not overcome. However, the acts of recognition upon which these processes have been based have also led to new sources of injustice. In many respects these new forms of injustice flow from the inability for the issue of cultural change over time to be taken seriously by some engaged in these processes of recognition. What we need to do then is approach these processes of recognition in the spirit with which they were created. To do otherwise is to merely replace one form of injustice with another.

References

Ballara, A. 1998. Iwi: *The Dynamics of Māori Tribal Organisation from c.1769 to c.1945*, Victoria University Press, Wellington.

Barcham, M. 1998. 'The challenge of urban Māori: reconciling conceptions of indigeneity and social change', *Asia Pacific Viewpoint*, 39 (3): 303–14.

Barcham, M. 2000. '(De)constructing the politics of indigeneity', in D. Ivison, P. Patton and W. Sanders (eds), *Political Theory and the Rights of Indigenous Peoples*, Cambridge University Press, Cambridge.

Buchan, B. 2002. 'Withstanding the tide of history: the Yorta Yorta case and indigenous sovereignty', *Borderlands*, 1 (2), (unpaginated), available at <http://www.borderlandsejournal.adelaide.edu.au/vol1no2_2002/buchan_yorta.html>.

Cane, S. 2002. *Pila Nguru: the Spinifex People*, Fremantle Arts Centre Press, Fremantle.

Fraser, N. 1995. 'From redistribution to recognition? Dilemmas of justice in a "post-socialist" Age', *New Left Review*, (July/August): 68–93.

Fraser, N. and Honneth, A. 2003. *Redistribution or Recognition? A Political–Philosophical Exchange*, Verso, London.

Glaskin, K. 2003. 'Native title and the "bundle of rights" model: implications for the recognition of Aboriginal relations to country', *Anthropological Forum*, 13 (1): 67–88.

Lavery, D. 2003. 'A greater sense of tradition: The implications of the normative system principles in Yorta Yorta for native title determination applications', *Murdoch University Electronic Journal of Law*, 10 (4), December (unpaginated), available at <http://www.murdoch.edu.au/elaw/issues/v10n4/lavery104.html>.

Maaka, R. 1997. 'The politics of diaspora', paper presented at the *Treaty of Waitangi: Maori Political Representation Future Challenges* conference, Wellington, New Zealand, 1–2 May 1997.

Morgan, M. 2002. 'The Yorta Yorta experience, paper presented at the *Outcomes and Possibilities Native Title Conference 2002*, Geraldton, Western Australia, 4 September 2002.

Strelein, L. (nd) 'Comment on the High Court decision', available at <http://ntru.aiatsis.gov.au/research/yorta_yorta/yorta_yorta.html> [accessed 15 October 2006].

Strelein, L. 2005. 'Culture and commerce: the use of fishing traditions to prove native title', in L. Taylor, G. Ward, G. Henderson, R. Davies and L. Wallis (eds), *The Power of Knowledge: the Resonance of Tradition*, Aboriginal Studies Press, Canberra.

Taylor, C. 1992. *Multiculturalism and 'the Politics of Recognition'*, Princeton University Press, Princeton.

12. History, oral history, and memoriation in native title

James F. Weiner

In the realm of native title, the distinction between 'traditional' and 'historical' people is one that is given official acknowledgement both by the courts of Australia and by Aboriginal people themselves. In the current guidelines for the production of native title connection reports (at least as construed by the State of Queensland) the anthropologist is required to address him/herself to the contrastive histories of such traditional and historical peoples—those who can demonstrate a connection to country that predates settlement, and those whose connection was established afterwards.

But the terminology here is anthropologically confusing. Would someone with a 'traditional' connection to land not also have a history of occupation of it? And would a 'historical' person have jettisoned any connection to a pre-colonial cultural world just because he/she is living on country other than that to which he/she was traditionally entitled? Anthropologists therefore have for the most part consistently criticised such a distinction. All anthropologists working in such places as the Pilbara, the Gulf country and adjacent Cape York and the eastern Northern Territory, insist that 'historical' relations to country are impossible to disentangle from … from what? What would we call such relations to country that we did not admit had a historical component?

Part of the difficulty in answering this question, or a source of the inability of history and anthropology to achieve an effective synergy, is the current rhetoric of Aboriginality itself. The requirements of the *Native Title Act 1993* (Cwlth), at least since the Yorta Yorta native title hearing in the Federal and High Courts, have obliged Aboriginal claimants to prove that they have retained traditional law and custom in some form. While admitting that such law and custom can undergo change over time, it must remain functionally and structurally recognisable as such. However, Aboriginal claims to the perdurability of the Law, its alleged unchangingness (see Sansom 2006), provide a narrower channel within which the anthropologist and historian can interpret the effects of event upon the structure of Aboriginal practices and world views. (It is hoped, of course, that both would see such attestations as themselves culturally-inflected utterances, generated from within a specific landscape of cultural, social and political positions).

Another difficulty, related to the one above, is that the various State Native Title Services' distinction between 'traditional' and 'historical' reflects in some important way—though with some distortion—the conventional disciplinary separation within Australian anthropology departments between 'traditional' and 'contemporary' Aboriginal society as distinct lecture courses—a regime in which status, approbation and the comfort of carrying out what Kuhn called 'normal science' accrued largely to postgraduates crafting degrees within the former and not the latter. It is hardly surprising that State and Federal legal departments, searching for what anthropologists had to say about Aboriginal society, found many examples from the former and far fewer from the latter.

But perhaps a more serious difficulty is that such a distinction has generated a corresponding professional division of labour between anthropologists and historians, a division of labour now given conventional sanction by the courts for the most part.

In the native title cases I have been involved in over the past few years, I have encountered the following:

1. A consultant historian is engaged to write a 'historical' report on the claim group for which an anthropologist is writing the connection report. The historical report is a compilation of passages gleaned from the State Aboriginal Archives, evidently generated by running a computer search on the names and surnames of the component claimant families.
2. Instead of an 'anthropological' report, an 'oral historian'—with no university qualifications in any discipline—instead produced several hundred pages of unedited interview transcript as 'connection material'.
3. An anthropologist confined him/herself to the elucidation of kinship and social organisational principles and other cultural 'rules', while a professional historian wrote a much longer and more detailed history of occupation of the claim area.

In the Karajarri claim, Geoff Bagshaw's monograph (2003) deals with the cosmogonic, mythological, and ritual foundations of Karajarri connection to country, while anthropologist Sarah Yu evidently authored a separate report dealing with history of occupation and the catalogue of physical activities constitutive of native title that members of the Karajarri claimant group have engaged in and presently engage in (Bagshaw 2003: 35). What is undermined by this strategy is the ability to assess the *historical dimensions* of a symbolically-constituted cosmology. This bifurcation of social science analysis prevents us from considering the cosmological, ritual and mythological domain of the Karajarri as a historically generated adaptation—and hence reinforces all of the negative stereotypes that have been made of anthropologists.

Such a distinction is in social science terms insupportable and factitious. In the first *De Rose* FC case, consider what O'Loughlin J concluded were the principles by which an Aboriginal person asserted the status of *nguraritja*, 'custodian' of a site or area. At 922, he affirmed the anthropologist Craig Elliott's account (at

349) that a person can become *nguraritja* through birth, long-time physical association, ancestral connection or knowledge of the area, and recognition by other *nguraritja*. The Aboriginal witnesses' statements made it clear that the applicants individually made use of one or more of these principles in different combinations to assert their status as *nguraritja*. These ways of achieving the status of *nguraritja* are completely historically constituted—although they occur against the background of cultural principles relating people and sites in general ways, they are contingent upon the particularities of personal sojourns in space and time. *Nguraritja* is *biographically* constituted even as it embodies the primary spiritual relation between person and place. What then is the substantive difference between these historically constituted attachments to place and the ones that other Indigenous people have achieved to various sites and pastoral properties throughout Australia?

In this brief paper, I am drawing attention to two analytic separations that have been engendered by the native title process. One is the contrast between society viewed as a static bundle of structural and normative laws and principles, and society as a historically-constituted community of persons associated both temporally and spatially. This has led to the recognition of distinct anthropological and historical contributions to the demonstration of proof of native title, a distinction that has been more detrimental to anthropology than to history.

The second analytic separation is analogous, in that it has to do with the separation of anthropology and history, but has been wrought by disciplinary competition and revision rather than as an effect of the judicial interpretations of social science boundaries. Separating anthropology's commitment to the structural and structural-functional from its historical dimension leads to an overly particularistic history. Removing the social and cultural from a consideration of the historical production of the subject has allowed history to insert its own version of subjectivity, the self as a node of memoriation, rather than as an inter-subjective, culturally constituted self.

Both of these distinctions are products of the devaluation of the structural and the cultural in Aboriginal anthropology, and both are responses, in different ways, to the dilemma of drawing attention to the phenomenon of 'loss of culture' in many of Australia's Aboriginal communities in settled Australia. The judicial interpretation of native title has forced anthropologists to make judgements on the degree of retention of 'traditional law and custom' among contemporary Aboriginal communities. While some anthropologists may be hesitant to discuss the possibility of loss of culture, it is more difficult to countenance the loss of history or memory, which then becomes the safer academic terrain upon which to confront 20th century Aboriginal continuity.

History vs anthropology

As Geertz suggested, what has helped undermine the difference in subject matter between historians and anthropologists 'has been a change in the ecology of learning that has driven historians and anthropologists, like so many migrant geese, on to one another's territories' (2000: 121). There is nowhere in the world these days (nor I suspect for most of the last 100 years) where an indigenous village or community has been left out of the flow of global events and influences, so that such history becomes at least a necessary prelude to the identification of more conventional anthropological problems.[1] And historians, again for longer than we would care to admit, have known that places like Indonesia, West Africa, and Polynesia have fully their own complement of documentary sources, sources that allow the historian to write about these places in the same way they have written about European ones. 'Culture' is certainly a way of speaking about the varieties of coherence of human social life, but it emerges within a historically construed horizon of time and place, not apart from it.

So, anthropology is and was already a historicised mode of social analysis—social formations unfold through time and therefore proper anthropological inquiry in the field is a process that has to be situated diachronically, that is, across an interval of time. There have been dominant modes of anthropological analysis that have stressed the importance of synchronic analysis (that is, confined to a single moment in time)—for example, structural analysis, structural-functionalism and certain forms of symbolic anthropology. These methodologies illuminate the important aspects of systemicness that are part of all cultural forms. But anthropology also acknowledges that cultures and social systems make themselves visible as temporally-constituted social phenomena.

Human cultures everywhere thus recognise the historical and biographical dimensions of human life. The anthropologist Marshall Sahlins (1981) reminded us that social and cultural structures are reproduced through events, an approach that critiques the methods employed in allocating different historical and anthropological tasks in the connection report process. He went on to suggest that events of major culture contact had the power to more sharply illuminate the structures of society and its reproduction—for all parties to the contact.

But this alone does not make history and anthropology difficult to distinguish today. Even as Sahlins was arguing for a more historicised structural anthropology, anthropology has more recently thoroughly disengaged itself from *any* structuralism, disengaged itself from the notion that *a* culture is (or

---

[1] This perception itself has a very long anthropological life. It was Evans-Pritchard's ground-breaking study of the Sanusi cult of Cyrenaica, that demonstrated, according to Cohn, 'the process by which a lineage-based society developed centralized political roles and institutions' (1968: 442). Cohn (ibid.) termed it a 'model for the study of the process of internal structural change ... under the impact of foreign rule.'

ever was) a coherent and systemic entity that was susceptible to description as formulaic or as rule-governed—a complaint also levelled at anthropology by Sutton (see for example Pannell and Vachon 2001). Whereas Lévi-Strauss once confidently spoke of the 'death of the subject', we have recently seen the subject and subjectivity become the centre of social analysis. Subjectivity has become largely an effect of narrativity, a reflection, perhaps, of the rise of textualism generally as a model for social and psychological life.

If the self is today largely a narrative project, it becomes more closely associated with other textual projects—such as mythopoeia. History and anthropology have become increasingly harder to draw, not because there has been any significant unification of social science theory—although others might wish to argue otherwise—but because, I think, of the increasing acceptance of the project of mythopoeia in western public life. As Faubion (1993: 44) put it: 'If, in the last two decades, history has itself become anthropologically indefinite, that is in part because the lines between the reproduction and invention of tradition, between mnemonics and conjuration, and between myth and *historia*' have grown increasingly less distinguishable. As Faubion (ibid.) suggests, our current attitude towards the Human Condition 'is nostalgist even when at its most futurist and has virtually sacralized history, even if in sacralizing and making an essence of it, it has also done violence to it ...'. In other words, anthropology jettisoned structuralism, and history jettisoned the event; the very conjunctural ground that Sahlins tried to stake out. Having abandoned this ground, the two disciplines found themselves competing over the right to authorise a version of *memoriology*.

History, narrative, ethnohistory

The dangers of memoriology lead me to my final observation on the methodological problems generated by native title for the social sciences. For one of the ways in which contemporary social science has repaired the lack of indigenous voices in conventional history is to embark on a wholesale project of *oral history*. *Oral history* has become the methodological substitute for the almost complete absence of reliable records of the words, theories and analyses of Aboriginal social action at the threshold of colonisation: 'Ethnohistory might address the native reception of events. It made plain that peoples purportedly without history had histories after all. It occasionally found in their oral tradition the glimmer of some crude art of memory' (Faubion 1993: 42).

But Faubion never confused this with the art of *historia*. The contrast that has emerged within native title research in recent years is not so much between the disciplines of history and anthropology—for as I have suggested such was always a factitious opposition within anthropology in the first place—as between the objective validity of the documentary record and claimants' counterposed 'oral history'. 'Oral history' is not an exclusively anthropological methodology, and never was, even though methodologically it was not differentiated from some anthropological modes of questioning. But to call claimants' self-narratives 'oral history' is to conceal the fact that it is not history as such—it is a congealed form of *memoriation*. Much of the 'oral history' I read has been obtained by people who evidently see memory as a form of text and who 'treat memory as a set of documents that happen to be in people's heads rather than in the Public Records Office' (Fentress and Wickham 1992: 2).

From this perspective, memoriation brings a view of history into an already-defined and accepted history of the subject. It commonly becomes a story about how the subject has achieved an identity and subject-position, rather than constitutes a 'history of the person' per se. The sociologist Stuart Hall writes, however, that identities are themselves 'the names we give to the different ways we are positioned by, and position ourselves in, the narratives of the past' (quoted without citation in Huyssen 1995: 1). In other words, identities emerge as an effect of a self located in and acting within a social field, a field which is temporal, spatial and human simultaneously. Aboriginal people's construction of memory and oral history is an identity-building practice, fully culturally constituted. It is not disengaged from other cultural practices, such as that of being a native title claimant, but it is insufficiently accounted for in the current repertoire of 'laws and customs'.

As *social processes themselves*, the human acts of recalling and remembering are selective and interpretational processes and in important methodological respects distinct from the historian's task of constructing an objective account of the past. Historians Christine Choo and Margaret O'Connell thus say: 'Historical narrative goes beyond chronology because it imposes *a discursive form* on the events; transforming the events into a story, it gives meaning to the events by presenting the events, agents and agencies as elements of identifiable story types' (2000: 2; emphasis added). If these stories are subjective in their origin and meaning, then they are contiguous with other social phenomena that constitute the community and are therefore within the domain of anthropological analysis. By the same token, such stories that a community authors for itself are not a preferred alternative to other historical accounts, or to the record of documented events. They themselves are another culturally-constructed gloss on such events and documents, and it is, as both Sahlins and Sutton concur (e.g. Sutton 2003: 19) in the mutually constitutive relation between event and its human apperception that cultural accounts are forged.

But the contrast between 'objective history' and 'oral or ethno-history' is itself a highly political one, and is used to deliberately polarise the Aboriginal and non-Indigenous positions in the national debate on Indigeneity and Indigenous rights. So I return to a consideration of the way the rhetoric of Aboriginal and non-Aboriginal self-makings, and the attempts on both sides to maintain their epistemological divide via appeals to 'tradition' and 'history', have contoured disciplinarity in native title. I make two observations, one about history and the other about culture.

First, the effective contrast is between a previous 'official' colonial history, in which a strong mythographic component is apparent, and a history which seeks, through an appreciation of the course of a total social world, to re-insert previously invisible persons, classes, races and occupants of that colonial world, an approach made famous by E. P. Thompson in his landmark history of the English working class. Anthropologist Jonathan Hill has used the term *ethnogenesis* to describe 'peoples' simultaneously cultural and political struggles to create enduring identities in general contexts of radical change and discontinuity' (1996: 1).[2] Its investigation is founded in 'historical approaches to culture as an ongoing process of conflict and struggle over a people's existence and their positioning within and against a general history of domination' (ibid.).

But a historical anthropology of the conjuncture between indigenous and non-indigenous histories is where a suitably defensible *anthropological* account of connection should start (see for example Merlan 1998). The anthropological sensibility in this approach is admirably expressed by Sutton's forthright assessment of pastoralism as 'the form of colonisation most compatible with the maintenance of traditional Aboriginal connections to land' (2003: 35). Not only did the pastoral industry itself develop a requirement for permanent seasonal Aboriginal labour, Aboriginal forms of subsistence ensured that they remained on properties during the wet season of work lay-off—Sutton thus remarks, 'the viability of the granted leases was in some measure enhanced by, if not dependent on, the maintenance of Aboriginal foraging' (2003: 33). The methodological implications of this observation are also clearly understood by Sutton: 'it is the lawyers' chronologies of official tenure changes, and the anthropologists' diachronic accounts of indigenous laws and customs giving rise to customary rights and interests in land and waters, that form the crucial historical evidence' (2004: 4).

The second point I want to make concerns the restricted field in which we are more or less obliged to locate the evidence for 'the history of connection', and the manner in which we fail to distinguish between discursive and praxical connections to a life world. In settled Australia, 'connection to country' lies chiefly in knowledge of past activities, and it is this knowledge that is transmitted, rather than the repertoire of subsistence skills per se. Further, in settled Australia, much evidence on behalf of native title claims is elicited from informants in their houses, not on country. Anthropologically this produces an attenuated and weakened account of social process, since the interviewer is not

---

[2] Jones and Hill-Burnett (1982, cited in Beckett 1994) used the term 'ethnogenesis' in the Aboriginal Australian context in 1982, defining it as 'the process whereby a "common culture" comes about and the manner by which it is defined'.

observing the *social practice of story-telling and narration among group members*, but is merely subjecting the informant to a series of questions that itself does not derive dialectically from the observation of social action at all, or does so in an extremely artificial and factitious context. Many native title anthropologists consequently become oriented towards what their interlocutors were able to *tell* them and insufficiently attuned to the way they *behave* in a culturally-patterned way. I am not disparaging 'oral history' as such. We can characterise Aboriginal society as an 'orally' rather than 'literarily' based culture—but this should orient us towards a description of *the social practices and behaviours by which they transmit and construct knowledge among themselves by way of speech*,[3] rather than indiscriminately to any utterance an Aboriginal person produces, especially in highly-polarised intercultural encounters among anthropologists, lawyers, NTRB personnel and claimants. It is therefore not simply a question about how much or how little people know, but of obtaining an anthropologically respectable account of how such accounts are transmitted and the role of such transmission in current Aboriginal cultural practice.

Unfortunately, anthropologists and other native title researchers have neither the time nor the resources for the kind of participant-observation—a cornerstone of anthropological methodology—that would lead to a description of the social practice of narrative and oral communication. Paradoxically, although the architects of current native title interpretation insist on the historical verifiability of accounts of connection to country, they have been unable to infer from such a demand the anthropological requirement of observation across and within a temporal interval. Without this temporal dimension, however, we can achieve no real anthropological understanding of how society is constituted normatively, for we are unable to construe the social work of interpretation through which people reconcile human behaviour with its idealised rule-governed portrait. Such integral features of anthropological theory and methodology are so far considerably beyond the capacity of legal practitioners to turn into guidelines for practice. In the meantime, anthropology on behalf of native title will be able to bring only a denatured version of its own analysis to bear on the topic.

---

[3] In settled Australia where the transmission of pre-contact Aboriginal cultural and linguistic practices has been severely impaired by dislocation, removal, migration and other factors, many Aboriginal families rely heavily on existing documentary evidence in order to learn about their predecessors' life histories, their places of habitation, their culture and their language. Collections of such documentary evidence become resources that are invoked, publicly shown, deliberately withheld, tactically alluded to, and so forth, in confrontations between Aborigines and non-Aborigines, and between disputing groups of Aborigines themselves.

References

Bagshaw, G. 2003. The *Karajarri Claim: a Case-Study in Native Title Anthropology*, Oceania Monograph No. 53.

Beckett, J. (ed.) 1994. *Past and Present: the Construction of Aboriginality*, Aboriginal Studies Press, Canberra.

Choo, C. and O'Connell, M. 2000. 'Historical narrative and proof of native title', in *Land, Rights, Laws: Issues in Native Title*, 3 (2), (unpaginated), Native Title Research Unit, Australian Institute of Aboriginal and Torres Strait Islander Studies, Canberra, available as <http://ntru.aiatsis.gov.au/ntpapers/IPv2n3.pdf>.

Cohn, B. 1968. 'Ethnohistory', in D. Sills (ed.), *International Encyclopedia of the Social Sciences*, Macmillan, New York, pp. 440–8.

Faubion, J. 1993. 'History in anthropology', *Annual Review of Anthropology*, 22: 35–54.

Fentress, J. and Wickham, C. 1992. *Social Memory*, Blackwell, Oxford.

Geertz, C. 2000. *Available Light: Anthropological Reflections on Philosophical Topics*, Princeton University Press, Princeton.

Hill, J. (ed.) 1988. *Rethinking History and Myth: Indigenous South American Perspectives on the Past*, University of Illinois Press, Urbana.

Huyssen, A. 1995. *Twilight Memories: Marking Time in a Culture of Amnesia*, Routledge, London.

Jones D. and Hill-Burnett J. 1982. 'The political context of ethnogenesis: an Australian example', in M. C. Howard (ed.), *Aboriginal Power in Australian Society*. University of Queensland Press, St. Lucia.

Merlan, F. 1998. *Caging the Rainbow: Places, Politics and Aborigines in a North Australian Town*, University of Hawai'i Press, Honolulu.

Pannell, S. and Vachon, D. 2001. 'Notes and queries in the native title era', *The Australian Journal of Anthropology*, 12: 238–44.

Sahlins, M. 1981. *Historical Metaphors and Mythical Realities*, University of Michigan Press, Ann Arbor.

Sansom, B. 2006. 'The brief reach of history and the limitation of recall in traditional Aboriginal societies and cultures', *Oceania*, 76 (2): 150–72.

Sutton, P. 2003. *Native Title in Australia: An Ethnographic Perspective*, Cambridge University Press, Cambridge.

Sutton, P. 2004. 'Social scientists and native title cases in Australia', *General Anthropology* (Bulletin of the General Anthropology Division of the AAA), 11 (1): 1–4.

CAEPR Research Monograph Series

1. *Aborigines in the Economy: A Select Annotated Bibliography of Policy Relevant Research 1985–90*, L. M. Allen, J. C. Altman, and E. Owen (with assistance from W. S. Arthur), 1991.

2. *Aboriginal Employment Equity by the Year 2000*, J. C. Altman (ed.), published for the Academy of Social Sciences in Australia, 1991.

3. *A National Survey of Indigenous Australians: Options and Implications*, J. C. Altman (ed.), 1992.

4. *Indigenous Australians in the Economy: Abstracts of Research, 1991–92*, L. M. Roach and K. A. Probst, 1993.

5. *The Relative Economic Status of Indigenous Australians, 1986–91*, J. Taylor, 1993.

6. *Regional Change in the Economic Status of Indigenous Australians, 1986–91*, J. Taylor, 1993.

7. *Mabo and Native Title: Origins and Institutional Implications*, W. Sanders (ed.), 1994.

8. *The Housing Need of Indigenous Australians, 1991*, R. Jones, 1994.

9. *Indigenous Australians in the Economy: Abstracts of Research, 1993–94*, L. M. Roach and H. J. Bek, 1995.

10. *The Native Title Era: Emerging Issues for Research, Policy, and Practice*, J. Finlayson and D. E. Smith (eds), 1995.

11. *The 1994 National Aboriginal and Torres Strait Islander Survey: Findings and Future Prospects*, J. C. Altman and J. Taylor (eds), 1996.

12. *Fighting Over Country: Anthropological Perspectives*, D. E. Smith and J. Finlayson (eds), 1997.

13. *Connections in Native Title: Genealogies, Kinship, and Groups*, J. D. Finlayson, B. Rigsby, and H. J. Bek (eds), 1999.

14. *Land Rights at Risk? Evaluations of the Reeves Report*, J. C. Altman, F. Morphy, and T. Rowse (eds), 1999.

15. *Unemployment Payments, the Activity Test, and Indigenous Australians: Understanding Breach Rates*, W. Sanders, 1999.

16. *Why Only One in Three? The Complex Reasons for Low Indigenous School Retention*, R. G. Schwab, 1999.

17. *Indigenous Families and the Welfare System: Two Community Case Studies*, D. E. Smith (ed.), 2000.

18. *Ngukurr at the Millennium: A Baseline Profile for Social Impact Planning in South-East Arnhem Land*, J. Taylor, J. Bern, and K. A. Senior, 2000.

19. *Aboriginal Nutrition and the Nyirranggulung Health Strategy in Jawoyn Country*, J. Taylor and N. Westbury, 2000.

20. *The Indigenous Welfare Economy and the CDEP Scheme*, F. Morphy and W. Sanders (eds), 2001.

21. *Health Expenditure, Income and Health Status among Indigenous and Other Australians*, M. C. Gray, B. H. Hunter, and J. Taylor, 2002.

22. *Making Sense of the Census: Observations of the 2001 Enumeration in Remote Aboriginal Australia*, D. F. Martin, F. Morphy, W. G. Sanders and J. Taylor, 2002.

23. *Aboriginal Population Profiles for Development Planning in the Northern East Kimberley* J. Taylor, 2003.

24. *Social Indicators for Aboriginal Governance: Insights from the Thamarrurr Region*, Northern Territory, J. Taylor, 2004.

25. *Indigenous people and the Pilbara mining boom: A baseline for regional participation*, J. Taylor and B. Scambary, 2005.

26. *Assessing the evidence on Indigenous socioeconomic outcomes: A focus on the 2002 NATSISS*, B. H. Hunter (ed.), 2006.

For information on CAEPR Discussion Papers, Working Papers and Research Monographs (Nos 1-19) please contact:

>Publication Sales, Centre for Aboriginal Economic Policy Research, The Australian National University, Canberra, ACT, 0200

>Telephone: 02–6125 8211
>Facsimile: 02–6125 2789

Information on CAEPR abstracts and summaries of all CAEPR print publications and those published electronically can be found at the following WWW address:

>http://www.anu.edu.au/caepr/